JIMMY CLIFF

JIMMY CLIFF
An Unauthorized Biography

David Katz

Interlink Books

An imprint of Interlink Publishing Group, Inc.
Northampton, Massachusetts

First American edition published in 2012 by

INTERLINK BOOKS
An imprint of Interlink Publishing Group, Inc.
46 Crosby Street, Northampton, Massachusetts 01060
www.interlinkbooks.com

Library of Congress Cataloging-in-Publication Data

Katz, David, 1965-
Jimmy Cliff : an unauthorized biography / by David Katz. -- 1st American ed.
  p. cm.
Includes bibliographical references and index.
ISBN 978-1-56656-869-2 (pbk.)
1. Cliff, Jimmy. 2. Singers--Jamaica--Biography. 3. Reggae musicians--Jamaica--Biography.
    I. Title.
ML420.C566K38 2011
782.421646092--dc23
  [B]   2011029752

The author and publishers would like to thank the following for permission to reproduce their material: Extracts from the film *Jimmy Cliff: Moving On* by Hélène Lee and François Bergeron, reproduced by permission of Hélène Lee; "Jimmy Cliff In Paradise" by Roger Steffens, in the *Beat*, Vol. 5, No. 4, 1986, p19, reproduced by permission of Roger Steffens; "Jimmy's No Dreamer" by Ray Connolly, from *Daily Express* 22 July 1972 with permission of *Daily Express*; Jimmy Cliff Interview, conducted by Dave Rosencrans and Jeremy Marre, 30 January 2000, for the Experience Music Project, Seattle, reproduced by permission of Experience Music Project. If any copyright holders have been omitted, please contact the publishers who will make the necessary arrangements at the first opportunity.

The author and publishers would like to thank the following for permission to reproduce their photographs: Courtesy of Verden "Terry" Allen p58; Getty/Chris Morphet/Redferns p107, Getty/Michael Ochs Archives pp78, 98, 117, Getty/Jim Steinfeld/Michael Ochs Archives p146, Getty/David Redfern/Redferns p145; Flora Gil (courtesy of Liminha) p125; © *Gleaner* p33, © *Gleaner* 1967 p24, © *Gleaner* 1975 p88, © *Gleaner* 1980 p129, © *Gleaner* 1989 p178, © *Gleaner* 1997 pp119, 182, © *Gleaner* 2003 p192, © *Gleaner* 2005 pp4, 197; Courtesy of Douglas Graham/The Palace Amusement Co. (1921) Ltd p18; Courtesy of João Jorge p169; © David Katz pp21, 39, 63, 132; Rex/Geoff Wilkinson p48, Rex/Everett Collection p72, Rex/Warner Br/Everett Collection p154. Picture research by Gill Metcalfe.

Cover photograph by Getty/Michael Ochs Archives

Printed and bound in the United States of America

Contents

Acknowledgements vii
Introduction x

1 Better Days Are Coming: From Somerton to Kingston 1
2 Daisy Got Me Crazy: The Professional Debut 13
3 Hurricane Hattie: Arrival at Beverley's 23
4 Ska All Over the World: First Steps outside Jamaica 37
5 Aim and Ambition: Arrival in England 47
6 Wonderful World, Beautiful People: South American Revitalization 61
7 The Harder They Come: From Muscle Shoals to the Silver Screen 71
8 Brave Warrior: The EMI/Reprise Years 85
9 Meeting in Africa: Journeys in the Motherland 105
10 Roots Radical: Early 80s Rasta Resurgence 121
11 American Sweet: Commercial Success Stateside 141
12 Rebel in Me: Breaking Free from the Majors 153
13 Samba Reggae: The Salvador Phase 171
14 Higher and Higher: The French Connection 179
15 Black Magic: Furthering the Journey in the New Millennium 187

Select Discography 203
Select Bibliography 212
Select Videography 215
Index 216

Acknowledgements

A great many people deserve thanks for their assistance in the creation of this book. First, the many musicians and music industry personnel that shared their memories of working with Jimmy, including Howard Albert, Verden Allen, Esther Anderson, Gladdy Anderson, Derek Austin, Wally Badarou, Noel Bailey, Dave Barker, Family Man Barrett, Chris Blackwell, Ken Boothe, Dougie Bryan, Watty Burnett, Nonato Buzar, Squidley Cole, Ansel Collins, Sidney Crooks, Santa Davis, Denzil Dennis, Béco Dranoff, Sly Dunbar, Pepe Felly, Gilberto Gil, Zéu Góes, Senyah Haynes, Perry Henzell, Bongo Herman, Clive Hunt, Rick Iantosca, Jackie Jackson, Wayne Jobson, João Jorge, Ini Kamoze, Chris Kimsey, Bunny Lee, Byron Lee, Lloyd "Bread" McDonald, Nelson Mireilles, Derrick Morgan, Gibby Morrison, Aurelia Msimang, Mutabaruka, Stefan Paul, Lee "Scratch" Perry, Ernest Ranglin, Mikey "Boo" Richards, Edward Seaga, Roy Shirley, Chinna Smith, Trevor Starr, Maxine Stowe, John Stronach, Sticky Thompson, Phil Wainman, Bagga Walker, Philip White and Sidney Wolfe.

The fellow journalists, authors, photographers, and editors that shared memories of interacting with Jimmy and helped with fact checking include Olivier Albot, Bruno Blum, Geoff Brown, Stephen Davis, Hélène Lee, Jeremy Marre, Elena Oumano, Mark Paytress, Peter Simon, CC Smith and Roger Steffens, while Dana Smart, formerly of Universal, went beyond the call of duty in supplying missing titles from the back catalogue and generally helping fill in the blanks. I am also grateful to Jasen Emmons of the Experience Music Project and Dave Rosencrans, formerly of EMP, and to Douglas Graham and Eileen Thomas of the Palace Amusement Company and Lloyd Alberga, formerly of Palace, for allowing access to archive material.

In seeking to better understand Jimmy's time in Brazil, I was given invaluable assistance from musician Marcus Paulo Cientista of Rio's Digital Dubs crew, Nelson Mendes, Cultural Director of Olodum, Gilberto Monte, Musical Director of the Cultural Foundation of the State of Bahia, São Paolo-based journalist Otávio Rodrigues, and Laura Guimarães and Leo Vidigal of the Federal University of Minas Gerais. I am also grateful to Dr Mike Turner for helping me forge links in Brazil, and to Ligia Teixeira and Celeste Gattai for helping with the intricacies of Brazilian Portuguese.

Further links and fine-tuning were provided by Karen Bortcosh, Michael Cheeseman, Roland Clare of Procolharum.com, Doug Heselgrave of Writeous Word, Hannes A. Jonsson, Mike Kellie of Spooky Tooth, Norman Reid, Quinton Scott of Strut Records, Bazz Smith of Not So Blue, Cathy Snipper of Island Outpost, Ray Watkins (aka Kwayko Blandella), Lois Wilson of Mojo and Klaus "Selector K" Winter of Nicetime International.

James Ferguson, series editor of Caribbean Lives, deserves special mention for understanding the worth of this book's subject matter, while Nick Gillard, Annie LaPaz and Louisa Browne at Macmillan and copy editor Nicole Foster helped make the pre-publication process as trouble-free as possible. Chris Salewicz, a writer whose work I have long admired, made astute comments on an early draft that helped shape the book's final form. Additionally, Paula Johnson, Awards Secretary of the Authors' Foundation at the Society of Authors, encouraged me to apply for a grant that enabled the completion of this book, and her assistance, as well as that provided by the grant, is most gratefully acknowledged.

I am also grateful to friends and family for their support and encouragement, particularly Dr Claudia Bernard, my long-standing partner, for her continual patience, editorial suggestions, and other expressions of love, as well as fellow writers Garth Cartwright, Jon Lusk, Chris Menist and Ollie Sanders, and photographer/press officer Adrian Thomas. Similarly, Steve Barrow, David Hill and Ray Hurford are among the peers that have always supported my work, while the late Colin Moore of Fencebeater Records, whose tragic passing came shortly before the completion of the first draft of this book, provided important links that yielded key collaborative testimony (Colin, you left us too soon, but are certainly not forgotten). I would also like to thank anyone else not already mentioned that helped in some way, including select members of the Cliff clan; you know who you are and your contribution is appreciated.

My final word of thanks is reserved for the man to whom this book is a testament, none other than the Honorable Dr Jimmy Cliff, OM, for giving us so much incredible music during the last half-century, and for being living proof of mankind's positive potential.

Introduction

Jimmy Cliff is one of a handful of iconic figures to emerge from the Jamaican music scene in the last half of the twentieth century. In a career that has spanned more than fifty years, Cliff has recorded over twenty-five studio albums, pioneering new styles of music by merging the rhythms of his native Jamaica with various forms of overseas pop, helping several of his fellow countrymen make their first steps toward stardom in the process. He has also starred in feature films and documentaries, and circled the globe several times over, not only as a touring performer, but also as an African descendant who has perpetually sought new ways of understanding his ancestry and the rightful place of black people in the world. And although he is clearly an outstanding example of the kind of talent that a place like Jamaica is brimming over with, Cliff has never been blinded by the star trip, channelling his energies into charitable activities rather than getting lost in the perils of substance misuse or idol-worship folly. Indeed, Cliff's powerful messages of righteousness and self-determination have drawn the admiration of many world leaders, leading to familiarity with prime ministers, kings and presidents in several continents; yet Jimmy has never distanced himself from common folk. His undeniable talent and obvious conviction in fighting for truth and rights have led to dozens of official awards, including an honorary doctorate and an Order of Merit, Jamaica's third highest civic honor. All of which is certainly incredible, given that the man started life with literally nothing, growing up in a tiny shack in the Jamaican countryside.

Jimmy Cliff's story is a fascinating and heartening one, involving the political and spiritual awakening of a man, as well as his stupendous musical blossoming. Yet, as is the case with other Jamaican musicians, there is much that has been written about Cliff that is simply untrue. Indeed, his very date of birth is still regularly misquoted, and although some scribes would have you believe that Jimmy's musical experiments have kept him perpetually out of favor in his native Jamaica, the converse is actually the case: with the exception of the brief period when he remained off the island for a few years in the mid-1960s, Jimmy's work has always been lauded in the land of his birth, even when the styles of his recordings were far from the reggae idiom. Similarly, in South America and Africa, audiences really took to Jimmy's message, understanding intrinsically the optimism and direct political criticisms that have marked his greatest works. As is fitting for an artist who has consistently pointed out that humanity shares a universal experience, his work remains popular with audiences all over the world, who draw inspiration from his unifying messages.

Although dalliance in other forms like pop and soul have sometimes displeased reggae purists, Jimmy Cliff has always been aware that he need not be pigeonholed or solely constrained by the reggae format. And if any mistakenly believe that he was ever in the shadow of Bob Marley, it is worth remembering that Jimmy was the one that brought Marley to the attention of producer Leslie Kong in the first place, leading to Marley's very first recordings. Were it not for Jimmy Cliff, Bob Marley probably would never have made it into our public consciousness, yet it is wrong to think of the two as rivals, as they remained a pair of friends who admired each other's work. In any case, we should keep in mind that Jimmy scored a number of hits some years before Bob did, and he has continued to enjoy a successful career decades after Bob's unfortunate passing.

Like so many others outside of Jamaica, my first introduction to the music and culture of the island came through *The Harder They Come*, the landmark of Caribbean cinema that cast Jimmy Cliff in the lead role. At the time, I was an impressionable teenager, living in a small town in northern California, with very few Jamaicans anywhere nearby. But Jimmy's semi-autobiographical performance as an innocent country boy, corrupted by the oppression of the city, was so naturalistic and the story so universal that my friends and I could easily relate to the tale, while the music was so stunning that I hunted down a copy of the soundtrack as soon as I could. I began tuning into reggae radio on a daily basis, and was soon reaching for *Reggae Bloodlines* (one of the first serious explorations of reggae in print), attending reggae concerts and amassing reggae vinyl with increasing frequency, leading to a lifelong fascination with Jamaican music and culture. Such early experiences formed stepping stones that led me to London in the 1980s, where I was appointed Lee 'Scratch' Perry's biographer, resulting in several lengthy trips to Jamaica and elsewhere in the region. Thus, if not for Jimmy Cliff in *The Harder They Come*, my residence and profession would probably be entirely different.

Back in the days of our youth, my friends and I returned to *The Harder They Come* time and time again, as it was often screened at art-house cinemas. Yet when we purchased Jimmy's albums of the 1970s and 80s, we could not fathom why the music was often so different from the dynamic reggae he performed on the soundtrack of the film. In time, I would come to understand that Jimmy's affinity with diverse forms would often confound his critics, yet a trawl through Cliff's extensive catalogue yields an incredible array of exemplary creations, many of which are unjustly overlooked.

I first had the pleasure of meeting Jimmy Cliff when I was researching my second book, *Solid Foundation: An Oral History of Reggae*, and was instantly struck by the man's openness and obvious honesty. Additionally, despite the overriding confidence and shining aura that emanates from a man who is aware of his talent, Mr Cliff was clearly a very down-to-earth person who cared deeply about all mankind. Of course, at that time, neither he nor I was aware that I would one day write this book, but when the Caribbean Lives series was launched and editor James Ferguson suggested Jimmy as a potential candidate, it was clear to me that the man deserved a book that examines his life and work more fully, and I am very pleased to see it published during his lifetime, which seems particularly fitting, because Jimmy Cliff remains very much a contemporary artist of the present, both in the studio and live performance arenas; his ecstatic performances are still capable of bringing tears to adult eyes in the audience.

Although I have made every effort to check the facts stringently, a book like this is bound to have errors, and I apologize for them in advance. Additionally, there may be certain intentional omissions, left out in an effort to be sensitive to Jimmy and his family. It is also worth pointing out that, unlike my Lee Perry biography, this book was not the idea of the protagonist, and I am aware that a non-Jamaican writer like myself, who is not of African-Caribbean heritage, may not have been his first choice of author. Furthermore, Jimmy Cliff has always been an intensely private individual who has sought to avoid the intrusive enquiries of the media into his private life; although some family members have already garnered media attention, I have thus made a conscious decision to focus on the man's music rather than family matters, in an effort to respect such wishes. Although recent artistic activity has sparked a flurry of print and radio interviews, Mr Cliff seems to have often shied away from meddlesome press attention, more out of the frustration of having been repeatedly misunderstood on the rare occasions when he has actually granted extensive interviews. There have been all kinds of misinterpretations regarding Jimmy's views on faith, race relations, the use of marijuana, and personal relationships, and the resultant quagmire of confusion has sometimes taken away from the true meaning and worth of his musical creations, which is why I have tried to avoid spurious speculation about Jimmy's personal motivations in the portions of the text where I was not able to glean a first-hand explanation.

In any case, my intention is to celebrate a very uncommon and highly gifted individual who has brought about much positive change through music. Jimmy Cliff is a true Caribbean original; in highlighting his many achievements, this book ultimately seeks to place his life and work within their proper context.

1

Better Days Are Coming:
From Somerton to Kingston

When Jimmy Cliff was born, the island of Jamaica was experiencing a period of particular uncertainty. The Second World War had been raging for five solid years and, although the battlefields of Europe were thousands of miles from Jamaica's Caribbean shores, the war was the overriding concern affecting daily life.

As Jamaica was still a Crown Colony, thousands of young Jamaican men left the island to fight the Nazis on behalf of the British "Mother Country"; others were recruited into the Royal Canadian Air Force or seconded to American military bases in the region, while Jamaican women were also sent overseas in significant numbers as members of the Auxiliary Territorial Service, though most of them at least avoided the front lines. American GIs also became part of the fabric of Jamaican society, as three American military bases were established on the island. Several thousand evacuees from Gibraltar and Jewish refugees from elsewhere in

Europe were housed in a purpose-built camp on the outskirts of Kingston, while an airport was constructed south-east of the capital to allow for the refueling of Allied bombers searching for enemy submarines. Censorship was imposed on the press, telephones, letters and telegrams; staple foods were rationed and a ban on imported meat resulted in the popularity of "dip and fall back," a stew that replaced animal protein with mackerel or salted cod.

Even though Europe was an entirely unknown entity for most Jamaicans, the island's newspapers were filled with reports from European battlegrounds; movie theaters screened nothing but war films, propaganda and war bulletins; and those lucky enough to have access to a radio were treated to daily dispatches from the front on ZQI, then Jamaica's sole radio station. The threat of invasion by the Germans and their Axis partners felt very real, particularly as Japanese submarines were torpedoing Jamaican banana boats bound for Britain, and the daily lists of Jamaican casualties publicly posted in Kingston brought home the tragic results of war with terrifying clarity.

At the same time, the bitter labor disputes that erupted on the island during the late 1930s continued unabated, with trade union leaders Alexander Bustamante and Norman Washington Manley galvanizing the public into dramatic action, lobbying the island's colonial rulers to consent to a living wage for the entire populace, the great majority of which had inherited a life little better than the slavery their ancestors endured during the centuries of British rule that had followed Spain's fleeting control of the colony. And although the two leaders were distant blood relatives united in certain ideals concerning wages and human rights, with Manley even taking charge of Bustamante's union during the latter's imprisonment, each had very different ideas about the kind of governance a free Jamaica should engage. Manley favored a version of Fabian socialism while Bustamante believed in the free market; thus the seeds of the island's independence movement were already fraught with a divisive conflict when Manley founded the People's National Party (PNP) in 1938, from which Bustamante broke away five years later to form the rival Jamaica Labour Party (JLP).

As negotiations with the colonial authorities continued, universal suffrage was granted to all adult citizens in 1944. At the end of the year, due largely to the charismatic Bustamante's vociferous call for better wages, the JLP won the island's first general elections by a huge margin, making Bustamante the leader of the country's first democratically elected Executive Council, though the elections had been marred by stone-throwing and stabbing incidents among party supporters, particularly in Kingston's ghetto areas.

Meanwhile, as British and Russian soldiers were closing in on Nazi aggressors in Poland and France, and Mahatma Gandhi and Muhammad Ali Jinnah were negotiating the partition of India to enable the creation of Pakistan, Jamaica was gradually becoming more industrialized: the island's railway switched from steam engines to diesel fuel, and the first bauxite extracts were shipped abroad to investigate the potential for mining; roads were constructed along the north coast and agricultural concerns were expanding, particularly in the dairy sector. But as increasing numbers of the unskilled traveled to the USA to engage in seasonal farm work or to toil in munitions factories, life in the Jamaican countryside continued much as it had done for countless generations: by day, the people bore the brunt of back-breaking labor in sugarcane fields and on banana plantations; by night, men quarrelled over women and sought solace in rum, with music and dancing being among the only elements to bring some form of release. For most, life was inevitably hard, and there was little else to sustain them other than a fervent belief in God and the promise of a better life to come.

It was into such a world that Jimmy arrived on Sunday, 30 July 1944. He was born James Ezekiel Chambers at Adelphi Land, an impoverished hilltop community above Somerton, an underdeveloped town in the parish of St James, located about twelve miles southeast of Montego Bay, the most populated port on Jamaica's north coast. Jimmy's father, Lilbert Chambers, was a tailor who also farmed the land; greatly respected in the area, he was often deferred to for judgement when disputes arose and he would even influence which candidate the locals cast their votes for, giving him the status of the district's "lawyer," despite being a man of limited means. Jimmy's mother, Christine, was a domestic worker descended from the Maroons, fiercely independent runaway slaves who formed impenetrable communities in remote mountain areas, from where they launched attacks on plantations to free others, often resulting in the deaths of white planters and colonial militia. A treaty brokered in 1739 had granted the Maroons a certain degree of autonomy, and although the British defeated them during the Maroon War of 1795, Maroons have maintained their traditional way of life in a handful of communities that are somewhat separate from the rest of Jamaican society.

From the very start of Jimmy's days on earth, it seemed that fate was threatening to throw obstacles in his path. Indeed, a mere three weeks after his birth, the north coast was struck by a fearsome hurricane, with 120-mile-per-hour winds whipping in from Port Maria, and although they had slowed to 80 mph by the time the storm passed directly over Somerton and exited Montego Bay, the coconut crop had been entirely decimated. The neighboring parish of St Mary suffered most, but there was widespread flooding in the Somerton

Somerton, St. James: Jimmy Cliff's birthplace

area and considerable damage to many homes in the district.

Life did not get any easier after the storm. For the majority of their childhood, Lilbert alone raised Jimmy and his older brother Victor in a tiny two-room dwelling. With only the bare earth as flooring, the wattle-and-daub shack had few amenities, other than a basic bed and homemade cupboard above it, with the nearby river providing the opportunity to bathe.

Yet despite the hardships of growing up poor in a village that had neither running water nor electricity, aspects of Jimmy's childhood were idyllic: on the way to and from the local spring from which drinking water was drawn, the lush, tropical environ-ment provided ample fruits for plucking, such as sweet, juicy mangoes and custard apples; there were guava, orange and grapefruit trees, as well as the prickly-skinned soursop, while tangy star apples and June plums were just as good to eat as to juice. There were also large breadfruit trees stretching over the hillside, providing an ample staple food, along with ackee, the fruit of which was used for a breakfast dish when ripened, and avocado, known locally as alligator pear, while the mineral-rich earth provided plenty of yams, Irish potatoes, cas-sava and other root vegetables, as well as peas and peppers. The abundant fruit and nectar-rich tropical flowers naturally attracted colorful bird life, their songs perpetually punctuating the air. Adelphi Land had the benefit of height, so in addition to the fantastic view over Somerton, there were also cooler breezes and less stifling hu-midity than in some of the communities below.

In general, Jimmy's early days were marked by a kind of Eden-like innocence involving a simple, naturalistic way of life largely untainted by pollution or negative influence; as he recalls: "I really enjoyed that period of my life because there were rivers to go to, and the beach."

The local Pentecostal church that formed the central focal point of the community was a place where he could exercise his vocal cords freely, though the sermons were terribly boring. As he ex-plains: "I enjoyed the singing of the church, but when the preach-ing came on, I slept."

In August 1951, not long after Jimmy's seventh birthday, Mother Nature made her presence felt in Jamaica in a very dramatic fashion, unleashing her fury on the hapless islanders in the form of Hurricane Charlie, which caused untold devastation all over the island. The storm was spotted in the Leeward Islands on 15 August, and was initially thought to be heading south of Jamaica, but instead it made a direct hit on the island's southern shore, battering it with 125-mile-per-hour winds from 9:30 pm on 17 August. The first forty-five minutes of impact were the most intense, but the winds continued wreaking havoc for another three hours, and torrential rain added to the misery when the wind finally died down. The damage was unprecedented, with the southeast coastal towns of Morant Bay, Yallahs and Port Royal completely flattened. Much of eastern Kingston was rubble, ships in Kingston Harbour had been smashed and Palisadoes Airport largely destroyed, while the island's banana and coconut crops were severely depleted. In all, over 150 people lost their lives in a storm that caused millions of dollars' worth of damage, and although the north of the island was spared the worst of the destruction, Jimmy and his family were among the thousands made homeless by the might of Charlie, their simple dwelling completely destroyed.

After Charlie, while his father began rebuilding, Jimmy went to live for an extended period at the home of an aunt who farmed the land along with her husband, growing crops like bananas and sugarcane, as well as rearing cattle, dairy cows, chickens and goats. The couple had six sons and Jimmy's grandmother also lived there. "I spent a lot of time with them," he recalls, "and I did quite a lot of things on the farm."

In addition to the farm work, Jimmy had many noteworthy experiences during the five years in which he was a member of his aunt's household, including his first encounters with color prejudice. His cousins were all much lighter skinned than Jimmy, whose complexion was very dark, and although he never faced maltreatment from any family member, it was while living with them that he first came to realize that skin color could determine different treatment in the wider society, based on the attitudes of neighbors.

As the young Jimmy grappled with these experiences, seeing himself in a different light, his grandmother, who was also very dark, revealed herself as a fountain of knowledge where race matters were concerned. She told Jimmy that her own grandmother had been a slave, noting that the woman was as dark-skinned as Jimmy and herself; she ultimately expressed to him that to be black was to be beautiful, and the wisdom she imparted through the special bond they fostered had dramatic effects as he grew older. She also became an ally where singing was concerned, as he would sometimes climb the large tree that stood near his aunt's home to sing out loud and long, and any complaints from the neighbors would be met by fierce scolding from his grandmother, who made sure to let all and sundry know how obvious it was that the young man was going to make something of himself, by virtue of his God-given talent.

Jimmy was a bright child who did well at Somerton All-Age School, but his mischievousness and constant questioning often brought the teacher's cane down on him. He was fond of teasing the other children and sometimes found it difficult to stop, while if another student attacked him physically, he would retaliate as necessary to avoid being victimized on account of his small stature. Mrs Robertha White became his favorite teacher, and he looked to her for the kind of guidance a mother would normally provide.

When he was cast in the starring role of a school play called *King Sugar*, everyone was impressed, particularly by his dramatic intonation of some adapted lines of William Cowper's poem "The Solitude of Alexander Selkirk": "I am monarch of all I survey, my right there's none to dispute. From the centre, all round to the sea, I'm Lord of the West Indies." Some of the pretty girls that attended the school told Jimmy they thought it was the radio they were listening to when they heard him rehearsing for the play, giving him the first real inkling of the seductive power of his voice. But singing was always his main preoccupation; according to Jimmy, he had already made up his mind to be a singer by the age of six.

In his early life, he encountered folk music such as mento, a uniquely Jamaican form that fused African rhythms with European melodies. Although its satirical and often ribald lyrics give it a similar feel to Trinidadian calypso, mento's distinctive instrumentation made use of what is known as a "rumba box," which is a kind of oversized *mbira*, and often featured homemade wind instruments fashioned from bamboo, along with a banjo and various forms of percussion. In addition to mento, neighbors would sometimes provide raw rhythm with just hand drums and an acoustic guitar. There were also the work songs ringing out from field hands, as well as the ring-game songs that children sang, but as Jimmy grew older, a more important source of music was provided by the occasional dances that took place next door at an upstairs juke joint, the Money Rock Tavern, where a sound system called Pope Pius blared Latin American music.

In the years immediately following the end of the Second World War, heavily powered sets of amplified equipment, known as sound systems, were becoming the rage on the island after Jamaican seasonal farm workers encountered music-filled outdoor block parties hosted by their black American co-workers. In Kingston, the first sound systems to appear were typically attached to downtown business places, their musical displays initially a lure to attract customers, but bigger sets were gradually established to provide inexpensive entertainment at outdoor events – the antithesis to the costly live jazz concerts that were the exclusive preserve of visiting tourists and the light-skinned upper class. From the dawning of the 1950s, most Kingston sound systems played a steady majority of rhythm and blues, bolstered by mento and other Caribbean forms; in the countryside, rhythm and blues took a little longer to become popular, and small country sets often had a weaker output, typically being powered by car batteries or feeble portable generators.

Pope Pius's speciality was Cuban rumba and merengue from the Dominican Republic, so these rhythms became part of young Jimmy's musical diet, along with the mento and calypso that were always around, until the raw sounds of American rhythm and blues swept into his consciousness with the force of a hurricane, thanks to a friend who sometimes had access to a radio. Jimmy was especially impressed by the New Orleans styling of Fats Domino and Professor Longhair, the raw excesses of the extravagant rock 'n' roll extrovert, Little Richard, as well as the gospel soul of Ray Charles and the ballads of Sam Cooke and Dee Clark. Elvis Presley's energetic early work and the emotive strains of Bobby Darin also inspired him, and he was aware of the huge influence of Louis Jordan and Smiley Lewis slightly earlier. But as his strict Christian father disapproved of such worldly sounds, deeming them "the devil's music," Jimmy had to enjoy their magic in secret: he would sneak out to the local bar, where there were dozens of songs to learn on the jukebox, and gladly sing any of them in exchange for a glass of soda, much to the delight of the older patrons.

After building a rudimentary guitar from bamboo, Jimmy wanted to try writing songs of his own. But first he needed to understand how a song was written. So one day, in his woodwork class, he asked the teacher, "How do I really write a song?"

"Well," replied the teacher, "you just write one!"

Jimmy's response was "I'll Go Wooing," a song that recounted his search for a fiancée, generally styled after rhythm and blues.

Jamaica experienced new levels of growth following the end of the Second World War, resulting in the construction of the University College of the West Indies in Mona, as well as various factories and agricultural processing plants. As the nation grew during the early 1950s and the independence movement strengthened, a new-found sense of optimism prevailed. Jamaica's rural development brought the widespread propagation of 4-H Clubs, initially part of the Jamaica Agricultural Service's drive to train farmers in the use of new agricultural methods, and the organization had a surprising role to play in the early musical development of James Chambers.

Jimmy was a member of his local 4-H club from the age of nine and often attended their summer camps; he sang regularly in the club and further developed his vocal skills at the camp, even toying with the name Jimmy Cliff at the time. "At the camps, they used to have little concerts, where I used to sing all Fats Domino's songs," he explains, "so I had to find a stage name. I was born in the mountainous part of Somerton, up in the cliffs, where I could see all of Somerton, so I thought, 'Why don't I use Cliff, because it's the heights.' And then my father used to call me Jimmy when I was a good boy and James when I was a bad boy, so, 'Why not use Jimmy?'"

Apart from his presence in the church choir and on the school stage, public recognition of James Chambers' vocal talent reached him at the age of fourteen, in April 1959. The occasion was National Achievement Day, part of a week of Easter events, the centerpiece of which was an island-wide competition held at the National Show Grounds in Denbigh, located on the outskirts of the town of May Pen, in which young 4-H clubbites displayed their skills in animal husbandry, pig-rearing and related agricultural arts, as well as basket weaving, food preparation, cake baking and other aspects of home economics, augmented by produce displays and machinery demonstrations, as well as a musical talent contest. For young country folk all over Jamaica, the day was greatly anticipated, particularly those in the 4-H clubs whose parishes had survived the elimination rounds that determined who would take part in the competition finals. Jimmy thus made his way across the mid-section of the island with great expectation, passing far beyond the other side of the impenetrable Cockpit Country that had been home to Maroons for centuries, to enter a couple of chickens in the poultry competition, which he won with flying colors.

But Jimmy was not content with this sole prize, and decided to up the ante by grabbing the microphone at the music competition, although it seemed that the entire island was present, the enthusiastic crowd partaking in the day's festivities being estimated at seven thousand strong. Nevertheless, exuding a very natural confidence, Jimmy took the stage with a grin on his face, belting out an impressive rendition of Fats Domino's "Be My Guest," accompanied only by his own vocal imitations of the song's driving instrumental backing. The crowd roared in appreciation, giving the young man his first taste of the endorphin rush that forms the immediate payback to a successful performance.

Thereafter, Jimmy would sometimes gaze down from the heights of Adelphi Land at a patch of ground in Somerton, where he pictured a large stage being built on which concerts and talent shows could be held. How wonderful it would be, he thought, if Somerton had somewhere at which live music could be performed regularly, as it was in Jamaica's larger towns and cities. The absence of such a facility was just another indication of what little opportunity there was for someone like him in the area, apart from the numbing reality of poorly paid plantation work.

During his schooldays, maps were another source of fascination. The young Jimmy would peer intently at the atlas, marveling at the many territories of the world and the huge rivers that flowed through them: there was America, with the Mississippi, which flowed past New Orleans; Brazil, with the massive Amazon, which cut across the entire country; Egypt, with the limitless Nile; and territories in the west and central regions of Africa had impressive rivers too. "I will travel to these lands and explore these rivers," Jimmy told his friends, "just you wait and see."

Through the encouragement of his father, Jimmy got a job selling the *Gleaner* and *Star* newspapers, singing out the headlines to attract customers. Although his profits were slim, he learned the art of saving from this time and was immensely proud when he opened his first bank account at the Post Office. But when Jimmy completed elementary school there were few prospects in sight, other than diving off the pier at Montego Bay to catch the few shiny coins that were flung into the water by the patrons of passing cruise ships. Of course, he could follow his brother Victor into an agricultural trade, or, like most in the locality, he could seek employment in the cane fields or banana plantations. Thankfully, Robertha White suggested he pursue a course in radio and television electronics at Kingston Technical School, and, understanding that his son possessed the intellectual aptitude and personal drive that would realize the potential for a better standard of living, Lilbert Chambers agreed that Jimmy should move to the capital.

Some time before the decision was made to send Jimmy to Kingston, Mr Chambers asked his son to make a choice: would he prefer that his father's meager savings were spent on private tuition, which might better prepare him for a respectable profession, such as that of a doctor or lawyer, or should the money be spent on a battery-operated radio instead? Naturally, his son chose the radio, as it would grant him direct access to his beloved rhythm and blues, typically through late-night broadcasts, when thinner airwaves made audible the play-lists of WNOE of New Orleans, WLAC of Nashville and, most consistently, WINZ of Miami. As Jimmy prepared to head to Kingston, the radio thus made him feel that he was getting even closer to the music.

2

Daisy Got Me Crazy: The Professional Debut

Kingston may have been only around 67 miles from Somerton as the crow flies, but it was worlds away in terms of everything else. The capital city was shockingly chaotic, unbelievably noisy and terribly overcrowded, with massive shopping arcades and sprawling street markets thronging the downtown area, which was littered with vagrants, pickpockets and street gangs. With so much to take in, it could be overwhelming, and there was much that the young man would need to get his head round, such as understanding the indications of a traffic light and knowing which streets to steer clear of. But the most important thing to get straight on arrival was exactly where he was going to live.

"When I got to Kingston, my father actually didn't have any place for me to stay," Jimmy recalls. "He just had a few ideas, like he knew this friend and that friend, and he was just checking them out. He started checking all the friends he knew, and most of them said no, until finally we got to one cousin in east Kingston, who just had a little single room. He said, 'I could accommodate him in my little single room, but that's all I have. How is his food and clothes going to be looked after?' We were just getting ready to go back home when this lady who lived in the same yard said, 'Oh, what a nice little boy, I'll take care of his food and his clothes,' so that was my luck."

Jimmy's benefactor, known as Miss Gwen, was the first of many Kingston women to take a shine to him, providing badly needed assistance just in the nick of time. Jimmy remembers that the yard was in one of the streets that fed off Windward Road, the main thoroughfare that connects the city to the island's eastern parishes, as well as to its main airport. Although poor, the neighborhood was not as rough as the ghetto areas of the west, meaning that life was relatively tranquil, despite being much more hectic than Adelphi Land. One thing Jimmy especially liked about the location was that it was close to the water, so swimming was always an easy option, though Kingston Harbour and its environs were obviously far more polluted than the rivers of Somerton.

Attending night classes at Kingston Technical School, Jimmy slowly became accustomed to life in the capital. Hanover Street, where Kingston Tech was located, was a very lively place indeed; its proximity to the port meant that sailors often frequented its illicit bars and brothels after nightfall. Jimmy was a green youth, freshly arrived from the countryside, but any tough that troubled him soon learned that he was not to be trifled with. Although possessing a thin frame and not being particularly tall, Jimmy was equipped with a muscular torso and had already mastered the art of self-defense in St James.

There was seldom enough food to go round at his cousin's, and the smell of fresh loaves from a nearby bakery sometimes became unbearable, tempting Jimmy to steal. However, knowing that his father would disapprove, he began gathering discarded bottles to sell for a few shillings' worth of sustenance instead.

On the more positive side, music was all around in downtown Kingston, and the might of the sound systems' massive equipment, as well as their continual battles, meant that rhythm and blues was often blasting from a nearby bar or open-air dance hall. Local talent was also increasingly becoming part of the picture, as a handful of forward-thinking entrepreneurs had begun recording Jamaican artists for exclusives that would be aired on their sound systems, pressing the more popular recordings after building up demand. In fact, such developments were happening in tandem with the growing independence movement, which was working toward a more definite goal, now that Bustamante was campaigning against Jamaica's membership in the Federation of the West Indies.

In 1958 the colonial authorities had brokered the short-lived Federation to join Britain's English-speaking Caribbean colonies as a controlled means to enact a staged, partial independence, with central governance to be administered in Trinidad. Although Norman Manley supported the Federation, Bustamante was now rejecting it in favor of full independence to be granted to Jamaica outright. Music was a part of the process, as Jamaican singers formed an increasing feature of the island's musical landscape; though most concerned themselves with ballads and love songs, several drew on tales of biblical retribution to make coded reference to colonial inequalities, and some directly addressed world politics. Thus, Laurel Aitken cut "Ghana Independence (They Got It)" in a percussion-laden calypso style when that nation broke its colonial yoke, while in the Jamaican variant of rhythm and blues, Bunny and Skitter spoke of "The Wicked" and Owen Gray warned that "Sinners Gonna Weep" when they face judgement day. Clancy Eccles also demanded "Freedom," and although his song actually called for the repatriation of black Jamaicans to Africa, the JLP co-opted it as their anti-Federation theme song of 1961, the year Jamaica seceded from the union.

When Jimmy heard Laurel Aitken's rhythm and blues hit "Little Sheila" on the radio, he was stunned. Aitken was a versatile singer who thrived in mento and calypso as well as rhythm and blues; he could even adapt foreign styles such as merengue, perhaps because he had spent his early years in Cuba. Yet Aitken was a Jamaican, just like Jimmy, living somewhere nearby in Kingston, and if Aitken could make a record that was played on the radio it naturally followed that Jimmy could make one too.

He started making enquiries about how to get recorded, and soon discovered that weekly talent contests, the "Opportunity Hour," were being held by journalist and popular stage actor Vere Johns at the Palace Theater, a huge landmark that Jimmy passed daily on his way to school, located as it was at a prominent corner of Victoria Avenue, the continuation of Windward Road. Highlights from the contest were broadcast on radio station RJR under the title *Opportunity Knocks*, leading to very real exposure for the winner, in addition to prize money. Auditions were held on Mondays and Thursdays at 3 pm, so one day Jimmy left home early to attend an audition, but when he tried to write his name on the list of prospective contestants he found too many competitors already in place. The same thing happened the following week, but the week after, upon spotting Vere Johns standing at the front of the stage, he thought fast on his feet, aiming to make a quick impact.

"Once I got close to the stage," he recalls, "I said, 'Mr Johns, my name is Jimmy Cliff,' and he looked down over his glasses at me, so I found that the name rang; it sounded like something to him, so he said, 'OK, you come on up.' And I went up and started to sing my Fats Domino songs."

On the night of the performance, vying for a prize pot of two pounds, Jimmy put his all into renditions of songs by Fats Domino and Sam Cooke, and was certain that he was the winner, since he sang much better than the other contestants. But the result was not as he expected.

"They booed me off," he laughs, "but how that thing used to work, the audience was the judge, something like what they have at the [Harlem] Apollo: after you sing, everybody stand in a line and Mr Johns hold the two pounds over your head, and he goes down the line and the one who gets the most applause wins. Most people told me that I was the best on the show that night, but I didn't have friends in the audience to applaud for me; what the

Kingstonians used to do was to bring a lot of friends to make a big applause for them, so when they win the money, they share it among themselves. That happened to me all the way, so people said, 'Hey, this *Opportunity Knocks* goes on at another theater in west Kingston, why don't you try it in west Kingston? You may be lucky there.'"

The "Opportunity Hour" was held at various theaters in Kingston on different days of the week, so on another evening Jimmy traveled along Spanish Town Road, nearly two miles to the west of the downtown area, passing the May Pen Cemetery and the Denham Town ghetto on the way, to reach the imposing land-mark of the Majestic Theater, situated right at the corner of Max-field Avenue. There he joined the hopefuls for another go with Vere Johns, this time hitting the crowd with a rendition of "Sinners Weep" by Owen Gray. Even though Gray's voice was considerably deeper than Jimmy's, young Mr Cliff tackled the number with considerable aplomb, so when the prize was held over his head in the post-performance line-up, he bagged it by a long margin, using the money for a new pair of trousers and some food, the remaining portion going to his cousin.

Getting his songs recorded was a major preoccupation, espe-cially after pianist Frankie Bonnito, the leader of the *Opportunity Knocks* backing band, recognized his talent and encouraged him to begin recording. But finding the way was difficult, and there were other hurdles to overcome.

"After a while, I had to leave my cousin," Jimmy explains, "be-cause the room wasn't working out with him and his girlfriend, so after about two months I really had to leave. My father came up and we decided we'll have to go back to the country again, but on the way back, he just said, 'Oh, let's visit this friend I know.' Country people are like that, or my father was very much like that, so we stopped by this lady that my father knew, and he said, 'Well, James come to Kingston to go to school, but we can't find a place, so we're going back to the country.' And she said, 'Well, we don't have any place here, but if you bought a little bed, we could stick him in the corner there.' So luck shined again. It looks like women are always good to me. That was right in the center of west Kingston, just opposite what was then called Back-O-Wall."

West Kingston was far less developed than east Kingston, and the tenement Jimmy shared with his father's friend and her husband was part of a cramped, poorly constructed yard at 63¾ Spanish Town Road, its flimsy wooden walls interspersed with rusty zinc fence sheeting. The yard faced the slum of Ackee Walk, part of the broader Back-O-Wall community, a sprawling squatter camp of lawless dwellings hastily erected between the railway line, May Pen Cemetery and the main road, which merged farther down into the Dungle, bordering on the municipal garbage dump. As more and more migrants poured into the city from the countryside in search of work, Back-O-Wall and its neighboring slums continued to grow, becoming ever more overcrowded, volatile and dangerous.

Living in one of Kingston's harshest ghettos, Jimmy was faced with a whole new way of life. Sound systems were all around, meaning that Jimmy was constantly surrounded by music; indeed, a noted venue called Carnival Lawn was just behind his tenement on the other side of the zinc fence, being at the end of North Street that intersected with Spanish Town Road, while Chocomo Lawn, the largest and most popular venue of all, was just a few yards away

The Palace Theater with its twin bandstands

on Wellington Street. Jimmy seldom had the money to contemplate paying the entry fee to the dances, but the sheer power of the sound systems meant he did not really need to, as the music was clearly audible throughout the entire neighborhood, keeping him up to date with which sounds were hot.

Then there were the ecstatic drumbeats emanating from the Rastafarian camp established by Prince Emmanuel Edwards at Ackee Walk, stunning sounds that resonated with the rhythms of Africa. During the 1930s and 40s the Rastafari movement had slowly grown among the Jamaican poor, following the crowning of Ras Tafari Makonnen as Emperor Haile Selassie I in Ethiopia, which was interpreted as a fulfillment of biblical prophecy indicative of Selassie's divinity. The Rastas believed that the rightful place for black Jamaicans was Africa and that repatriation was an inevitable necessity; most also venerated marijuana as a holy herb, did not trim their beards and wore their hair in matted dreadlocks as a symbol of their faith, all of which made them social outcasts in a colonial Jamaica that had a hierarchy based on skin tone, equating blackness with backwardness and denigrating anything seen as African. Prince Emmanuel, head of a sub-group known as the "Bobo Dreads," emerged as a significant leader in 1958, when he gathered several thousand followers at his Ackee Walk camp.

Jimmy had encountered a Rasta in Somerton and was intrigued by the man's dreadlocks, as well as the way he spoke about Africa, the gravity of his words heightened by a raspy baritone. But everyone in the district had shunned the man, except for Jimmy's father. Now, in western Kingston, Jimmy was drawn to the drums of the Rasta camp, and he eventually smoked his first spliff at Ackee Walk, the strong herb putting his mind into a whole different headspace.

Unfortunately, there was also a lot of badness in Back-O-Wall. Tear gas was regularly fired into the vicinity by police, particularly when political rallies erupted into violent demonstrations, so Jimmy sometimes had to hide under his bed in an effort to escape the noxious fumes. Jimmy had become a devotee of violent spaghetti westerns at the downtown movie theaters, but here the threat of violence was all too real: street gangs ran riot, and as allegiance was a crucial element of survival, it was perhaps inevitable that he would make the acquaintance of rough characters that were not necessarily on the right road. But, despite the many pitfalls all around him, the young James Chambers knew that betterment was possible, as long as he concentrated on the ultimate goal.

Jimmy had been trying to find a way to get recorded since his months in east Kingston, and moving west put him right in the midst of Kingston's Tin Pan Alley, the sound-system owners that were emerging as Jamaica's top record producers all having premises close by. One of his first ports of call was the liquor store owned by Duke Reid, a former policeman, whose Trojan sound system was the biggest on the island. Jimmy went there because he had been greatly impressed by the recordings local singers Derrick Morgan and Eric "Monty" Morris were making for Reid.

Influenced by the sounds he encountered in west Kingston, as well as by rhythm and blues and the music he grew up with in the countryside, Jimmy auditioned with a song about seeking a return to his African homeland.

Unfortunately the song was not greeted with much enthusiasm; nor was "I'll Go Wooing," Jimmy's early effort about needing a fiancée. The story was the same at Reid's rivals, such as King Edwards the Giant, whose sound system was one of Jamaica's most powerful; Simeon Smith, whose Little Wonder sound system was based farther up Spanish Town Road, at a haberdashery near the Majestic Theater; and Clement "Sir Coxsone" Dodd, a family friend of the Duke who had set up his Downbeat sound system just east of Orange Street, at the corner of Beeston Street and Love Lane.

Eventually, after five solid months of unsuccessful attempts, Jimmy finally found someone willing to take the gamble on his vocal ability, namely a sound-system operator called Count Boysie the Monarch (aka Jeremiah McIntosh), whose set was based at West Street, near the bottom end of Spanish Town Road, his claim to fame being a popular sound-system hit called "Babylon Downfall." When Jimmy appeared with a Little Richard-styled original called

"Daisy Got Me Crazy," Boysie liked what he heard, so a rudimentary recording was arranged at Federal, then the island's only proper recording facility. Jimmy was thrilled to finally commit his voice to tape, but the thrill proved short-lived, as his request for payment drew anger from the Count, who initially summoned some tough associates to dispatch violence to the young singer. Then, when the anger subsided, he offered only meagre recompense.

"Count Boysie offered me a shilling as bus fare to go to school," Jimmy laments, "and I said, 'This is not right.' I heard about people getting £50 and £100, and he's offering me a shilling? Something's not right here, so I didn't accept the shilling."

Adding insult to injury was the fact that the song was retained only as an acetate for exclusive airing on Boysie's sound system; it was never given an actual release, and Boysie's sound later faded into obscurity. But this early disappointment did not quell Jimmy's urge; if anything, it spurred him onwards more forcefully, as he knew that succeeding in music was a real possibility.

Somewhere along the way he joined forces with another aspiring singer, in the hopes of making it as a duo. "One day I met one guy

Early inspiration: the pioneering Jamaican vocalist Derrick Morgan

from the countryside, his name was Keith Smith," Jimmy recalls. "He also was a singer and he wants to record too, so he said, 'Why don't we sing together?' So we became a duo and started writing songs together, and the name of the duo was Cliff and Swift."

The pair would rehearse at the beach, practicing their harmonies together, but Smith was somewhat unreliable, leaving Cliff to focus on his own development. In fact, Smith suggested the duo audition for Sir Cavalier, a sound-system operator based in nearby Jones Town, who had established a small record label called Hi Tone, working with backing musicians such as noted drummer Arkland "Drumbago" Parks and harmonica player Charlie Organaire (aka Charles Cameron), but when Smith repeatedly failed to turn up at the appointed hour, Cliff eventually did the honors on his own. The audition took place about six months after his run-in with Boysie, and he struck lucky this time with a rhythm and blues original called "I'm Sorry," in which Jimmy apologized to a heartbroken girlfriend for his errant ways.

"Sir Cavalier was new in the business," Cliff recalls. "He had just recorded one big song called 'Times Are Going' by a duo called Martin and Derrick, and the song was a big song in Jamaica. Swift said, 'Hey, let's go try Sir Cav, because I live close to him,' but every day we decide to go, [Swift] didn't go, so I just went on my own."

"I'm Sorry" was released on Hi Tone and even found its way to the UK without Jimmy's knowledge, through a licensing deal Cavalier brokered with Blue Beat Records, though it never achieved popularity in either territory. In truth, Cliff's unpolished, quavering voice sounds somewhat amateurish on the record, while the minimal musical backing of stand-up bass, mouth organ and handclaps was not mixed properly, recorded as it was with every-one crowded around one microphone. At least Cliff was paid for his efforts this time, reaping a £15 reward, which was immediately spent on new trousers, a hat and a pair of boots, as well as an en-tire chicken, which he devoured in one sitting, the source of the food making the meal taste all the more sweet.

3

Hurricane Hattie: Arrival at Beverley's

At the end of Jimmy's first year in Kingston, he decided not to continue with his studies, certain that he would make his career in music. When his father found out, he was livid, decrying Jimmy's actions as foolhardy and reckless. "You're on your own now," said Lilbert decisively, cutting him off from parental support.

The rejection was painful, but Jimmy was determined to stick to his decision, despite the very real hardships he faced on a daily basis in Back-O-Wall. He earned meager wages working on a vegetable truck for a time, but at one point things got so bad that he contemplated robbing a bank, though the thought of his father finding out ultimately deterred him. Then, as 1961 gave way to 1962 and independence loomed ever closer, everything changed one evening when, pounding the streets of downtown Kingston in search of the way forward, Jimmy Cliff found himself a few streets from home at 135 Orange Street, the site of an ice-cream parlor, cosmetics shop and record outlet called Beverley's, which also had real estate offices upstairs. Pots, Cecil and Leslie Kong, three Chinese Jamaicans, were the businessmen that ran the place, though no one can recall the origins of its name.

Once again, Cliff thought fast at the front door of Beverley's: if he came up with a song that made use of the name Beverley, maybe he could convince the proprietors to record him. So he started to put lyrics together in his head, based partly on a girl he knew in Somerton. Then, once the song was fully formed, he returned the following evening to present it.

"I thought, maybe if I write a song called 'Beverley's,' I could probably get my foot through the door," he recalls. "They said they are closed and I said I have a song, and they said, 'Well, we don't do recording,' and I said, 'Can you just listen?' and I forced my way in. There were three Chinese brothers there, and they said they're not into recording, and I said, 'But I think you can get into recording,' and I sang the song 'Dearest Beverley'."

When Jimmy was through, Pots and Cecil laughed out loud, but Leslie Kong's reaction was different. "I think he has the best

Award-winning producer Leslie Kong (second left), founder of Beverley's Records

voice I've heard in Jamaica," he exclaimed, telling the singer to return the next day.

On Jimmy's return, Kong said he would be happy to record him, as long as certain conditions were met. The first hurdle, he explained, was that Jimmy needed to seek out the better-established Derrick Morgan, and present the material to him. If Morgan liked it, Cliff should bring the singer back to Beverley's with him, and arrangements would be made for him to record. As an astute businessman, Kong's extra precaution had a dual purpose: if Morgan liked the singer, it meant that he was truly ready to record, and if Kong was going to take the plunge into the unknown arena of record production, it would probably be better to have an established pro on board as well, since Jimmy was still completely unknown and relatively inexperienced.

Jimmy was a big fan of Derrick Morgan, really knocked out by his song "Fat Man," which grafted Morgan's grainy rhythm-and-blues baritone atop a bolero beat. In fact Morgan's early success was one of the reasons Jimmy had first approached Duke Reid, as Morgan was then one of Reid's most successful performers.

On the ghetto grapevine Jimmy learned that Morgan lived in a big yard where Orange Street met North Street; when he approached the singer as Kong instructed, Morgan was impressed by the youth's vocal tone, and the melody of "Dearest Beverley" greatly pleased him. But Morgan pointed out that the song was unlikely to be popular because its pace was a little too sluggish; after all, the sound that was increasingly capturing the nation's imagination was ska, and the ska beat was anything but slow.

Ska was a unique hybrid that blended elements of big-band jazz and swing with Caribbean cadences to yield something uniquely Jamaican, and the unbridled optimism of its melodies and full-steam-ahead pace of its rhythm were linked to Jamaica's impending independence. The style had sprung up spontaneously at late-night jazz jams held at the Rasta camp established by master hand-drummer Count Ossie in the Wareika Hills overlooking east Kingston, through innovations fueled by gifted horn players such as the visionary but mentally unstable trombonist Don Drummond and his protégé Rico Rodriguez, as well as trumpeter "Dizzy" Johnny Moore, tenor saxophonist Roland Alphonso, guitarist Jerome "Jah Jerry" Haines, bassist Lloyd Brevette and drummer Lloyd Knibb, all of whom would eventually form the Skatalites, the premier band of the ska era.

In the late 1950s there had also been innovations in the studio, most notably by pianist and vocalist Theophilus Beckford, whose song "Easy Snappin'"was a milestone that pointed toward ska. Prince Buster, a former boxer who had broken away from Clement "Sir Coxsone" Dodd's Downbeat set to establish his own Voice of the People sound system and group of record labels, also played a big part in the development of ska, not only through the recorded material he was producing by himself and with peers such as Monty Morris and Derrick Morgan, but also through the development of the dance moves that went with the music, which mimicked household chores and specific actions such as rope-pulling or boat-rowing. As the nascent form emerged during the early 1960s its most important delineation came in accentuated after-beats, with the second and fourth beats of every measure given emphasis by staccato horn puffs or choppy guitar licks.

When Derrick Morgan complained that "Dearest Beverley" was too slow, Jimmy responded with another number called "Hurricane Hattie," a clever ditty that warned a girlfriend not to misbehave, lest he lick her with the wrath of the hurricane that had been heading for Jamaica, but which ultimately destroyed British Honduras on 31 October 1961, changing course at the last minute. Derrick and Jimmy then went back to Leslie Kong, and arrangements were quickly made for a recording session.

"He asked me, 'How does Jimmy sound?' and I told him, 'Very good,'" Morgan explains. "He said, 'What about you, you no have anything fi sing?' I say, 'Yes, I have a song named "She's Gone,"' and I told him about Drumbago and the All Star band, and he said he would like to see them. Drumbago was living right at King Street, so I went there and tell him about Leslie. Drumbago take me and Jimmy to Greenwich Farm to rehearse at a place with just a piano there; we went with the rest of the musicians and go to Federal studio the following day."

Now with a full band behind him, "Dearest Beverley" was cut as a gentle rhythm-and-blues ballad, in which Jimmy softly implored Beverley to return to him, despite his erroneous ways, the verses broken up by a lengthy saxophone solo. The same session also yielded "Cinderella," sung by Derrick's friend, Monty Morris.

Kong's second session, arranged soon after, turned out to be pivotal, as it brought forth exceptional material. On arriving at Federal, Morgan found his friend and rival, Owen Gray, putting some lyrics together; the resultant love song, "Darling Patricia," was voiced for Kong, inspiring Morgan to retaliate with the boastful "Be Still," in which he claimed to be "superior" to Gray. Morgan also voiced a song called "Sunday Monday," and Jimmy voiced "Hurricane Hattie," not quite in the mode of full-blown ska, but as an understated number with a pleasant up-tempo rhythm, Jimmy's boasts and warnings nicely framed by mouth organ and lead guitar licks.

When "Hurricane Hattie" and "Dearest Beverley" were pressed back-to-back on a single, "Hattie" was the hit that took off. "Be Still" was also massively popular, alternating with "Hattie" for the number-one position at the top of the Jamaican charts in March 1962, followed soon after by "Darling Patricia." Leslie Kong was rapidly rising as one of the island's formidable record producers, and Jimmy Cliff and Derrick Morgan played a big part in his ascendancy, as they were in charge of auditions and assisted with musical arrangements, in addition to providing the producer with hits of their own. For Jimmy, reaching the number-one spot on the charts felt like crossing a major hurdle; over the moon, he felt justified in defying his father.

Being based at Beverley's allowed Jimmy to develop his musical skills dramatically. At rehearsals and recording sessions he rubbed shoulders with highly talented musicians and singers, such as Drumbago, bassist Lloyd Mason, guitarists Jah Jerry and Dennis

Sindrey (the latter an Australian that played in the Caribs, the house band at the Glass Bucket club), pianist and arranger Theophilus Beckford, tenor saxophonists Stanley "Ribs" Notice and Roland Alphonso, alto saxophonist "Deadly" Headley Bennett and a younger peer called Lester Sterling, trumpeter Raymond Harper, and singer Frank Cosmo of the duo Cosmo and Dennis.

After moving to west Kingston, Cliff had learned some rudimentary guitar skills by hanging out at a barber shop in Trench Town, but the learning was painfully slow because Jimmy was left-handed; no one knew how to string a guitar for a lefty, so he initially tried playing upside down. Now, at Beverley's, he learned much more about the formal structure of music, as well as vocal harmony and timing.

"Beverley's had a piano at the back of the restaurant," he recalls, "and that's where I learnt to play piano. I didn't know anything about it, but Derrick Morgan was one of the first who showed me how to hold C. He said, 'See that Jimmy? That's it,' and I just picked up from there. I watched people, and we used to go to the back and rehearse. Every time that we wrote a song, we work it out on the piano; everybody get their turn to learn how to play, but some could play better than others."

As Jimmy continued honing his skills at Beverley's, he quickly became an important feature of the live music scene, thanks in part to the patronage of Edward Seaga and Byron Lee.

Seaga, a Harvard-educated anthropologist primarily of Lebanese and Scottish origin, whose parents ran a lucrative travel agency, had an unusual career trajectory that took him from anthropology to the music industry and then into politics. Despite being from the island's social elite, between 1952 and 1955 Seaga conducted field research in the remote village of Buxton Town and the west Kingston ghettos, effectively becoming part of the communities he studied for the duration, resulting in early anthologies of Jamaican folk music and African-Jamaican religious practices, issued by Smithsonian Folkways. Then, after working as a distribution agent for American record labels such as Columbia, Atlantic, ATCO and Epic, Seaga established the West Indies Records Limited recording studio as competition to Federal, issuing notable records on the WIRL label such as "Manny Oh" by Trench Town duo Joe Higgs and Roy Wilson, and "Dumplins" by Byron Lee and the Dragonaires.

As the 1950s gave way to the 1960s, Seaga abandoned business for politics, joining the JLP to represent western Kingston. Knowing that music was a crucial element that would help him to connect with his constituents, Seaga purchased Chocomo Lawn and began holding public meetings there. He also bought musical instruments and other equipment for a local band called the Victors, who would shortly evolve into the Techniques, one of Jamaica's most prominent harmony groups, and Jimmy Cliff was one of the budding young hopefuls who took part in the im-promptu live sessions backed by the Victors at Chocomo.

Although his connection to Seaga was tenuous, Jimmy's link with Byron Lee was far more concrete. Of mixed Chinese and African-Jamaican parentage, Lee was born in the village of Chris-tiana, Manchester, moving to Kingston at eight years old. The product of elite Catholic boarding schools, where he was taught music as a means of keeping him away from the female students, Lee was briefly a star soccer player before forming the Dragonaires band, one of the leading club acts of uptown Kingston.

Lee, who succumbed to cancer in 2008, claimed to have been the first person in the Caribbean to play an electric bass. He was also the man that took ska uptown to try to broaden its acceptance, which is ironic, for although his band had talented players, such as trombonist Vernon Muller, guitarist Rupert Bent, saxophonist Sammy Ismay, and three keen trumpeters led by Frank Anderson, the Dragonaires had built their reputation playing cover versions of foreign hits and middle-of-the-road material. Ska was typically frowned upon by the middle- and upper-class elite, due to its un-couth ghetto connotations, and the Dragonaires had only turned to ska after being encouraged to do so by Edward Seaga, who rec-ognized the music's unique potential as an artistic expression of independent Jamaica. Almost instinctively, Seaga understood that ska was a marketable commodity and believed that Lee was best suited to raise its profile uptown.

"Eddie Seaga, he was the politician in whose constituency ska was," Lee once explained. "He knew that the music need help, and he wanted to be the Minister of Culture who said, 'I have given you a music from the ghettos of Kingston to celebrate our sovereignty of independence.' It was 1962 when he sent us down there to study the music, because another music was around called mento, and Carlos Malcolm was playing mento, so he said, 'Carlos, you go; Byron Lee, you go.' He knew for himself that it's ska he wanted, because ska is from west Kingston."

Thus, when Byron Lee launched his ska offensive in May 1962, Jimmy Cliff joined fellow vocalists Derrick Morgan, the Blues Busters, Hortense Ellis, Tony Gregory, toaster Count Prince Miller (then riding high with his hit interpretation of Frankie Laine's novelty number "Mule Train") and harmonica player Roy Richards for a ten-date tour of theaters stretching right across Jamaica, from Annotto Bay, Port Maria, Ocho Rios and Duncans on the north coast to Savanna La Mar, Santa Cruz and Old Harbour on the south, as well as interior locations such as Linstead and Spanish Town. The Kingston dates that bookended the tour featured a number of special guests: on 25 May, at the Majestic Theater, the entourage was joined by rising vocal stars the Jiving Juniors and comedian Ranny Williams; then, at an early morning show held at the Carib on 2 June, they were joined by Lord Superior and Lord Invader, two of Trinidad's top calypsonians. The dates were all arranged by Danny Sims, a black American entrepreneur who had run a restaurant called Sapphires in Times Square, putting him into contact with entertainers such as Sidney Poitier, Harry Belafonte and Johnny Nash, the black Texan pop singer who achieved stardom in his teens. Sims eventually formed a partnership with Nash and began promoting concerts in the Caribbean through a company called Concert Artists, which regularly booked prominent dates for Byron Lee.

Two months after the first tour, toward the end of July, Jimmy was one of the featured artists on the "Twisting To Independence" revue held at four Kingston theaters, along with Alton Ellis and Eddie Perkins, Alton's sister Hortense, Higgs and Wilson, Count Prince Miller, pioneering ska trombonist Don Drummond, and saxophonist Roland Alphonso and his Upsetters, as well as dancers Persian and Gillie, with their "atomic kneecaps," and "rhumba dancer" Doreen. In August, an "Independence Jump Up" tour was arranged by Concert Artists with a similar line-up to the first, this time taking in theaters in Falmouth, Grange Hill and May Pen, and culminating in an expanded revue at the Carib on 1 August, a mere five days before the British flag was finally lowered and the black, gold and green emblem of the newly independent Jamaica was unveiled.

After the end of the island-wide independence festivities, and directly following the swearing in of Alexander Bustamante as the nation's first Prime Minister, Jimmy and his peers were part of a farewell performance for the Blues Busters, which took place at the Montego Bay Palladium on 12 August, with musical backing this time provided by the Vagabonds, another popular show band led by brothers Colsten and Phillip Chen. He also appeared with the Vagabonds on 18 September as part of a gala concert held at the Palace Theater, a farewell performance for Derrick Harriott of the Jiving Juniors (who was also traveling to the USA). Jimmy then opened for American soul giant Ben E. King at Kingston's massive State Theater the following day, and at the Tudor in Mandeville the day after. Then, on 29 September, he performed with the Vagabonds at Curphey Place for the "Summer Spectacular," another multi-band revue that also featured a fashion show.

Meanwhile, he continued recording at Beverley's, seeking a follow-up hit to "Hattie." His next single, "Miss Jamaica," a jaunty ska bridged by a trumpet solo, had Jimmy proclaiming that a girlfriend from his underprivileged neighborhood was just as beautiful as an official contest winner. Although locally popular, it did not quite reach the heights accorded to "Hattie," while the

B-side, "Gold Digger," was a risqué ditty about a girl trying to dig Jimmy's gold with her hands "deep down" in his pants, its rhythm mid-way between ska and Jamaican rhythm and blues. Another single, "I'm Free," was seemingly addressed to a controlling lover, but also referenced Jamaica's new-found independence, noting as it did that the singer was "a free man, living in a free country." "Since Lately" also decried a girlfriend's mistreatment, bolstered by a fine saxophone solo, while "My Lucky Day" placed honking ska horns over a strolling rhythm-and-blues backbeat, as Jimmy regaled the girlfriend he was fortunate to call his own.

Though Jimmy Cliff failed to find much success with these early efforts, every day at Beverley's brought valuable experience. One day a young welder called Desmond Dacres presented himself for audition. Derrick Morgan recognized him from the nearby marketplace as an orphan who had been partly raised at the Alpha Boys School, the Catholic charitable institution on South Camp Road that had been a training ground for many of Jamaica's best horn players. Jimmy was very impressed with the youth's voice, which, like Jimmy's, was high and subtle, yet held considerable power, but it still took several attempts for the teenage Dacres to pass an audition successfully. Renamed Desmond Dekker, he thus went into the studio with Jimmy, Derrick, Monty Morris, Frank Cosmo, and the duo of Andy and Joey to voice his first single, "Honor Your Mother and Father," a smash hit that went straight to the top of the Jamaican charts. Dekker quickly became an important part of the Beverley's stable, providing backing vocals on a lot of material as well as recording further hits of his own.

In addition to assisting with Dekker's career, Jimmy's input had very pertinent results after Dekker mentioned Jimmy to a co-worker who was also an aspiring singer; the totally unknown youth was none other than Bob Marley, who would later be hailed as Jamaica's most famous son and the first "Third World Superstar." As Cliff told the Experience Music Project, "Desmond Dekker went back to Bob and said, 'I've found this guy, Jimmy Cliff, and I got my songs passed, and I'm going to record, so you should go and see him.' So I was there playing the piano one day, and in walked Bob Marley, behind me, and said something like, 'That sound good.' And I knew if he could just walk in straightaway and knew it sounded good, it had to be somebody really sensitive, who had a good sense of music. He said he came to audition and told me about Desmond and sang some of his songs, and among the songs that he sang, three of them I chose, and then when Derrick come, he liked those as well, which was 'One Cup of Coffee,' 'Judge Not' and 'Terror.' And at Leslie Kong's next session, he

Derrick Morgan's farewell show

recorded those three songs. And that was the start of Bob Marley."

Unfortunately, these early singles were entirely unpopular, so Marley moved away from Beverley's, concentrating on honing his harmony skills in Trench Town with Joe Higgs. He eventually formed the Wailers, initially known as the Teenagers, with his step-brother, Neville "Bunny" Livingston, and friends Peter McIntosh, Junior Braithwaite and Cherry Green. Although Marley later emerged as a potential rival to Cliff, like Dekker he never forgot that Jimmy gave a helping hand at the very start of his career; all three remained friends despite the competitive nature of the music business.

As 1962 drew to a close, Cliff appeared on some very notable live events, of which a particular highlight was opening for legendary soul singer Ray Charles at the National Stadium on 30 October. Then, after performing a solo spot with a band called the Rivals at the Majestic on 9 December, before the screening of *The Lonely Man* (starring Anthony Perkins and Jack Palance), he formed part of the "All Star Spectacular" revue that featured on another set of dates promoted by Concert Artists, traveling to Mandeville, Linstead, May Pen and Kingston's Ritz Theater for concerts at each end of the New Year holiday, continuing to the Race Course, Duncans and Port Maria two weeks later and then on to St Ann's Bay, Savanna La Mar, Spanish Town and Old Harbour the week after, finishing on 25 January at the Majestic. Two days after, Cliff was a featured artist at the Palace Theater with the Vagabonds for a farewell performance for his friend and mentor Derrick Morgan, who was departing for London, leaving Jimmy largely on his own at Beverley's.

The gigs tapered off a bit in the early part of 1963, as Jimmy concentrated on recording, though he received top billing at the "Stars On Parade" show staged at Kingston's Deluxe Theater on 17 February with the Vagabonds, who also backed him on the concert section of an awards ceremony for Jamaica's Athletes of the Year, held at the Regal Theater on 5 March. Toward the end of May he was back on the road, traveling around the country with

Byron Lee for an eight-date tour, this time in support of "The Mighty Samson," whose "unbelievable rituals" made use of "superhuman feats of strength"; in the midst of the Samson tour, on 26 May, Cliff also did a guest spot at the Palace Theater with uptown club band Kes Chin and the Souvenirs. He was also the featured artist at the Carib with Byron Lee on 14 July, and was part of the "Independence Spectacular," featuring the Vagabonds, held at the theater on 5 August. Finally, at the end of the year, he formed part of the 1963 "Christmas Joyride" events held at the Carib on Christmas morning.

Of the handful of Jimmy Cliff singles issued by Beverley's in 1963, "King of Kings" was by far the most successful. Laden with hidden symbolism, the song had been put together in Derrick Morgan's yard through the help of a neighbor, Courtney Green, who contributed the initial concept and lyrics. Speaking of the hierarchy of jungle creatures and aided on the record by mighty roars, it venerated the lion as king in a coded reference to the Rastafarian belief system, as Haile Selassie's self-appointed title was King of Kings, Lord of Lords, Conquering Lion of the Tribe of Judah, though the reference may have been largely lost on most of his audience – indeed, Cliff concedes that his own Rastafari consciousness was "not so high" then, noting that the song also echoed a popular Kingston street phrase which stated that one needed the strength of a lion to survive.

"Derrick Morgan and Courtney, they started writing the song and said I should sing it, and I finished writing the song," he explains. "I had consciousness of Rastafari before I leave Somerton, and when I went to west Kingston at Back-O-Wall where lots of Rastas were, my consciousness became higher, but [the song] wasn't inspired because of that."

Regardless of its inspiration, "King of Kings" was certainly popular, and although it did not scale the heights achieved by "Hattie," it was another of the early hits that made Cliff a household name in Jamaica. It even sparked a reply from Prince Buster, "The Lion Roars," in which Buster claimed a speechless lion could never be

King, being one of a series of critical songs aimed at singers loyal to Leslie Kong.

Other notable Jimmy Cliff singles to surface that year included "One Eyed Jacks," a defiant number that was inspired by one of Cliff's detractors, who had burst into Beverley's during a rehearsal session to claim that the singer was washed up. Titled in reference to the popular film starring Marlon Brando, it featured an introductory snippet of racetrack commentary, because Jimmy and his peers saw the rampant competition of the Kingston music scene as similar to a frantically fought horse race. There was also "The Man," a woeful track that warned of how man's inhumanity can turn friends into murderous enemies; "You Are Never Too Old," a meditation on a mother's proverbial advice; "Miss Universe," an alternate spin on "Miss Jamaica" that again had Jimmy crowning his girlfriend; and "The Prodigal," an autobiographical track in which he spoke of longing for the home left behind in Somerton and the distant father with whom he had fallen out of favor.

Life in Kingston had never been easy, and as revealed in "The Prodigal" it pained him to be far away from his family. But soon the music would take him even farther away, the stepping stones of his career leading to other lands.

4

Ska All Over the World: First Steps outside Jamaica

As Jimmy sought to increase his status on the Jamaican music scene, ska was beginning to impact overseas. In 1963, Chris Blackwell, the wayward son of one of Jamaica's most influential families, brought a sixteen-year-old singer from Clarendon called Millie Small to England to record a ska version of Barbie Gaye's obscure 1957 R&B release "My Boy Lollipop" with Jamaican guitar genius Ernest Ranglin. Licensed to Fontana, a subsidiary of the Dutch giant Philips, the song hit the number-two position on the British pop charts and reached number one in the USA and Sweden, reputedly selling over seven million copies worldwide. Prince Buster's "Wash Wash," recorded in London with rhythm-and-blues pianist Georgie Fame, was also a huge hit in England, and a guest appearance by Byron Lee and the Dragonaires playing calypso in the James Bond film *Doctor No* accentuated Jamaican music's currency.

Taking note of the growing ska craze, Atlantic Records' founder Ahmet Ertegum traveled to Jamaica with lawyer Paul Marshall to meet with Byron Lee, Ken Khouri and Edward Seaga at Federal, where a plan was hatched to launch ska in America via a musical delegation that would perform at the New York World's Fair, with American pressings of select ska singles to be released concurrently – most notably Monty Morris's ska adaptation of the hymn "Oil in My Lamp." Seaga, then Minister for Development and Welfare as well as MP for western Kingston, knew that in addition to making good business sense, Jamaica's presence at the World's Fair was certain to be positive, as the ruling JLP was generally reaching out to the USA, presenting the island as a potential home for foreign investment as well as a highly attractive tourist destination. He naturally chose Byron Lee's Dragonaires as the backing outfit as Lee was a close friend, whose mixed features would present an acceptable face of ska, despite the fact that the Dragonaires had appropriated the form from the black ghetto players of west Kingston.

Thus, on 15 April 1964, Jimmy Cliff boarded a jumbo jet with the Dragonaires, Prince Buster, Monty Morris and Lloyd Willis (better known as Teddy Charmers, as he began his career in the Charmers duo), along with a large entourage, including JBC radio announcer Alphonso Castro, who would introduce the acts, and Ken Khouri, who was to sort out the overseas record deals. Ronnie Nasrallah, the Dragonaires' manager, made the journey so that he could teach audiences to dance the ska along with Byron Lee's girlfriend, Janet Phillips, and fellow dancers Linda Jack, Beverly Neath and Selma Blake. The guest of honor was Carol Crawford, the 1961 Miss World winner, accompanied by her mother Edna.

American audiences were given their first taste of Jamaican ska on 16 April at Shepherd's, a posh Manhattan nightclub that hosted a very elite crowd; Swedish-American actress Inger Stevens was one of the notable guests dancing the night away during the Jamaican revue. The Dragonaires' floorshow was highly choreographed, the female dancers wearing costumes modeled on the styles of countryside peasants, their skirts embroidered with "Jamaican Ska" in bold letters, while the singers wore straw hats and sports shirts. In addition to their subsequent appearance at the Caribbean Pavilion of the World's Fair, held at Corona Park in Flushing Meadows, Queens, the revue also put in an appearance at the iconic Manhattan Center on West 34th Street.

Ken Khouri and Byron Lee had already spent significant time in New York, and Prince Buster had been to Miami more than once. But for Jimmy and the rest of the young singers, New York City was endlessly fascinating, especially the impressive Manhattan skyscrapers. Jimmy was astounded to learn that buildings could reach so much higher than a coconut palm and often had his neck craned upwards.

In addition to the live appearances, one of the highlights of the trip came when Prince Buster brought Jimmy and his peers to a nightclub at 125th Street in Harlem to meet the boxer Muhammad Ali. Buster had befriended Ali in London and subsequently visited him in Miami, where the pair attended Mosque 29 of the

World's Fair hero: ska pioneer Prince Buster

Nation of Islam, the black American separatist group then led by Elijah Muhammad. Ali's influence was largely responsible for Buster's indoctrination into their politicized version of the Islamic faith, leading Buster to take the name Yusuf Muhammad Ali in deference. Now, after meeting the ska delegation in Harlem, Ali made sure to send his Jamaican friends back downtown in a big limousine, heightening their experience of stardom.

Jimmy's first encounter with the Nation of Islam intrigued him, though its significance would take time to manifest. As he recalls: "The seed of Islam was planted from when I went to New York that first time in '64 for the World's Fair. I went to Harlem and I saw a lot of shows at the Apollo, and that's where I came into contact with some black Muslims; I read one of the newspapers, *Muhammad Speaks*, and I was very inspired."

Prince Buster has said that, where business matters were concerned, there was considerable tension during this brief trip to New York, largely surrounding the penmanship and copyright of the planned American ska releases. There was also more general tension between the management and some of the featured singers, heightened by social differences relating to skin tone. But the mini-tour was ultimately hailed as a success that brought ska into the US consciousness through exposure on television and in print. Indeed, *Variety* magazine placed ska on its front cover, *Billboard* and *Record World* raved about the World's Fair revue, while *Cashbox* singled out Jimmy for particular praise, noting that he "dramatizes his singing with cartoonistic motion," as he would bend backwards like a limbo dancer while performing, even dropping to one knee at select moments when singing Otis Redding songs, his vocals all the while infused with shades of the blues.

Jimmy has said that a number of record company executives approached him after the World's Fair performances, typically through Byron Lee, but the most notable offer, which was put to the singer directly, came from Chris Blackwell, the white Jamaican entrepreneur who was doing so well with Millie Small.

"Apparently he had his eyes on me in Jamaica," Jimmy recalls, "as I was one of the promising Jamaicans that looked like they could make it at that time."

Blackwell's mother, Blanche Lindo, was from one of Jamaica's most powerful families – whose fortune stemmed from rum – while his father, Joe Blackwell, was a former member of the Irish Guards and a major in the Jamaica Regiment, distantly related to the head of the Crosse and Blackwell foods empire. Although a secure job had been arranged for Chris with accountancy firm Price Waterhouse Coopers, the young Blackwell eschewed such a tedious career to forge a path in the music industry, launching Island Records in Jamaica in 1959 and subsequently making it the home of Jamaican music in the UK after shifting base to London when Jamaica achieved independence.

As Leslie Kong was a shareholder in Island, most of the releases on the Beverley's label were issued by Island in Britain. Blackwell says he became aware of Jimmy Cliff when "Miss Jamaica" first surfaced. Sensing his star potential on that and other releases like "King of Kings," he invited Jimmy for tea one afternoon in New York and offered to bring the singer to the UK.

"He was a very strong performer and had great dance moves on stage," says Blackwell, of the singer's appearance at the World's Fair, "very much in the vein of James Brown."

Knowing of the success Blackwell had achieved overseas with Millie, Owen Gray and popular balladeer Jackie Edwards, Jimmy was interested in the offer, but was reluctant to accept as he had already set his sights on moving to America. Blackwell pointed out that America already had an endless supply of black talent. It would be easier to break Jimmy in the UK, Blackwell reasoned, where there was a great demand for black music, but not so many black artists making music, the well-established Jamaican immigrant community in Britain being an obvious potential core audience.

Blackwell's offer made good sense but, first and foremost, Jimmy had some live engagements to fulfill in the Caribbean, and plans were already in place to record material for the American market. He and the rest of the ska revue thus returned to a heroes' welcome in Jamaica, being the featured artists performing with Stranger Cole and toaster Count Machuki on 1 May at the Glass Bucket, one of uptown Kingston's most exclusive venues.

Three weeks later Jimmy voiced "Ska All Over the World" with Byron Lee at Federal along with a new version of "The Man" titled "Trust No Man," at a session that also produced a re-cut of Lord Creator's "Don't Stay Out Late," as well as "No One," an original number by the Techniques; each would feature on the album *The Real Jamaican Ska*, compiled by soul legend Curtis Mayfield of the Impressions and acclaimed producer Carl Davis, released on Columbia Records' Epic subsidiary in September, though Jimmy's broken-hearted ballad "You're the One I Need," was left off. Soul singer Major Lance was involved in the sessions as well, having been brought to Jamaica by Davis to record some ska with Billy Butler, younger brother of Jerry Butler of the Impressions; unfortunately, work permit snags prevented Billy Butler's proposed ska foray.

The following month, a female advertising executive from the William Morris Agency named Frankie Katz came to Jamaica with fashion designer Roslyn Ross to view Jimmy and other ska acts, backed by the Dragonaires and Carlos Malcolm's Afro Jamaican Rhythms, in the hopes of designing a clothing line that would complement ska. An NBC television documentary was also mooted, drawing on live footage shot at the Glass Bucket and Sombrero, as well as a beachside venue (similar footage was broadcast in the UK on ITV).

Unfortunately, the ska craze failed to maintain any kind of momentum in the States, being a momentary diversion that never really caught on. "Oil in My Lamp," for instance, only reached the Top 100 for one mere week, barely scraping in at number 98. But in Britain the reaction to ska was entirely different, as the Jamaican immigrant presence had a much more direct impact on the nation's popular culture. British audiences appreciated ska and some of Jimmy's releases were championed by the Mods, an amphetamine-fueled, fashion-conscious youth movement, including the bouncing new versions of "King of Kings" and "One Eyed Jacks" that Jimmy had recently cut with Byron Lee, this time in the faster pace of full-blown ska, with each number featuring shouted backing vocals exhorting ska dance moves. The UK release, which issued the songs back-to-back in September, made Jimmy the first Jamaican artist on the Stateside label, the subsidiary of British giant EMI, established to showcase American talent.

Meanwhile, in Jamaica, the music scene was being shaken up by the newly formed Skatalites, a ska super-group drawn from the premier set of session musicians that were largely responsible for ska's creation, led by gifted saxophonist Tommy McCook. Toward the end of June, as his new version of "King of Kings" gained currency in Jamaica, Jimmy was among the artists to join them on stage at the Cosmo Theater in Clarendon, along with Derrick Morgan, who had recently returned to the island, and a child prodigy called Delroy Wilson. Cliff was also booked to open for versatile crooner Jackie Wilson the following month, but wound up being part of a touring revue with Monty Morris and Stranger and Patsy that traveled to Port Royal, Port Antonio and Linstead. Back in Kingston, on 1 August he joined the Maytals, Hortense Ellis and others to participate in an independence gala at the National Stadium that also honored Millie Small; two days later, he participated in a free concert at Coronation Market with Drumbago's band, which attracted over two thousand people; and the following night he was at another "Independence Jump Up," at the posh La Parisienne club, with the Vagabonds and balladeer Dobby Dobson.

The approach of the Christmas season brought further important live appearances: he and Byron Lee were the featured artists at the Sombrero on 7 November; he was one of the singers at a huge free stage show held at the Chinese Athletic Club's annual garden party on 6 December; he took part in the "Nuggets For The Needy" charity concert later that month; and he competed against Tony Gregory at the "Battle of the Giants," a Christmas Eve show at the Regal Theater that pitted the Dragonaires against

Carlos Malcolm's Afro Jamaican Rhythms. He also performed for five hundred orphaned children on Christmas Day and was back at the Regal on New Year's Eve for another spectacular gala, followed by an opening spot for the American harmony stars the Drifters, again at the Regal, on 4 January.

Ska had begun to attract attention in other Caribbean territories, so, one month later, Jimmy boarded another BWIA aircraft with Byron Lee and the band – this time with the Blues Busters duo, RJR radio announcer Radcliffe Butler, and fashion models Marguerite Wilson and Olga Lindo – for four days of performances on Grand Cayman, the largest of the Cayman Islands. A Jamaican ladies' netball team also made the journey to compete with a local side. As the first ska act to reach the Cayman Islands, the greatly anticipated entourage performed five times in four days, putting in three appearances at the newly opened Club Inferno on the northwest of the island, one night at the Galleon Beach Club, Grand Cayman's largest hotel, plus a Sunday matinee for teenagers at the Tortuga Club, a posh spot on the eastern side. The performances were very well received, with locals demonstrating their familiarity with the ska, and Canadian tourists also expressing their admiration of the band's abilities. And, although there had been recent reports of Jamaican migrant workers being mistreated in the Caymans, the entourage was officially welcomed by the Cayman Islands Administrator, His Honor John D. Cumber, who pledged to bring Jamaican acts to perform at regular intervals.

Back in Jamaica, in mid-April, Jimmy appeared in the record booth at the Grand Easter Fair held at Wolmer Girls' School in aid of the Boys Brigade, along with the Blues Busters, the Maytals, Lord Creator and Ken Lazarus, all signing autographs for their fans. The following week he appeared at the Copa with Byron Lee and the Blues Busters and took part in a massive gala at the Imperial Theater, the first of seven such performances to be given across the island, backed by the Mighty Vikings, who had been voted "Band of the Year" on both RJR and JBC.

Meanwhile, Jimmy continued his tradition of nurturing upcoming talent, giving a helping hand to Roy Shirley, a youth from Trench Town with a quavering vocal style who had made an impact at local talent contests. An original song called "Shirley," which Cliff helped him put together, began a long and fruitful career for the singer upon being issued by Beverley's in 1965.

Other prominent live engagements took place during the summer months. At the end of June, Jimmy flew to Miami with Byron Lee, the Blues Busters, Ken Lazarus and Keith Lyn to perform one night at the Island Club, before heading to New York, where another night at the Manhattan Center on 2 July would be followed by a two-month residency for Byron's band at the Lake George Inn, a holiday lodge in the Adirondack Mountains, about an hour's drive north of the town of Albany. During the residency another notable per-formance was given at the Manhattan Hilton, on 7 August in honor of Jamaica's independence.

Being back in the USA was more than just a pleasure for Jimmy. In fact, his return to New York brought certain things into per-spective, making Chris Blackwell's offer seem increasingly appeal-ing. Jimmy has said that he felt stifled by his situation with the Dragonaires, particularly after some of the musicians were singled out for mistreatment. The waning of ska in America also made other record deals seem a slim option.

Thus, upon returning to Jamaica, Jimmy had an intermediary write a letter to Blackwell on his behalf, to see whether the entre-preneur was still interested in bringing him to Britain. "At the time, the person who was advising him was a priest," Blackwell remembers. "I think that was the person he trusted and counseled with, and I got the feeling he was based in the parish where Jimmy came from."

As Chris Blackwell had never doubted Jimmy's ability, he quickly confirmed that his offer was still valid. Once the arrange-ments had been duly made to bring him across the Atlantic, Jimmy packed his bags once more, this time bound for London.

5

Aim and Ambition: Arrival in England

There was much to become accustomed to when Jimmy Cliff arrived in London in late 1965. Sometimes it was difficult even to understand what people were saying, since the clipped tones of BBC English, which Jimmy had been acquainted with via the radio, were not spoken by the general public. Many sounded as though they had marbles in their mouths and some littered their speech with cryptic slang. Plenty of locals had difficulty understanding Jimmy as well. To make matters worse, the greasy, overcooked food left a lot to be desired, and the terrible cold was so chilling as to be almost unimaginable, particularly when the wind drew dampness into his very bones. But in truth, Jimmy hardly had a moment to consider such elements, for shortly after he touched down, he had to take his music out on the road.

At first glance, London was fascinating, but highly alienating. And Jimmy encountered conflict right from the start, being con-

Island giant: Chris Blackwell, founder of Island Records

fronted head-on by the all-pervasive racism that was the daily reality for black people in Britain.

"When I first came, my agent booked me into a bedsitter, but
when the caretaker saw me, she said that I oughtn't to be there,"
Jimmy told *Express* journalist Ray Connolly in 1972. "Being just
over from Jamaica and very green, I didn't know what she meant.
She said it was okay that I stayed so long as I didn't let the landlord

see me. But after a couple of weeks, the landlord came banging on my door and gave me 24 hours to get out."

He soon found more permanent digs in Earls Court, a transient area on the western edge of central London; largely populated by Australians and New Zealanders, the district also had prostitutes operating from flats by the entrances to the Underground station. Jimmy was on his own there, but not entirely alone in the capital city, as a number of Jamaican artists were still in residence, including Laurel Aitken, Owen Gray and Derrick Morgan, so Jimmy's path naturally crossed theirs from time to time as he tried to find his way in the music scene, particularly at clubs like the Roaring Twenties on Carnaby Street, a thriving dive established by a friend of Prince Buster's called Count Suckle, or, later, at the Four Aces, a ramshackle venue in the East End, run by Jamaican immigrant Newton Dunbar. Having also shifted base to the UK, the Vagabonds were making an impact as soul performers, and Jimmy Cliff would soon make an important contribution to their recorded sound, but his most regular contact was with Jackie Edwards, then chiefly employed as an Island songwriter.

In fact, Jimmy reached London just as one of Edwards's compositions reached the top of the pop charts: "Keep On Running," the driving tale of a lover's determination to win his belle's heart, was written for the Spencer Davis Group, one of the more creative of the British "beat boom" acts that were trying to revitalize rock and roll through clever arrangements incorporating shades of soul within a rock framework. Put together in Birmingham and nominally fronted by the multifaceted Davis, the band's true creative engine proved to be the talented multi-instrumentalist Steve Winwood, who tackled organ and guitar, complemented by his brother Muff on bass. The song itself was an instant hit that became their first number one when released on Fontana in November 1965.

Shortly before Jimmy's arrival, Chris Blackwell had recruited a backing act, the Phil Wainman Band, a white soul group he hoped would help build up Jimmy's fan base in Britain. Wainman, a talented drummer who toured Europe with a Mod band called the

High Grades in 1964, was briefly a member of R&B act the Paramounts, but quit a few months before Jimmy's arrival, recording the song "Hear Me a Drummer Man" as a solo artist for EMI before forming his own band with organist Mick Fletcher, bassist Ron Thomas, a guitarist called Tony, and a small horn section. In the 1970s, Wainman would find tremendous success as a producer of "glam rock" acts, but at this point he was chiefly revered as one of the first drummers to use two bass drums in his kit, a technique that was subsequently adapted by Wainman's friend Keith Moon, the drummer of premier Mod act the Who.

Wainman says Blackwell recruited him just before the release of "Keep On Running," noting that the entrepreneur was carrying a test pressing of the tune when he caught Wainman's live set one night at a West End nightclub popular with music industry personnel.

"We ended up with a residence at Dolly's Club in Jermyn Street," Wainman recalls, "and Chris Blackwell came into that club and introduced himself as the managing director of Island Records. I'd never heard of Island Records, but I mentioned a label called Sue and he said, 'I import all that stuff,' so we struck up a friendship. At three o'clock in the morning, we were still chatting, and he said to me, 'I've got this little band that I've been working on, and if I don't have a hit with this, I'm gonna lose them.' Freddy Mac was the DJ there and I asked him to play the acetate, and it was 'Keep On Running' with the Spencer Davis Group. Finally, [Blackwell] said to me, 'There's a job waiting for you, whenever you want. I'm bringing in this guy called Jimmy Cliff from Jamaica, and we'd really love you to be the band to back him and tour with him.'"

After a few short weeks of rehearsals, Jimmy and the band appeared as the opening act for blues super-group the Steampacket (featuring Long John Baldry, future actress Julie Driscoll and young Mod vocalist Rod Stewart) at London's Marquee on 10 February, billed as the Jimmy Cliff Sound, returning to the venue on the 24th. Subsequently billed as Jimmy Cliff and the New

Generation, they hit the road to spread their sound all over the country, typically delivering sets of American cover tunes.

As Jimmy recalls: "When I went to England I had to make lots of changes in my career, because Chris suggested I get my band and tour the clubs, so I got an English band and started doing that, and some of my band didn't really know how to play ska. We played R&B and blues, so I was doing a lot of things that I didn't do in Jamaica."

"We used to do all the northern clubs," Wainman recalls, "that's when 'northern soul' really kicked off, and we were very much part of that, so we would be playing the Twisted Wheel in Manchester, which was like *the* club at the time, and we were playing Barbarella's in Birmingham, and everyone would be dressed accordingly. He used to come out to 'Uptight' by Stevie Wonder, to get the place jumping, and we'd be doing [Brenton Wood's] 'Knock On Wood,' [Wilson Pickett's] 'Midnight Hour,' Sam and Dave, all the R&B hits of that time."

Although Jimmy inevitably spent much of the year traveling up and down the country with the band in a run-down van, not long after arriving in London he managed to reach the recording studio to voice his UK debut. Island's in-house producer was then Jimmy Miller, a Brooklyn-born drummer and singer-songwriter who would help Blackwell break the Spencer Davis Group in America. After being summoned to the UK following the success of the Miller-produced "Incense," credited to the Anglos, Miller took charge of Jimmy Cliff's studio work, the first recorded single being an original, broken-hearted ballad called "Pride and Passion," issued on Fontana in the spring of 1966, its B-side a restrained version of Bobby "Blue" Bland's oft-versioned "Call On Me." Both tracks featured understated brass accompaniments, subtly arranged by Les Condon, a noted jazz trumpeter who had played on "My Boy Lollipop," but neither side was particularly popular. Later in the year, a rendition of Oscar McLollie and Jeanette Baker's R&B hit "Hey Boy, Hey Girl," recorded as a duet with Millie Small, was also included on the Island album *Ska at the Jamaican Playboy Club* (along with Jimmy's "King of Kings"), but as the disc was never released in stores, being only available at the club itself, it failed to significantly widen the potential audience.

Meanwhile, through Island's management, Cliff and the New Generation opened for the Spencer Davis Group at the Marquee on 8 March, and then appeared as opening act at the start of a tour of British theaters headlined by the Spencer Davis Group and the Who, commencing 14 April at the Gaumont Cinema in Southampton, with short-lived teen group Paul Dean and the Dreamers on the same bill.

"Pete Townsend [of the Who] said he couldn't wait for the curtain to go up when he heard our band," Phil Wainman recalls. "He was a fan of the band."

Jimmy and the Spencer Davis Group were back at the Marquee on 10 May and again on 14 June, the day after Jimmy James and the Vagabonds appeared at the venue. As the months rolled on, dozens of other performances took place up and down the country. Conditions on the road were extremely basic, earnings were minimal, and despite having been signed to Island, Jimmy was left to his own devices much of the time. Even though the band sometimes enjoyed week-long engagements at venues far from London, they often traveled back to London each night after performing, returning to the venue the following day, simply to save money on hotel fees. But because of Jimmy's drive and dynamism, the performances were always very well received, which was really his main preoccupation.

"The set had to be spot-on," Wainman emphasises. "He was a perfectionist, so it had to be right. One night we got to Birmingham, and the snow was a couple of feet deep. When Jimmy arrived, he flew out onto the stage, slipped, and fell down into the footwell with the stage lights, and I think he put out three or four of them, but it didn't go quiet – he was still singing, so the man was an absolute and total professional."

Despite the hardships, Jimmy was convinced he would achieve his goals. "He used to sit at the piano and sing us his three-chord songs, and he used to say, 'Phil, it's all out there, all you've got to do is go out there and get it.' That was his whole take on the world at that time, 'Go out and get it.'"

Toward the end of the year, after Jimmy provided backing vocals with Doris Troy on *The New Religion*, the second studio album by Jimmy James and the Vagabonds, Island Records placed advertisements in the music press to recruit a new backing band for Jimmy Cliff. Jimmy felt that things were stagnating with the New Generation, and certain incidents hastened his break with the band.

"We were playing in a beach hut in Grimsby," notes Wainman, "which was packed to the rafters with about eight hundred people; we used to play there once a month, because Jimmy went down an absolute storm up there. We used to stay in digs not very far away, and on top of the wardrobe, we found a black doll with curly hair and a black face, and we said, 'It's Jimmy's baby!' So we stuck it in bed with him when he was fast asleep, and about five or six in the morning, we could hear him cursing away. We didn't know, but Jimmy was a very religious person, so he smashed it to bits."

After a further dispute involving van repairs, things later soured completely, ultimately ending Jimmy's association with the New Generation. The new outfit to make the cut in the autumn of 1966 was the Shakedown Sound, a group of young West Country musicians known for a time as Lee Starr and the Astrals, then featuring drummer Sean Jenkins, guitarist Kevin Gammond, bassist John Best (aka Lee Starr) and organist Terry Allen (later known as Verden Allen). Although Jimmy was not alerted to the fact, Best was normally the group's lead singer and was not really a bassist, but as their regular bassist, John Leaver, was too young to travel, Best taught himself enough to fill in.

A few days after their successful audition, Jimmy and the band piled into another dilapidated van and headed across the English Channel to Paris, where they pitched up at the Hotel Ventimille, near Place du Clichy. Unfortunately, the journey destroyed the vehicle, forcing Island to send a replacement.

"Jimmy was on the verge of going back to Jamaica when he put the ad in and we turned up," says Terry Allen. "He wasn't sure whether to have us or not and we only knew three numbers when we got there. When the van blew up, he was shouting and bawling, but if I told him that the van wasn't any good, he probably wouldn't have gone."

Nevertheless, the group enjoyed a successful six-week residency at a lively nightclub in Montmartre (which also served as their rehearsal space), hitting the packed venue with rousing versions of soul hits such as Otis Redding's "It's Growing" and Percy Sledge's "When a Man Loves a Woman," along with a few of Jimmy's originals, like "King of Kings," added to the set once Jimmy had taught the band how to ska. With soul as the main medium, there was no problem with language differences for potential French fans, and since Jimmy choreographed the performances as well, getting John Best and Kevin Gammond to run back and forth across the stage in parallel with his own movements, the young French hipsters that flocked to the venue were typically screaming for more. A highlight of the tenure in Paris came in late September, when they shared the stage of the noted Alhambra club with Bill Haley and the Comets and the Spencer Davis Group, which helped widen their potential audience.

Having perfected their live act in Paris, the band returned to London, where the musicians rented a flat in Muswell Hill. Soon they were traveling all over the UK, often doing several performances at different locations on the same night.

"Jimmy was such a showman that I couldn't wait to get back to play, just to show off a little bit," Allen explains. "I remember we played at the Alhambra in Paris with the Spencer Davis Group, then we came back and played Kitchener's in Kidderminster, and we used to play in the Café des Artists in London, at the bottom end of King's Road. We used to do nine bookings a week, do allnighters at a nightclub in Leicester, and then go and do another gig afterwards in London. Plus, we would be up in the day, playing at the Birmingham Ice Rink, and then we'd go to another gig in the night. We were lucky to even have a day off!"

Toward the end of December, they headed back across the Channel for a series of gigs around France, including an appearance at the massive Eden Ranch in Loison-sous-Lens, near Lille, then a favorite haunt of British bands, as well as the Voom Voom club in St Tropez and other venues in Valbonne and Nice, reaching Corchevel in the French Alps at Christmas time.

Back in the UK in January 1967, they played to a packed house at the Black Horse in Hereford on the 19th, and soon started attracting the attention of the rock aristocracy, notably when opening for the Jimi Hendrix Experience at the Beachcomber Club in Nottingham on the 14th. Hendrix was also a southpaw who played his guitar upside down, the same way Jimmy used to string his axe when he first learned to play in Trench Town, but Hendrix's command of the instrument was awesome, so Cliff was particularly pleased to make his acquaintance after Hendrix attended other Shakedown Sound performances.

"We done the Dungeon Club in Nottingham and Jimi Hendrix was there, and the Beachcomber after that," says Terry Allen, "and then we played in the Bag O'Nails, in the West End, and there was all sorts of people there: Hendrix, the Stones, Lulu, the Animals, and two of the Beatles."

As interest in Jimmy Cliff continued to grow, through his ecstatic live performances and a regular residency at the Flamingo on Wardour Street, getting back into the recording studio was crucial. Although he voiced plenty of demos with the Shakedowns at Marquee Studios, the tracks were rejected by Jimmy Miller, who opted to use other session musicians to back Jimmy at Olympic Studios, where Hendrix and the Rolling Stones were also recording. The sound they were aiming for was one that would rival Geno Washington and the Ram Jam Band, a group led by a former soldier from Indiana, their full horn section helping make them one of London's most popular soul acts – so Miller made sure that brass players were also on board.

Jimmy Cliff's next single was the most momentous of his early days in Britain. "Give and Take," written during his last trip to

France and released on Island at the start of February, was an upbeat soul original that spoke of the reciprocal nature of love, marked out by bright horn blasts, while its B-side, "Aim and Ambition," was a slower soul groove with a choppy piano backline, that related Jimmy's determination to succeed. The buoyancy of "Give and Take" made it a favorite of the pirate radio stations that were broadcasting from ships to circumvent Britain's restrictive licensing laws, and when the song reached the Top 50 in the influential *Disc* music magazine it seemed that Jimmy was poised for a major breakthrough. But the glory proved short-lived. First, the government clamped down on the pirates, losing the single badly needed airplay; then, *Disc* magazine shortened their chart to include only 30 entries, and Jimmy's single somehow got lost in the shuffle, despite a televised miming performance of it on Germany's *Beat Club*.

"I was trying very hard to get him going in England," recalls Chris Blackwell, "and he came very close because of 'Give and Take.' It was moving up the chart and they cut their Top 50 to Top 30, and then it didn't make it into the Top 30. I remember that being a big disappointment."

Jimmy's next Island single, issued in May, was "I've Got a Feeling (and I Can't Stop)," a driving rhythm-and-blues love song, co-written by Jackie Edwards and Jimmy Miller, featuring a swirling organ and fully orchestrated horn section arranged by noted trad-jazz pianist Stan Butcher. Hidden away on the B-side was "Hard Road to Travel," a slowly creeping soul original with a spacious bass line, bluesy guitar riffs, mournful horn notes and staccato piano chords, giving it a rhythmic structure and pacing not entirely unlike "Time Is On My Side," Irma Thomas's 1963 soul number, which was a big hit when covered by the Rolling Stones the following year. Although largely inspired by his experience of racism, when his landlord gave twenty-four hours' notice, the song's title and repeated refrain were based on the lines of a Pentecostal hymnal:

It's a hard road to travel and a mighty long way to go
But Jesus the blessed Saviour will lead me all the way I know.

Over many a lonesome valley, where many dark waters flow,
It is a hard road to travel and a mighty long way to go.

On this initial version of "Hard Road to Travel," Jimmy's vocal recalled one of the emotive outpourings of Otis Redding or Wilson Pickett, his restrained delivery relating the desolation and emptiness he faced in an alien land so unlike that of his birthplace, where obstacles were many and he had little to take for granted. But the song's ultimate message, despite the allusion to faith, was one of self-determination, for whatever barriers might be in his way, he was certain that his goals were attainable.

Although "Give and Take" was by far his most successful single, when Jimmy's debut album was issued by Island, it bore the title *Hard Road to Travel*, perhaps because the song best summed up what Jimmy's music was all about. The front cover showed Jimmy in a pensive mood, clad in a brown leather jacket, white trousers and matching white boots, sitting forlornly against a chain-link fence, while the back had him flashing some intricate dance moves. In addition to the six sides that made up his first three singles, the album also contained "Your Reward," a driving original that again spoke of the terrible hardships one faced while striving to achieve greatness, and a lighter romantic number called "Let's Dance."

Unfortunately, a few cover tunes lacked conviction. Jimmy's take of Bobby Moore and the Rhythm Aces' "Searchin' for My Baby" was probably the most credible, but on his rendition of "Can't Get Enough of It," a Spencer Davis Group B-side, the hard-rocking rhythm sounds at odds with Jimmy's voice. Worse still was the overproduced cover of the Supremes' "All I Know About You" and, strangest of all, a faltering, guitar-free rendition of Procol Harum's Bach-influenced "A Whiter Shade of Pale," cut at Pye Studios, the only number on the album, incidentally, to feature the Shakedown Sound.

As Island Records was issuing select material through United Artists in the USA, *Hard Road* was later repacked for the American market as *Can't Get Enough of It* on UA's Veep subsidiary, with

"Whiter Shade of Pale" and "Searchin' for My Baby" replaced by the organ-led, rock-oriented tracks, "That's the Way Life Goes" and "Thank You." The songs, which were issued in October on an Island single in the UK and on Fontana in Europe, were produced by Muff Winwood, who had switched to A&R work after his brother Steve left the Spencer Davis Group to form Traffic. Using another chain-link fence photo, this time framed by multicolored 3-D squares, the Veep release likened Jimmy to Otis Redding, James Brown, Sam Cooke and Solomon Burke, but the comparisons failed to spark interest with US audiences.

Meanwhile, the Shakedown Sound were undergoing some changes, as Kevin Gammond quit to join Robert Plant's Band of Joy and was replaced by Mick Ralphs. Jimmy and the group played at the Plebeians Jazz Club in Halifax on 13 May, and when they enjoyed a residency at the Red Hill Ballroom in Hereford, Jimmy stayed with Terry Allen's parents for a week. On 1 June, with a full horn section in tow, they played before eight thousand spectators at the first International Festival of Pop Music, held at the Palais des Sports in Paris. The festival, which was later broadcast on French television, also featured notable British rock and pop acts such as Cream, the Troggs, the Pretty Things, the VIPs, John

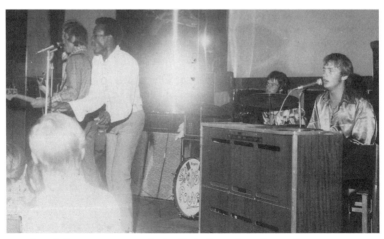

Hard road: live in Europe with the Shakedown Sound, 1976

Walker, Ronnie Bird and Dave Dee, Dozy, Beaky, Mick and Tich. Then, at the end of the summer, Jimmy was one of the featured acts at a packed all-nighter held on 8 September at the Chateau Impney, near Droitwich in Herefordshire, and on the 30th, he played at one of the last live events held at the Mojo Club in Sheffield, run by noted promoter Peter Stringfellow and his brother Geoff.

On 14 December, during another all-nighter at the Chateau Impney, Jimmy shared the stage with the Wynder K Frogg Band, featuring recent Island signee Mick Weaver, aka Wynder K Frogg, on Hammond organ. The group then also included bassist Alan Spenner, drummer Keith Rowland, guitarist Neil Hubbard (all active members of the backing band of Sheffield-born blues rocker Joe Cocker) and saxophonist Chris Mercer, along with a vibrant Ghanaian percussionist and sometime Traffic member called Rebop Kwaku Baah, whose rhythmic flourishes gave the group an added dimension. In early February 1968, two nights after Jimmy and the Shakedowns' appearance at the Grantham Catbalou on the 2nd, the Frogg Band and Jimmy again shared the stage at London's School of African and Oriental Studies.

As the two acts were increasingly on the same stage, and as both were signed to Island, it made sense for Cliff to recruit the Wynder K Frogg Band when things went pear-shaped with the Shakedown Sound, so soon Frogg was backing Jimmy all over the country. They hit the Marquee on 5 March, opening for Jimmy James, later performing at a venue in Malvern and at the Queen Mary Ballroom (located at Dudley Zoo in the West Midlands), reaching Glastonbury Town Hall on 4 May. Somewhere along the way, Mick Weaver actually left the band to pursue other interests, being replaced by a London College of Music graduate from Bristol called Derek Austin.

Although his live sets were almost always well received, Jimmy's debut album did not create much interest on either side of the Atlantic. After the great disappointment of "Give and Take," which had brought him to the edge of stardom without actually taking him across its threshold, both Jimmy and Island were really striving for a major breakthrough. Duets with Jackie Edwards, "Set Me Free" and "Here I Come' "made no impact when issued in June, and although "That's the Way Life Goes" was entirely unnoticed, Jimmy and Muff Winwood tried again with a cover of "Waterfall," an obscure pop song by an Island act called Nirvana, a psychedelic rock outfit that sometimes incorporated elements of baroque chamber music in their work, their phaser-laden song "Rainbow Chaser" reaching the UK Top 40 in May. More pop-oriented than anything he had tackled previously, Jimmy's version of "Waterfall," issued on an Island single in July (with "Reward" on the flip), featured full orchestration arranged by noted television composer Syd Dale, but the song sold poorly in the UK, its blatant commercialization and puffed-up production values failing to find a ready audience. Island felt that they were running out of options with Jimmy, while Jimmy felt that Island were not giving him the proper support to facilitate his climb to the next level.

"After some time in England touring, I hadn't met as much success as I had anticipated," Jimmy explains.

"Everything was in limbo a little bit," adds Chris Blackwell, "because one didn't really know where to go next."

Then, in late September 1968, an invitation came for Jimmy to travel to Brazil to participate in another international song contest, this time representing Jamaica. His first visit to South America would lead to all kinds of personal awakenings, providing exactly the kind of new inspiration that was so badly lacking in Britain.

6
Wonderful World, Beautiful People: South American Revitalization

When Jimmy Cliff reached Rio in late September 1968, he found a startlingly beautiful place, riven by irreconcilable contradictions. South America's largest nation had been ruled by a repressive military dictatorship for the last four and a half years, and although its foreign ministers were making diplomatic overtures outside the country, things were less straightforward for trade unionists or those expressing criticism artistically. Singers were especially suspect and vocalists that dared to challenge traditional mores, such as Gilberto Gil and Caetano Veloso, the leading lights of the Tropicália movement, would soon find themselves behind bars. In tandem with the repressive regime was a paradoxical economic boom, stemming largely from oil refining and mining concerns, yet hordes of the nation's rural poor continued to stream into urban areas, resulting in gigantic slums on the outskirts of most cities.

At first glance, Rio's ethnic make-up was also startling, as every shade and hue under the sun seemed present, but, unlike Kingston, there were more Brazilians of European descent clearly visible, compared to those with African ancestry. In fact, Rio felt almost like a tropical version of a European city, so it was all too clear to Jimmy that black people held a lower status in the social hierarchy. However, despite great differences in language, custom, culture and topography, there were aspects that reminded him of Jamaica, in the way that the women held rhythm in their hips on streets that pulsated with music, noise and energy. After so many months of cold, dark, uncertainty in anonymous London, arriving in Rio sparked a reawakening that reached the very depths of his soul.

Rio's third International Song Festival culminated in performances given at the Maracanãzinho Stadium on 28 September, before an audience of twenty thousand people. The European nations were fully represented, as were the USA, Canada, Mexico, Japan and Brazil. Most of the thirty-three entrants were totally unknown to the Brazilian public, though Paul Anka, who placed second, was somewhat familiar, as was Françoise Hardy of France.

Despite delivering an impressive performance of "Waterfall," backed by local musicians, Jimmy failed to place in the competition, but "Waterfall" somehow became a hit in Brazil, reaching the number-two position on the pop charts. "Waterfall" held great appeal for Brazilian audiences that were enthralled by the Tropicálistas' melding of psychedelic rock and soul influences with Brazilian samba and bossa nova. Brazil embraced Jimmy through "Waterfall," ultimately initiating a creative rebirth.

"When I went to Brazil, the people really loved me there, and it's like my whole career turned around," Jimmy explains. "I was inspired, due to the fact that they loved me in Brazil, so I started writing a lot of new songs."

His original intention was to spend ten days in Brazil, but the success of "Waterfall" and the incredible reaction of the Brazilian public led to an extended stay of over two months. In addition to the lyrics he was crafting, Cliff also went into a recording studio to cut some individual cover tunes of Brazilian hits, at the invitation of noted record executive Andre Midani, who appointed Nonato Buzar, an in-house producer for Polygram Brazil and pioneer of the relaxed "pilantragem" ("roguishness") vocal style, to oversee production. According to Buzar, the idea was to assemble an album that would merge the most potentially appealing of Jimmy's British recordings with new renditions of Brazilian pop songs. Jimmy selected a handful that he liked, which were duly

Innovative producer Nonato Buzar, arranger of Jimmy Cliff in Brazil

recorded with session players, though not all made the final cut. Once the lyrics had been translated into English, they were given additional poetic touches by Paul Anka and noted Broadway lyricist Sammy Cahn, who had attended the festival with Anka. The result was an album released in Brazil by Philips under the unimaginative title *Jimmy Cliff in Brazil.*

The album, its cover showing a delighted Jimmy on a Rio beach with the iconic Sugar Loaf Mountain behind him, opened with "Serenou" ("Calmed"), an up-tempo, orchestrated version of a traditional ring-game song about the morning dew, which Jimmy sang in Portuguese, backed by a harmonic chorus. There was also "With You, Without You," a rollicking soul ballad written by prominent bossa nova composers Edson Trindade and Antonio Carlos Duncan. "Andança (Me Leva Amour)" ("Travel [Leads Me to Love]") was a fitting choice of cover tune as it was the debut offering from Beth Carvalho, whose singing career was launched through her performance of the song at the festival; describing the protagonist's long sorrowful walk to a lover, the pace was speeded up for Jimmy's version, injecting a soul sensibility into what became an English duet between Jimmy and fledgling star Regininha, retaining its emotive expressiveness in a new framework. Buzar's "Vesti Azul" ("I Wore Blue"), here recast in English as "She's Something Else," was the most inspired choice, as it had been a huge hit the previous year for Winston Simonal, one of the first black Brazilian performers to gain widespread popularity. According to Buzar, Jimmy's rendition of "Vesti Azul" was also popular in Brazil.

Along with five earlier numbers from *Hard Road/Can't Get Enough of It* and the "Waterfall" hit, the album also included a spirited new track with full orchestral arrangement, "Hey Mister Yesterday," which implored the protagonist to get himself together and move on. Though ostensibly directed at one abandoned by a lover, it was symptomatic of Jimmy's general frame of mind, as he knew he needed to break with the stagnant past of England to move forward.

Jimmy was determined not to return to the UK without some hit material, so instead of heading back to London he traveled extensively throughout South America, performing to ecstatic audiences and constantly writing new songs. First he traveled to Chile, where the press hailed him as "the electric Jamaican"; in Argentina, his television appearances were so highly popular that he wound up with his own twenty-minute show, broadcast for three weeks straight on a national station. After further performances in Uruguay, Colombia, Panama and Mexico, he went back to Jamaica in early 1969 with an album's worth of new material to present to Leslie Kong, and enough money to purchase his first house.

Life back on the island was initially troublesome: he had left as a ska star of tremendous importance to seek greater fame abroad, but returned as a relative unknown whose accent and ways now marked him as a foreigner. And during Jimmy's time in London, Jamaican music had undergone dramatic changes. First, the furious pace of ska had slowed to the cooler and more spacious sounds of rock steady, a leisurely and less-cluttered dance music that took Jamaica by storm shortly after Jimmy left the island. Rock steady used smaller studio ensembles, often with American harmony groups such as the Impressions as role models, for smoothly atmospheric songs of romance, as well as numbers bemoaning the "rude boy" street toughs whose uncontrolled violence was increasingly problematic.

Then, just before Jimmy's return, a startling new sound took hold in late 1968, based on choppy organ chords and staccato guitar licks. Though the classic reggae style would later be even slower and more roomy than rock steady, its initial bursts were frantic, jumbled affairs that thoroughly appealed to Jamaica's dancing public.

The top band of the rock steady era was the Supersonics, a group of exceptional musicians whom Tommy McCook put together as the house band at Duke Reid's Treasure Isle studio, following the demise of the Skatalites. One of the band's defining players was bassist Jackie Jackson, who became the key element of the most in-demand reggae session group, known initially as the Beverley's All Stars, because Leslie Kong was the first to request them for sessions. Other notable members included pianist Gladdy Anderson, who was also the chief arranger, and organist Winston Wright, occasionally supplanted by Neville Hinds or Theophilus Beckford. Of the various drummers, Winston Grennan was one of the most creative, though an army camp veteran known only as Drummie was often in his place, as well as the younger Paul Douglas. Hux Brown was one of the group's most expressive guitarists, along with reliable players Radcliffe "Dougie" Bryan and Ranny Bop, while the gifted Trinidadian migrant Lynn Taitt also occasionally contributed. Collectively, these players were responsible for countless hits for various producers, not least of all for Kong himself, being featured on all-time classics such as Desmond Dekker's "Israelites" and "Ah It Mek," the Melodians' "Sweet Sensation" and the Maytals' "Monkey Man," to name but a few.

Harnessing these musicians during their prime at the studio formerly known as WIRL but now called Dynamic Sounds – the best-equipped recording facility in the entire Caribbean region following Byron Lee's acquisition and refurbishment of it – Jimmy set to work on the album that would bring his career to the next level, particularly for audiences outside Jamaica. It also healed his rift with Chris Blackwell, as Leslie Kong convinced Cliff that Blackwell was best placed to issue the material overseas. Jimmy thus traveled to New York with the unmixed master tapes to meet with Blackwell, who was very impressed by what he heard. Blackwell drafted in the gifted arranger Larry Fallon to help shape the final product with slight orchestral arrangements for the most radio-friendly numbers, then standard practice when aiming material toward a wider overseas audience. Several numbers also featured gospel-tinged backing vocals, giving them a more soulful dimension, and after Blackwell requested another number to complete the album, a non-reggae track was even built from scratch in New York with the Swampers (drummer Roger Hawkins, bassist Dave Hood, guitarists Tippy Armstrong and

Jimmy Johnson, and keyboardist Barry Becket), session players from Muscle Shoals, Alabama, who were often used by Jerry Wexler for Atlantic Records' hit releases.

As Island Records was becoming increasingly associated with rock music, Blackwell delegated the UK issue of the album to Trojan, the grassroots reggae label aimed at the Jamaican immigrant community, which he initially established as an Island subsidiary, but which was now being run chiefly by his former London landlord, an Indian-Jamaican accountant called Lee Gopthal. In the USA, Blackwell was now channeling material through A&M, the independent label founded by trumpeter Herb Alpert and his business partner, Jerry Moss. Trojan's late 1969 issue bore the eponymous title *Jimmy Cliff*, the album's front cover showing Jimmy with an ivory snaggletooth around his neck, while the better-known A&M release, issued in January 1970, appeared as *Wonderful World, Beautiful People*, showing a defiant-looking Cliff in a fringed leather vest, standing before an image of a giant hand making a peace sign.

One of the songs Jimmy wrote in Brazil, "Wonderful World, Beautiful People" spoke of the need to move beyond the petty squabbles that were keeping people apart from each other, ultimately calling for the unification of all mankind to aid the betterment of humanity. To emphasize the urgency of the message, toward the end of the song Jimmy directly addressed world leaders by name, including US President Richard Nixon, British Prime Minister Harold Wilson, and French President Georges Pompidou. Following an appearance at the UK's first Caribbean Music Festival, held at the Empire Pool in Wembley on 21 September 1969, with Jimmy second on the bill below Johnny Nash, the single reached the number-six position in the UK pop charts on 25 October, remaining in the charts for a full three months; it reached number 25 in the US charts shortly thereafter, making it among the very first Jamaican recordings widely aired outside Jamaica. It also reached the Jamaican pop charts in January 1970 and surfaced on a Philips single in Uruguay as "El Bello Mundo de la Bella

Gente," with Cliff singing the lyrics in Spanish. Parisian pop star Claude François even cut a French version for Philips as "Le Monde Est Grand, les Gens Sont Beaux."

In March 1970, "Come Into My Life," an entreaty to a reluctant paramour that featured a strong female chorus, also reached the US Top 100, as well as the Jamaican Top 10, just as "Vietnam" reached the UK Top 50. This hard-hitting number, marked out by an organ melody and rim-shot drumbeats, described a soldier's tragic death shortly before the end of his conscription, incongruously backed on a Trojan single by the sensuous "She Does It To Me Right." "Vietnam" proved highly influential among the rock and folk aristocracy, with Bob Dylan reportedly rating it an exceptional protest song and Paul Simon being inspired to travel to Jamaica to cut "Mother and Child Reunion" with the same backing band, after being turned on to the track by Dylan. Later, the Rolling Stones, folk-rock troubadour Cat Stevens, and soul singer Roberta Flack would follow suit, heading to Dynamics to capture some of the magic that permeated *Wonderful World*.

The rest of the album was thoroughly excellent. There was a new, up-tempo version of "Hard Road to Travel," now in the more fitting meter of full-throttle reggae. The opening number, "Time Will Tell," was a driving track that flashed back to the singer's youthful days and the lessons life had taught him along the way, while "Use What I Got" was another number that spoke of Jimmy's determination to use his God-given talents to succeed, despite whatever obstacles lay in his path. Like the title track, "Suffering in the Land" referenced many of the world's terrible inequalities, while Jimmy's rendition of Lou Rawls's "My Ancestors" was given extra depth through its vibrant percussion, heightening the message of the lyrics. The weakest link in the chain was probably "That's the Way Life Goes," its rock orientation and swirling organ sounding somewhat out of place with the rest of the disc. But a truly outstanding moment was provided by "Many Rivers to Cross," a stunning ode to determination, that stemmed from the years of frustrating toil in London; the extra track put together in New York at Blackwell's request, the song had been half-written considerably earlier, but was only properly completed while Jimmy was on the way to the studio to record it. The song's exceptional atmosphere came through the chilling organ chords and blues guitar of the Muscle Shoals players, being a particularly fine example of all that Jimmy was capable of, though it would not really enter the public's consciousness for quite some time.

Wonderful World, Beautiful People brought Jimmy Cliff to another level of popularity, the acclaim that had so long been denied him arriving at last. And there were other successes along the way, as Cliff's song-writing skills yielded hits for his peers at Beverley's Records, first through Desmond Dekker's popular version of Jimmy's determined "You Can Get It If You Really Want," which peaked at number three in the British charts in August 1970 (totally surpassing the original, which Trojan issued in June), just as Jimmy's masterful version of Cat Stevens's "Wild World" was competing with it for chart space. An inspired collaboration between the two singers, "Wild World" sounded almost as if it had been written for Jimmy and was given further credibility by Stevens' keen musical arrangement and piano playing. The song reached the number-eight position in the UK charts in September, and might have done as well in the USA had its popularity not been eclipsed by Stevens's own version. The B-side, "Be Aware," pointed to the spiritual questioning that was increasingly on Jimmy's mind as he strove to find greater truth and meaning.

With Dekker's version of "You Can Get It If You Really Want" reaching the pop charts, Jimmy was given another major boost on 8 August when he topped the Split 70 Light Music Festival in Yugoslavia, winning the $4,160 first prize for his performance of a sentimental original called "The Song We Used to Sing," the basis of another Top 10 hit for Desmond Dekker when he covered it toward the end of the year.

Traveling between Kingston and London, with side trips to New York and Miami as required, Jimmy recorded diverse singles throughout 1970. One of the most notable numbers was an expressive cover of Swamp Dogg's critical "Synthetic World" that Jimmy recorded at Miami's Criteria studio, again backed by the Muscle Shoals players, with former Yardbirds bassist Paul Samwell-Smith sharing production duties with Blackwell (who was credited under the alias John Kelly). Issued on an Island single in November with a sloppy soul track, "I'll Go to Pieces," the song unfortunately failed to make any impact.

Although *Wonderful World, Beautiful People* provided the breakthrough he had long been searching for, Jimmy knew that the pop world was fickle, and the future somehow seemed very uncertain. Still seeking to reach the kind of solid footing that was only afforded one who had truly made it, he pondered on exactly which way to turn. The catalyst would ultimately come from a most unexpected place, and the process was anything but immediate.

7

The Harder They Come: From Muscle Shoals to the Silver Screen

In the latter half of 1970, Jimmy Cliff was back at Dynamics, fine-tuning a follow-up album to *Wonderful World, Beautiful People* that would lead with the hit single "Wild World." Though the album was eventually shelved, it was during its construction that Cliff first met Perry Henzell, a white Jamaican filmmaker, who asked whether the singer thought he could provide the music for a film he was planning.

"What do you mean, 'think'?" replied Jimmy incredulously. "I can do anything."

An unorthodox, intuitive and intensely creative person, Henzell was raised twelve miles outside Kingston on the Caymanas sugarcane estate, one of the last bastions of the plantocrats, who had held significant economic power in Jamaica since slavery days, but, like many prominent Jamaicans, Henzell's background was complex.

Publicity poster for The Harder They Come

His paternal grandfather, descended from wandering Huguenot glassblowers who had fled France after suffering religious persecution, married into an old Antiguan family involved in sugar production, but although he was part of Jamaica's social elite, Henzell rejected his privileged status early.

Like his friend Chris Blackwell, Henzell was sent to an exclusive English boarding school, but absconded to hitchhike round Europe. Presenting himself at the BBC to gain directorial experience, he was saved from outright rejection by working as a stagehand, and on returning to Jamaica in the late 1950s he began directing commercials, initially for cinema and later for Jamaican television. As early as 1966, after making over two hundred commercials, some of which featured non-acting street people, he set out to create "a little crime film set in Jamaica" that would use an entirely Jamaican cast, gradually convincing leading Jamaican dramatist Trevor Rhone to come on board as co-writer.

Henzell was first drawn to Cliff after seeing the *Jimmy Cliff* album cover, in which Jimmy appeared a tough, rebellious winner on the front, and a forlorn sufferer on the back. The film he envisaged would update the tale of Rhyging – aka Ivanhoe Martin, aka Ivan Brown – the "two gun killer," a notorious Jamaican gangster who became a legendary anti-hero for evading capture and taunting police, despite engaging in rape, murder and wanton violence during the late 1940s.

Recasting Ryging in contemporary times, Henzell turned him into an aspiring reggae singer. He originally had Johnny Nash in mind for the part, but was pointed elsewhere by Island staffer Esther Anderson, a Jamaican-born actress who was a confidante of Henzell and a former girlfriend of Chris Blackwell (and who was later romantically linked with both Bob Marley and Marlon Brando). Anderson had been giving Jimmy managerial assistance for a time, and suggested that he was the natural choice for the lead, so about four months after their initial meeting, Henzell sent the singer a screenplay via Blackwell. When Jimmy then passed a screen test, he was officially cast as Ivan O. Martin, Rhyging's reggae reincarnation, in a film that was provisionally entitled *Hard Road to Travel* and ultimately released as *The Harder They Come*.

After more recording work in Miami (where he put the finishing touches to an album that was given a catalogue number by A&M, but not released), Jimmy returned to Jamaica on 8 October to await the start of the film production, which began toward the end of the month for an initial period of six weeks. It would take over a year for the filming to be completed, the production being a stop-start affair as funding was often a problem. Although Henzell told Jimmy that he needed to lose the cockney twang cultivated in London, the singer slipped right into his screen role. Indeed, since many of Ivan's experiences matched those of his own, Jimmy was a natural for the part; he influenced the outcome of several scenes by using spontaneous dialogue and actions, drawing on events from his own life.

During a break in the filming, Jimmy made a few notable live appearances at select high-profile events, including top billing at

"Skating with the Stars," held at Kingston's Skateland on 5 December. He was also among the dozens of acts that appeared at Jamaica's first Pop Swingaree, a three-day musical marathon held at the Island Inn Hotel in Ocho Rios the following weekend.

Apart from working on the film, early 1971 saw the issue of a number of singles aimed at different markets. These included the nostalgic Trojan release "Those Good, Good Old Days," backed by a rock-oriented track called "Pack Up Hang Ups," whose musical arrangement was reminiscent of a Rolling Stones song. On Beverley's, there was "Going Back West," a cross-genre tale of the perils of the music industry, issued with the broken-hearted "My World Is Blue" (later covered by Desmond Dekker), and, best of all, a sublime roots reggae recording called "Bongo Man," a percussion-filled ode to Prince Emmanuel Edwards that held all the energy of a Rastafari niyabinghi "groundation," in which oppressive forces are attacked through drumming and chanting.

"After I had a hit with 'Wonderful World,' I found out the best thing for me to do was to keep going back and forth to Jamaica to do my recording, because I get the feeling there," Jimmy explains. "So 'Bongo Man' came out of one of those recordings. Niyabinghi music was something that I had been into since I lived in west Kingston, when Prince Emmanuel was at Back-O-Wall, and my Rastafarian influence grew from those times, especially with the drums."

Although "Bongo Man" reached the Jamaican charts, its UK release on Trojan's Summit subsidiary failed to have an effect, perhaps partly because it bore Jimmy's given name, James Chambers. But if such songs were unjustly overlooked at their time of issue, Jimmy could rest safe in the knowledge that his songwriting and production skills continued to bear fruit for his peers at Beverley's, with Millie Small's take on a song Jimmy had written, "Honey Hush," being a minor local hit in 1970, followed by Desmond Dekker's version of "The Song We Used to Sing," which went down well in Britain, while the Pioneers' rendition of Jimmy's "Let Your Yeah Be Yeah" ultimately became one of the biggest British reggae hits of 1971.

The overall goal was still a greater permeation of overseas audiences, and, after noting the keen artistic result on "Many Rivers to Cross," Chris Blackwell hatched a plan to bring Jimmy to Muscle Shoals itself, so that the singer could craft an album making use of the studio's session players within their own natural habitat. Jimmy thus traveled to Alabama in May 1971 to begin working at Muscle Shoals studio on the *Another Cycle* album, bringing with him songwriter and co-producer Guillermo Bright-Plummer, aka Guilly Bright, a Panamanian of Jamaican extraction who Jimmy had recently met at a song contest held in Mar del Plata, Argentina; at the event, Jimmy placed tenth with "Another Cycle," facing stiff competition from former Beatle John Lennon, LA rock favorites the Doors, Canadian folk-rock vocalist Joni Mitchell, Australian pop hopeful Olivia Newton-John and Catalan folk singer Maria Del Mar Bonet.

When the album surfaced on Island in September, *Another Cycle* saw Jimmy heading in different directions. There was gospel, bluegrass, country-tinged rock, and straight-up blues – not necessarily genres that reggae fans thought the singer should pursue.

"After I recorded *Wonderful World, Beautiful People*, I wanted to do different kinds of recordings," Jimmy explains. "After *Wonderful World*, they started giving respectability to reggae in England, so that was good, but by then all the blues and R&B that I had been doing while playing clubs in England had become a part of me, so I welcomed the opportunity to record in Muscle Shoals, and it was a very positive experience. *Another Cycle* was really different from the reggae things that I was doing. Lots of people thought that it was a bad move, because I was doing good with reggae, so why change and go into a different kind of thing?"

In addition to the multiple genres, the album's focus comprised philosophical odes of contemplation and songs of romantic entanglement. In terms of lyrics, the strongest numbers were honest utterances from the soul, such as the opening "Take a Look At Yourself," with its impressive gospel choruses, and the title track, which built to an erupting climax as Cliff alluded to very personal experiences, a searing guitar adding to the urgency. Like "Be Aware," "Please Tell Me Why" questioned why teachers, preachers and parents had tended to omit aspects of the truth when educating the youth, while the rocking "Inside Out, Upside Down" was an autobiographical outpouring, voicing the confusion that so often beset him. The message of "Opportunity Only Knocks Once" was basically, "Strike while the iron's hot," but the crowded production, with its overpowering choruses, distracting slide guitar and warbling horn lines, made it easy for the idea to get lost. The adulterous theme of "My Friend's Wife," one of two songs written by Guilly alone, was too lightweight to take seriously, while the bluegrass of "Oh, How I Miss You" somehow seemed unbalanced; Jimmy also sounded unconvincing against the blues backing of "Our Thing Is Over," the other Guilly Bright solo composition. The best of the bunch was the quietly contemplative "Sitting in Limbo," which Jimmy had begun writing in London in 1970, but which Guilly helped him finish when they met in Argentina, another autobiographical track that expressed an unyielding determination to succeed, nicely framed by electric piano, flute riffs and brass.

In some ways, *Another Cycle* was ahead of its time, placing a Jamaican singer within an unfamiliar milieu. But the album lacked the confidence and coherence of *Wonderful World, Beautiful People*, and was also missing the protest numbers that made that album so popular, while the fact that *Another Cycle* was entirely devoid of reggae was another strike against it. Although Jimmy savored his time in Muscle Shoals, the album he recorded there was largely dismissed.

When Jimmy finished recording *Another Cycle*, he embarked on an extensive Caribbean tour, playing Georgetown, Guyana, toward the end of June, as well as towns along the Demerara River, with Count Prince Miller in tow, going on to Dominica, the US Virgin Islands and Trinidad, where he appeared at Port of Spain's prestigious Queen's Hall on 12 July. Meanwhile, Island began issuing material from the Muscle Shoals sessions, pairing an optimistic, bluegrass-tinged number called "Goodbye Yesterday" with another track called "Breakdown," though its American issue on A&M, which surfaced in June, was backed by a socially conscious Guilly Bright composition, "Let's Seize the Time," delivered as a slow blues.

In August, just when the Jamaican music scene was shaken by the sudden death of Leslie Kong from a heart attack, Island released "Sitting in Limbo" on a single, with a heavily orchestrated number called "The Bigger They Come, the Harder They Fall" on the B-side; this driving track, whose rhythm was cut at Dynamics during the movie project, used a proverb to convey the idea that oppressive big-shots typically meet terrible ends. Of course, the better-known alternative version voiced by Jimmy during the film production as "The Harder They Come" is one of the defining statements of his career; the fantastic scene in which he voiced the track – the actual first vocal attempt committed to tape – would become one of the most iconic moments of Perry Henzell's film, ultimately released under the same title. But for the moment, "The Bigger They Come" was issued only as an obscure single B-side, the screeching violins and commercial brass drowning out its serious message.

In truth, none of this material sparked much interest at its time of issue, and when *Another Cycle* was released by Island at the end of the year, it flopped. A&M decided not to release it, and they also shelved an alternative album of recent reggae recordings, led by "Wild World" but filled largely with older soul tracks. However, a similar set was issued in Jamaica on Beverley's as *Two Worlds*, which paired the best of Jimmy's recent Jamaican creations with some of the more notable overseas recordings. Thus, in addition to "Wild World," "My World Is Blue," "Synthetic World," "Going Back West," "You Can Get It If You Really Want," "Goodbye Yesterday" and "Breakdown," the album featured "Better Days Are Coming," a brilliantly optimistic number framed by niyabinghi drum beats, the critical "I'm No Immigrant," a bubbling reggae groove in which Cliff demands his birthright, and a desolate number called "I've Tried." And although the tracks would not be issued

Hero never dies till the last reel: Jimmy as Ivan in The Harder They Come

on album in Britain for some time, Island made the most of the newer singles material by issuing it in Holland as *Goodbye Yesterday,* an album handled by the Benelux subsidiary of the German conglomerate Ariola; a related release, titled *Wild World,* was issued by Island in France, devoid of the earlier soul tracks and with "Let's Seize the Time" as a centerpiece.

Pleased with the broad success of "Wild World," Island again paired Jimmy with Cat Stevens for a complex rock creation called

"Trapped," whose sterling arrangement was greatly aided by Stevens's concrete input. Issued by Island in March 1972 with a stop-start reggae called "Struggling Man" on the flip, the single was also unjustly ignored, though "Trapped" would later enjoy popularity as a cover tune.

By this point, Jimmy Cliff had already joined the Nation of Islam, though it would take time for the fact to become public knowledge. Reading Malcolm X had further expanded his mind, as the radical activist's autobiography expressed so eloquently the legacies of slavery that lingered in the present, which Jimmy had experienced throughout his life; there was also the overt and covert racism that ruled the West, and the liberating aspects of Islam, which Jimmy found deeply inspiring. Recalling his first encounters with the group in New York, and after further contact with other adherents, Jimmy began attending Nation of Islam functions and soon adopted the faith for his own, being known for a time as Jimmy X in NOI circles, before taking the name Naim Bashir (Naim signifying "Blessed by the Divine," Bashir being "Bearer of Good Tidings"), although he would not publicly go by this new name for some considerable time.

In many ways, Jimmy's embracing of the Nation of Islam grew out of his long-standing frustration with elements of Christianity, as represented by his Pentecostal upbringing. There were aspects of Christian doctrine, and the manner in which it was imparted, that he found lacking, contradictory, or inappropriate, particularly in relation to the denigrated status of black people in the West, and to which the Nation seemed to provide the perfect antidote.

"So many people, especially in Jamaica, where there is every sort of church, still have this spooky idea of dying and going to heaven – it's like a brainwashing process," he told Ray Connolly shortly after his conversion had prompted some in Britain to label him anti-white. "I don't think they should sing hymns in church at all, because they help to excite the emotions, which cause illusions. I used to see them all getting worked up and 'getting the spirit.' Getting all spooked up."

Although Jimmy's membership of the Nation may have seemed like an outright rejection of the Christianity of his childhood, it was, in fact, merely part of his ceaseless quest to find the truth. From an early age, Jimmy knew that the preacher was not necessarily telling him everything he needed to know; reaching the Nation of Islam and hearing its teachings thus felt like discovering a hidden body of knowledge whose existence he had always suspected.

"My father was Christian and had very strong moral principles that stayed with me all my life," Jimmy explained in the 1996 documentary *Moving On*. "After I reject religion at a very early age, when I was leaving Somerton, I went through many doors, searching for the reality of myself... and after *The Harder They Come* came out, my values changed, and I went in to study Islam; that was one point where I dive into something."

In terms of his professional career, after so many false starts and disappointing responses to his recorded material, a moment of true glory finally came when Jimmy was flown to Jamaica to attend the opening of *The Harder They Come*, held at the Carib Theater on 2 June 1972. Expectations were running high, with lines for an 8 pm screening forming in the early afternoon; by 7.30, a multitude had descended on the Carib, making downtown Kingston one big roadblock. The theater's 1,500 seats simply could not accommodate everyone, so the rampaging crowd forced entry, destroying the surrounding fence and breaking down the theater doors to squeeze the maximum bodies possible into the venue. When the screening finally began, the scene inside was that of joyous bewilderment: at last, Jamaicans were seeing themselves on the silver screen, with scenes of their ordinary lives reflected, rather than foreign fantasies.

At the beginning of the film, the death of Ivan's grandmother forces him to trade the tranquility of the countryside for Kingston's volatile chaos; Ivan seeks out his mother, whom he has not seen since infancy, but she ultimately rejects his presence. As soon as he arrives in the capital, baffled by a stop light, his few belongings are pilfered, and later he nearly gets his hand chopped off trying to steal food at Coronation Market. Temporarily housed by a priest, who discharges him after Ivan makes romantic approaches to the priest's female ward (portrayed with feeling by radio actress Janet Bartley), Ivan runs into trouble when he injures another of the priest's lodgers in self-defense, leading to his arrest and a brutal beating from a policeman wielding a tamarind switch. He then comes under the influence of a hustler called Jose (brilliantly portrayed by Carl Bradshaw), who soon inducts him into the ganja trade. At the same time, when Ivan tries to establish a name for himself as a recording artist, he faces another kind of exploitation, and it is only when he takes up the gun and gets press coverage while on the run that he is able to gain radio airplay; the swift and gory demise that follows feels terribly inevitable.

A veritable landmark of Caribbean cinema, *The Harder They Come* had countless incredible touches that enhanced its pervasive feeling of authenticity. In addition to Jimmy's naturalistic performance, there was Ras Daniel Hartman's appearance as a sympathetic Rastaman called Pedro, a guest cameo by Prince Buster as a sound-system selector, and singer Alton Ellis as Jimmy's double in a fight scene, while the market stalls, church halls, gambling dens and ganja yards were actual trade premises and not stage sets. Production assistant Beverly Anderson also portrayed the wealthy housewife who berates Ivan when he appears at her door seeking work. It was another masterful piece of casting, as Anderson was shortly to marry Michael Manley – the socialist-leaning son of Norman Manley – who had been elected Prime Minister in February 1972; quickly revealed as a challenging figure in Caribbean politics, Michael Manley's Leftist policies and friendship with Cuba were ultimately seen as problematic by the Nixon administration in Washington.

In addition to its stunning visuals and the fine art direction and wardrobe choices supplied by Perry's wife Sally, *The Harder They Come* also had an exceptional soundtrack, though most of it was hastily assembled from Island's back catalogue after Jimmy, due to time constraints, had failed to deliver a requested track listing.

Faced with major gaps in the soundtrack, Henzell thus selected fitting incidental material to illustrate key scenes, such as the Slickers' "Johnny Too Bad," Desmond Dekker's "007 (Shanty Town)," the Maytals' "Sweet And Dandy," the Melodians' "Rivers of Babylon," plus "Draw Your Brakes" from deejay Scotty. Although the idea of Jimmy recording new versions of the tracks was mooted, the decision was made to use the original versions, as all feature superb performances. The Maytals also appeared in the film, recording "Pressure Drop" at Dynamics, and there were also select numbers from Cliff's recent career, including "You Can Get It If You Really Want," "Many Rivers to Cross" and "Sitting in Limbo." According to both Cliff and Henzell, only "The Harder They Come" was written especially for the film.

At the Cork Film Festival, held at the end of June, Perry Henzell gained an award for Best Editor with *The Harder They Come*. Then, at the Venice Film Festival, the film won the Best Young Cinema award and the soundtrack was also given an award; the film was also positively received at the Locarno Film Festival in August. However, reactions were lukewarm at the London debut screening, held on 2 July at the Brixton Classic, leading Henzell to hand out leaflets at Brixton Underground station in an attempt to raise its profile. Some expatriates objected to its gritty portrayal of Jamaican poverty and corruption, though it was eventually lauded by George Melly and other leading British film critics, who hailed the universality of its storyline and the general originality of its deliverance.

Although it would eventually be deemed a cult classic, playing in over forty different countries, the film took time to establish itself, particularly in the USA, where it was not given a proper release until 1975, despite opening at the Embassy in New York's Time Square in February 1973, with Cliff once again present for the occasion. Largely through Perry Henzell's direct actions, *The Harder They Come* opened in August 1973 at the Orson Welles Theater in Boston, where it enjoyed an unprecedented seven-year run, and later, in coastal cities such as San Francisco, the film would gain regular screenings on the art-house circuit for decades to come. Its exceptional soundtrack also formed the first experience of reggae for countless overseas listeners, proving to be a particular revelation when eventually issued in the States. However, it took over six years for the film's investors to break even.

In Jamaica, *The Harder They Come* immediately elevated Jimmy Cliff's status. The single release of "The Harder They Come" theme song hit the Jamaican Top 10 toward the end of July 1972 and remained in the charts for several weeks. On 15 October, Michael Manley announced that Cliff had made the Honors list and, along with Perry Henzell, was to be awarded the Order of Distinction the following year – making Jimmy Cliff much more of a household name on the island than he had been during the ska years. Unfortunately, the process was much slower overseas. And there were elements associated with *The Harder They Come* that displeased Jimmy. He could not understand why the soundtrack had not yet been released in territories where he had a strong following, such as South America, or places where he was trying to gain a wider following, like the USA, and there were financial aspects that he also found lacking, leading to dramatic changes.

As Chris Blackwell explains: "I thought it would be a great idea for him to do the film, because it was another shot for him to find his way, so I pushed him into doing that, which ended up being the reason that he left Island. He was going to leave Island earlier, because he was offered $50,000 by RCA Records, and I talked him into not leaving Island, because I said we would definitely be able to do better than that, he would earn better than that over the period of time, but when you do a low-budget, independent film, you don't get very much money for it and it uses up a hell of a lot of time. So he never made as much as he would have done if he'd taken the money from RCA, and so, when another opportunity came from EMI, that's when he decided that he would leave. I was devastated, because I felt very close to him, and I felt I knew how best to market him, which was to follow his image from *The Harder They Come*."

Jimmy Cliff could not have known that just as he was leaving Island in the latter half of 1972, Bob Marley and the Wailers were seeking Chris Blackwell's patronage. Blackwell signed the Wailers just after Jimmy's departure and slotted Marley into the image that Jimmy had fashioned with *The Harder They Come*, ultimately facilitating Marley's emergence as the first reggae superstar. But, regardless of such external factors, for Jimmy, it was simply time to move on.

8

Brave Warrior: The EMI/Reprise Years

When Jimmy Cliff left Island, he brokered deals with different record companies to allow greater penetration of the international market: in the UK and Europe, his material was handled by EMI, the major label that was home to the Beatles, while his American outlet became Reprise, the semi-autonomous pop subsidiary of Warner Brothers, founded by Frank Sinatra. Jimmy's EMI output was also issued in Jamaica via Total Sounds, a label and distribution service established by Australian immigrant Herman McDonald, while EMI's strong distribution network made the material available to new audiences in the developing world, particularly West Africa, thanks to the company's Nigerian pressing plant.

The first album to surface was *Unlimited*, released overseas in the summer of 1973 and in Jamaica the following November. EMI's issue spared no expense with the packaging, designing a weighty gatefold sleeve with Jimmy's clean-shaven face displayed within an illuminated star on the front cover, which drew on the pivotal studio scene in *The Harder They Come* where Jimmy voiced the title track in a star-emblazoned T-shirt – though, this time, Jimmy's close-cropped hairstyle, conservative suit and bow tie, as seen on a portrait of the inside sleeve, reflected the dress code of the Nation of Islam. Recorded at Dynamics with engineer Karl Pitterson, it featured the core of the band that had backed him at Beverley's, now augmented by a great horn section centered on trumpeter Bobby Ellis, who arranged several tracks, along with saxophonist Tommy McCook and trombonist Ron Wilson. The album also featured some of Jamaica's best backing vocalists, including the Heptones, Judy Mowatt, Bunny Wailer's common-law wife Jean Watt, and Bob Marley's wife Rita, as well as Nora Dean, a talented former member of Rita's group, the Soulettes, that had debuted in the late 1960s with a series of risqué hits.

Although the presence of such talent greatly enhanced the material, portions of the album were spoiled by gratuitous keyboard overdubs that were terribly intrusive. Some songs made use of a mellotron, the keyboard of choice for progressive rock, which sounded out of place on a reggae album. The layers of unnecessary synthesizer sounds that overpowered certain tracks were presumably employed in the hopes of broadening the album's appeal to international audiences, but such overblown production techniques had the unfortunate effect of appealing to neither serious reggae lovers nor rock fans, and actually lessened the album's overall appeal. And as had been the case with *Hard Road* and *Another Cycle*, the album held a sense of unevenness, veering as it did between straightforward reggae, experimental rock and other, more pop-oriented, styles.

Overall, the lyrics were surprisingly angry and critical, not only of the slanted mechanisms of the music industry, but more broadly of racial inequality and historical injustices. Such content was the result of the great personal changes that were gradually having an effect on Cliff, particularly where matters of faith were concerned; Chris Blackwell's plan had been to market Jimmy as a rebel outlaw, but on *Unlimited* he came across more as a judicious soothsayer and spiritual seeker.

The disc starts off strong with two of its greatest efforts. "Under the Sun, Moon and Stars" was a spirited number with an upbeat melody that disguised its outrage. Driven by Bongo Herman's African-styled percussion and Leslie Butler's swirling organ lines, it decried the unpaid work that Jimmy's forefathers were forced to perpetually endure; by demanding immediate recompense, Jimmy refutes the promise of a pie-in-the-sky heavenly reward, as proffered by Christianity, insisting instead that he be granted proper pay for the work he does "right here on earth." Then, a minor masterpiece unfolds: the rhythmically complex "Fundamental Reggay," which was issued as an EMI single in October, begins with sparse percussion from Denzil Laing atop drumbeats from session player Neville Grant, as Jimmy paints a picture of all that is inspiring about the music, heightening the diverse beats and melodies that help give reggae its universal appeal. Another strong track is the closing "Born To Win," which is marked by Cliff's characteristic optimism, stating that no matter how hard the struggle or bitter the battle, he is surely going to succeed. The song was issued by Reprise as the album's anticipatory single in May 1973, backed with the rousing "Black Queen," an excellent number that celebrated the resilience and moral fortitude of black women, their courage belying the unjust deprivation they continually face.

The rest of the album is more varied. The patriotic "Oh Jamaica," a deep reggae groove that EMI issued as a single in July, symbolically explored the island's perilous history, while its B-side, "On My Life," used a rock drumbeat as the grounding for a song of romantic devotion, though its overdubbed flute seems off-kilter. And although the blues-influenced "Be True," which requested a lover's fidelity, has more synthesized strings than are necessary, the fine backing vocals were a strong enhancement – even if Jimmy flubs the high notes in the third verse, in a vain attempt to show off his vocal range. In contrast, punctuated by more fantastic percussion and bolstered by female choruses, "Rip Off" warned of the

Bow-tie buddy: new-look Jimmy in live action

unscrupulous nature of the music industry. Keyboard overdubs truly ruin the pertinent "World of Peace," its serious message getting lost beneath cheesy synths and annoying xylophone lines; likewise, "The Price of Peace" is drowned in synthesized strings and other useless overdubs, clouding the song's very weighty exploration of the legacies of slavery. The extremely personal "I See the Light" suffers from a similar problem: the song apparently speaks of the spiritual awakening that pointed Cliff toward the Nation of Islam; the superfluous overdubs really take away from his vocal delivery, though Hux Brown's lead guitar licks inject a strong element of soul. Thankfully, the bluesy "Poor Slave" relies on horns and percussion instead of keyboards, leaving the mix relatively uncluttered, as Cliff ponders the concept of mental slavery in which the descendants of slaves are still symbolically bound. But strangest of all is "Commercialization," whose disco-funk arrangement would not have seemed out of place on a "blaxploitation" film soundtrack – which perhaps followed a kind of logic, as *The Harder They Come* was marketed as such in the USA.

Expectations for *Unlimited* were high, but reactions were mixed. *Cashbox* suggested the album summed up all that was potentially positive in reggae and *Stereo Review* gave it an Honorable Mention in their Record of the Year awards, but in *Rolling Stone*, respected journalist and early supporter Charlie Gillett wrote that *Unlimited* paled in comparison to *Wonderful World*. Despite much initial interest in the UK, USA and the Eastern Caribbean, sales figures were ultimately disappointing.

Unlimited faced unanticipated competition from the August 1973 issue of *Struggling Man*, an odds and ends compilation of outdated out-takes and single B-sides, hastily issued by Island in an effort to pip EMI and Reprise to the post. The blueprint for the album, which bore a flat cartoon drawing of Jimmy on the cover, was an unreleased set assembled for A&M in late 1971 – rendering its sound generally passé – and the hodge-podge assembly lacked any sense of continuity. Which is not to say that the material was low quality; the songs themselves were not bad: in addition to the title track, "Going Back West," "Those Good, Good Old Days," a remixed "Better Days Are Coming" and "Let's Seize the Time," there was another bluesy Muscle Shoals track, "Can't Live Without You," and the equally bluesy "Can't Stop Worrying, Can't Stop Loving You," written by guitarist Dave Mason of Traffic, as well as an edgy track called "Sooner or Later," plus a percussion and horn-filled ode about life's trials and tribulations called "When You're Young," delivered with typical Cliff optimism, together with a well-executed soul cover, "Come On People." Unfortunately, the disparate sources made the set feel too random to be a proper album, and the age of the material also made it seem like an afterthought, though the title track proved popular in African territories.

Despite the music industry tussles, Jimmy was still enjoying other accolades and reverences, most notably being awarded the Order of Distinction on 25 October by the Governor General, Florizel Glasspole, as part of the National Heroes Day honors awarded to the island's "Nation Builders."

Although Jimmy was now traversing the streets of London in a gold BMW, in truth, career demands made his life generally stressful, and during 1973 and early 1974 he spent a lot of time in the air, traveling between Jamaica, Britain, and other territories as necessary. For instance, in May 1973, there was a brief UK tour with a band of UK-based Jamaicans (including Jackie Parris of the Sensations on drums), during which he shared the stage with the Wailers and soul star Inez Fox in Leeds and Birmingham, followed by engagements in Montserrat, Antigua and Dominica. He had also used the popular live act the Cimarons as backing band for a brief tour of UK bingo halls and cinemas, and later assembled a full Jamaican band, featuring bassist Jackie Jackson, pianist Gladdy Anderson and organist Winston Wright of the Beverley's All Stars, plus drummer Neville Grant, guitarist Radcliffe "Dougie" Bryan of the Sensations, and saxophonist Tommy McCook, to perform a series of live dates abroad, some of which were featured on a BBC television special. While overseas, they met jazz flautist Herbie Mann, who subsequently traveled to Jamaica to record with the band at Dynamics, around the same time that Jimmy and company were laying down the tracks for a follow-up set to *Unlimited*. Jimmy was also on the island for Jackie Edwards's performance at the Flamingo Hotel in April 1974, the occasion being a happy reunion for the pair, who had not glimpsed each other for years.

Jimmy's new album surfaced in July, bearing the title *House of Exile* in Europe and *Music Maker* on its American issue. Thankfully, the album felt more cohesive than *Unlimited*, and the few overdubs it carried were tastefully executed, though, this time, EMI's front cover had also been downgraded to a mere cartoon drawing, while the Reprise issue skirted bad taste with its incongruous image of a woman in a wet T-shirt. But there was no faulting the music, most of which was pointed more firmly in a reggae direction.

"House of Exile" was one of the most outstanding tracks, a complex, finely crafted creation that used biblical allegory to warn that the mighty may fall. Although "Brother" also drew on the Bible, recounting the story of Joseph being sold into slavery in Egypt by his brothers, to illustrate mankind's mistrust and abuse of those perceived as threatening or different, the song was actually a rejection of religious dogma, as revealed by lines that asked whether the listener was content to be spoon-fed lies by preachers. Several songs drew on folk melodies, Pentecostal hymns and mento, heightening their Jamaican feel, as heard on "You Can't Be Wrong and Get Right" and the devotional "My Love Is Solid as a Rock." Similarly, "I Want To Know" adapted a spiritual to suit Cliff's own purposes; after noting that man devised guns and bombs, while God created plants, beasts and people, Jimmy concludes that, as God made man in his own likeness, then God must be man, echoing concepts that the Rastafari and Nation of Islam both espoused, namely that God is represented on Earth by a living man, or that God dwells inside each of us. The weighty "I've Been Dead 400 Years," one of the album's most moving numbers, also drew from the melody of a Pentecostal hymn, using vibrant niyabinghi percussion, blues guitar licks and soulful horns to drive home its bittersweet contemplation of the ongoing legacies of slavery.

The rest of the album pointed in different directions: "Long Time No See" was a slow, romantic creeper edging toward rock and soul, while "Foolish Pride" was a bit too sluggish to make an impact, and "Music Maker" too clever for its own good, claiming as it did that Jimmy was "recovering" from a "psychedelic shock," his soul "feeling low" because of an overdose of "rock-and-roll stew." Faring somewhat better was the driving "Money Won't Save You," in which Jimmy extolled the virtues of truth and righteousness. The most unexpected track was the rollicking "No. 1 Rip-Off Man," aimed squarely at the head of the unnamed Chris Blackwell: Cliff swore retribution on the "stinking old liar" whose empire he had helped build, along with named peers such as "uncle Ernest" (Ranglin), "brother Jack" (Edwards), "sister [Millie] Small" and "brother Bob" (Marley), the end result being surprisingly provocative. There was also a confusing hybrid called "Look What You Done To My Life, Devil Woman," which lay somewhere between reggae and soul, with full female choruses, vibrant percussion, and a fuzz-box lead guitar contrasting with its skanking rhythm. The song spoke of a temptress who ruined the protagonist's life by luring him away from his family.

Just as Jimmy's album releases during this period were confusing, confounding critics and fans alike, so was there considerable disorder in his life, as he was traveling continually across the Atlantic and contemplating a new spiritual path. Nevertheless, in Jamaica, there were further accolades. In May 1974, during a presentation for the Prime Minister of Lesotho, Rex Nettleford, director of the National Dance Theater Company of Jamaica, announced that the company was to pay tribute to Jimmy Cliff in their forthcoming Season of the Dance. Thus, when independence celebrations took place in August, Jimmy was delighted to return to Jamaica to view their vibrant interpretations of "The Price of Peace," "On My Life," "Sitting in Limbo" and "Many Rivers To Cross." He was also interviewed at length on television by noted broadcaster Neville Willoughby.

It was an exceedingly busy time for Jimmy, as he kicked off a brief UK tour at London's Rainbow Theater, titled "The Jimmy Cliff Extravaganza," with dynamic vocalist Dave Barker (of hit-making duo Dave and Ansel Collins) as opening act, backed by the seven-piece Dansak Band, a London-based outfit that included several former members of popular backing band Greyhound, such as keyboardist Sonny Binns, guitarist Errol Dunn and bassist Trevor White, together with drummer Jesse Green, a fellow St James native, who had played with Desmond Dekker and the Pioneers, and guitarist Trevor Starr (aka Trevor Brown), a Kingstonian who had come to London in the backing band of Dave and Ansel Collins and who had already backed Jimmy in the Cimarons.

In the autumn, the same band backed him on select dates in far-flung territories: in addition to a debut performance at New York's Carnegie Hall, there was a triumphant return to Trinidad, and, more importantly, a two-week tour of Nigeria, where songs like "House of Exile," "Fundamental Reggay" and "Under the Sun, Moon and Stars" were virtual anthems.

Jimmy's performance at Carnegie Hall on 16 November garnered mixed reviews. Dressed in white and ecstatically dancing all over the stage, as usual, his set lasted nearly an hour, but some critics felt the tone was too serious. As far as they were concerned, reggae was supposed to be "feel-good" music, so they had difficulty understanding the anguish Jimmy sometimes imparted. But then, reggae was still largely a "novelty" in America, the market a particularly tough one for reggae performers to crack, as Bob Marley and others would later discover.

In contrast, Jimmy's arrival in Lagos was momentous, as it made him the first reggae singer to perform on the African continent. On a personal level, it was also revelatory: here, at last, was the Africa of his ancestors, where he could see near-mirror images of himself everywhere. It is unlikely that he could have been prepared for the type of all-encompassing tropical heat that washed over him in intense waves the moment he stepped out of the airplane, nor for the noise and general chaos of the capital city, which made downtown Kingston seem almost like a quaint village. In the aftermath of the Biafran war, Nigeria was still run by a military dictatorship, so soldiers formed an intimidating presence, and, although there were open drains in much of Lagos, which was incredibly overcrowded and largely impoverished despite the nation's great oil wealth, there was a certain majesty in the civilization that resonated deeply within him. After all, here was a black city in a black nation at the heart of the African continent, with a gigantic mosque at its center, all of which heightened the feeling that he had somehow come home.

Although he was given a hero's welcome, Jimmy's arrival in Lagos was not without its peculiarities. In his book *Music Makers of West Africa*, musician and author John Collins recounts that Jimmy Cliff's highly anticipated performance at the 45,000-seat National Stadium was brought to a premature end by the arrival of the radical Nigerian musician and political activist Fela Kuti, who was hoisted onto the crowd's shoulders and paraded around the soccer ground the moment he entered the stadium, causing the audience to desert the stage area.

Despite the momentarily stolen thunder, after the Nigerian rebel had invited the Jamaican band for dinner, Cliff and Kuti forged an instantaneous bond, sharing as they did many of the same ideals and personal tastes: like Jimmy, Fela queried the colonial mindset of black people in the post-colonial age, the divisive shortcomings of religion, and the failure of governments to adequately provide for the people; he also had a fondness for the liberating qualities of spliff, as well as for beautiful women. At the Shrine, the nightclub that also functioned as a meeting point for his disciples, Fela worshipped his ancestors through music, melding free-form jazz and funk to African beats during intense jam sessions that lasted all night; there were also regular lecture sessions, in which Fela criticized the government and discussed broader current affairs. Presiding over a large compound in the Mushin district, which he proclaimed the Kalakuta Republic, surrounded by the rag-tag band of social outcasts that were his most ardent supporters, Fela called for political, spiritual and sexual liberation, his direct censure of governmental corruption resulting in frequent harassment by the authorities and brutal beatings. Cliff and Kuti took each other for kindred spirits, and thus cultivated a long-standing friendship.

During his weeks traveling around the country, Jimmy was given a tumultuous welcome, the audience response in cities such as Lagos, Port Harcourt, Benin City, Jos, Kadu and Kano simply overwhelming. He met many impressive musicians along the way, with rising juju star Sonny Okosun being one of the more noteworthy.

At the end of the Nigerian sojourn, however, a serious problem arose when it was time to leave the country: according to guitarist

Trevor Starr, instead of taking the band to Kano Airport, the security guards who had previously acted as escorts held them captive, summoning the police and the army, who threw Jimmy Cliff into jail. The problem stemmed from a previous invitation to the singer that Jimmy had ultimately declined; following disagreements relating to alleged loss of income, the promoter had Jimmy arrested for supposed breach of contract, along with the road manager. After a couple of days' detention, the situation was rectified and the captives were freed, but being imprisoned was a very negative way in which to end the symbolic homecoming.

"Our equipment spend four years in Nigeria, before we get it back," laments Trevor Starr, "and when they came back, they were broken up. But the audience response was beautiful. Jimmy Cliff was crowned as a god."

By the end of the year, Jimmy had already begun working on *Brave Warrior*, the only album handled in Europe by EMI not given an American release by Reprise. Although recorded in stages during late 1974 and early 1975, with various musicians in different locations, *Brave Warrior* felt somewhat more cohesive than *House of Exile*, retaining a generally harder edge, even though half of the tracks were in "fusion" territory, due to the presence of Latin jazz session players.

The straightforward reggae numbers were given their overall definition by key members of the Wailers band, including bassist Aston "Family Man" Barrett, drummer Carlton Barrett, keyboardist Bernard "Touter" Harvey and percussionist Sticky Thompson, bolstered by former Wailer Peter Tosh on rhythm guitar. During sessions recorded at Harry J studio with engineer Sylvan Morris, conducted around the time of Bob Marley's *Natty Dread*, the Barrett brothers give a palpable tension to tracks like "Bandwagon," aimed at record company executives that were flirting with reggae without being truly committed to it, as well as the self-explanatory "Action Speaks Louder than Words." The I Threes harmony trio of Marcia Griffiths, Judy Mowatt and Rita Marley, who were then in the process of becoming Bob Marley's permanent backing vocalists, were also fully present, making a particularly strong impact on the title track, a finely crafted ode that was issued as a single, on which Jimmy spoke of the ongoing struggle facing musical and spiritual warriors like himself.

The final reggae track on the disc, "Every Tub," had a strange genesis: built around the proverb "Every tub has to sit on its own bottom," which points to the need for self-determination, the song was first recorded with the Aggrovators, the ace team of session players led by Tommy McCook that normally recorded for Bunny Lee, featuring the "flying cymbal" style that was then ruling Jamaica, centered on an open-and-closed high-hat cymbal pattern. And although a single surfaced in Jamaica with the Aggrovators backing, for the album, Jimmy had Carlton Barrett overdub a new drum line, and a flute melody was also added to flesh out the tune, courtesy of Ghanaian brass master George Lee, the man who played alto sax on Marley's "Natty Dread."

The rest of the album was put together with memorable figures from the New York Latin jazz and funk circuits, including drummer Steve Berrios, a veteran of Mongo Santamaria's group; keyboardist Rogers Grant, who was then playing for Willie Colon; percussionist Emanuel Rahim, who had played on John Coltraine's *Live at the Village Vanguard*; funk guitarist Bobby Whitehead; and backing vocals by Orenzia Grant and Helena Walker, the latter featured on Olatunji's *Drums of Passion*. Morphing the album in another direction, this team gave shape to the Latin jazz cadence of the introspective "A Million Teardrops" and the quietly unfolding "Don't Let It Die," which builds to a climax as Cliff implores the listener to keep love alive on our planet, while "Save a Little Loving" was delivered as a slow and soulful blues. Opening and closing the album were two versions of the censorious "My People," which spoke of the broader divisions and differences of humanity that seemingly cannot be rectified, as filtered through Cliff's personal life experiences.

As had been the case with his previous EMI recordings, the album was greeted by mixed reviews overseas. And although it was not a particularly strong seller in Europe or Jamaica, it again helped solidify his growing status in the territories of the developing world, most notably in West Africa and South America.

After gradually spending more time in Jamaica, Jimmy Cliff decided to make his exit from London and return to the island full time. He thus installed himself in a sprawling property at Lady Musgrave Road, a relatively tranquil part of uptown Kingston, close to the British High Commission and the American Embassy, but still just a stone's throw from the downtown recording studios. In addition to spacious living quarters, the property had enough room for an office and the compound's garage allowed for a rehearsal space. Cruising around the island in a gold VW Beetle, the closest thing to a luxury item that he could afford, in this period, Cliff was a regular fixture at the mosque opened by the Nation of Islam on Wildman Street in downtown Kingston.

Almost immediately after Cliff moved in, the Lady Musgrave Road residence became the home of Sunpower Productions, the publishing company and record label established as the Jamaican outlet for his work. The earliest releases on Sunpower were heavily roots oriented: Nora Dean's "Album of My Life" recounted the hardships of her childhood, and one can almost visualize the tears in her eyes as she sings mournfully of walking six miles to school, her bare feet scorched by the burning sun; similarly, Studio One veteran Freddy McKay's "The Wound May Heal" (aka "Help Me") implored for assistance from the Lord, while its flipside, "Your Cup Is Full," was a chilling roots record, warning that evildoers would be summarily punished. There was also a sensual one-off single from harmony group the Willows, "Baby Let Me Feel It."

Aiming for a more authentic Jamaican sound for his own material, but one that would allow for complex musical arrangements, Cliff recruited the assistance of the veteran singer Joe Higgs, mentor of the Wailers and countless other local stars, after a chance meeting on a Kingston street, when Higgs offered to write a song for Jimmy. In the ska era, the duo of Higgs and Wilson had really impressed him, and Cliff had often seen Higgs schooling singers like Ken

Mega-star at the microphone: greater glory after The Harder They Come

Boothe and Stranger Cole in Boys Town, the district that lay just below Trench Town. Higgs had recently released the stunning *Life of Contradiction* album, as well as impressive work with his former students the Wailing Souls (under the name Atarra), and was anything but a spent force. Cliff thus asked Higgs to coach his new backing band, and to assist with vocal harmony and percussion on an upcoming tour. The first incarnation of the band, which Jimmy called the Jamaican Experience, featured drummer Carlton "Santa" Davis and guitarists Earl "Chinna" Smith and Tony Chin of the Soul Syndicate, a hit-making band from the Greenwich Farm ghetto whose members sometimes moonlighted in the Aggrovators, along with bassist Errol "Bagga" Walker, a Trench Town resident who had backed Ken Boothe in the Graduates, plus Bagga's friend (and fellow member of the Rastafari sub-group the Twelve Tribes of Israel) keyboardist Paul "Pablo Black" Dixon, who had been active in a steel band called the Advocates, as well as club acts, the Youth Professionals and the Rotations.

After briefly rehearsing at Lady Musgrave Road, which was still an empty shell with no furniture apart from a few chairs, Jimmy and the band headed east, across the Greater Antilles, for performances in St Thomas and St Croix in the US Virgin Islands, with noted keyboardist Ossie Hibbert in attendance as sound engineer.

"It was very successful tour," remembers Tony Chin. "On some of the shows we had police escorts. But after the shows, you would rarely see Jimmy; he was a very disciplined and spiritual person, and he tried to avoid some of the distractions that musicians face. He was serious about the music, as he would keep group meetings after every show to review it and make changes as necessary, and he was open to feedback from all the musicians."

Ossie Hibbert was then one of the key personnel at Channel One, the recording studio opened by the Hoo-Kim brothers in the heart of the Maxfield Park ghetto, and as its status was on the rise, Jimmy made use of the facility and its leading session players for the bulk of *Follow My Mind*, issued by Reprise in the USA in November 1975 (shortly after the soundtrack of *The Harder They Come* was finally released stateside). At Channel One, Jimmy brought together the immensely talented drummer Sly Dunbar, of leading club act Skin Flesh and Bones, and his bassist friend Robbie Shakespeare of the Aggrovators, for some of their first-ever collaborative work, bolstered by guitarist Dougie Bryan, as well as veteran Studio One drummer Leroy "Horsemouth" Wallace on certain tracks, voicing most of the material at King Tubby's tiny front-room studio in the Waterhouse ghetto, yielding a robust core of roots reggae. However, other elements were then added at a Burbank, California, facility by Trevor Lawrence, a sax player who had worked with Stevie Wonder and Marvin Gaye at Motown, including notable keyboard work by Beach Boys collaborator Van Dyke Parks, Motown session guitarist Dennis Coffey, and backing vocalist Jim Gilstrap from Stevie Wonder's band, pulling the material into the realm of international pop and soul, resulting in yet another complex album framed by differing musical styles.

One of the album's strongest tracks was its opener, "Look At the Mountains," another of Cliff's driving odes to self-determination. Other winners formed part of his live act in this era, especially "I'm Gonna Live, I'm Gonna Love," which had a cool reggae groove behind Cliff's highly personal musings, boosted by a catchy chorus, while the meditative title track had the kind of insistent rhythmic structure that could easily get stuck in your head.

Two outstanding numbers were co-written by Joe Higgs, namely the anguished "Who Feels It (Knows It)" and the celebratory "Dear Mother," the latter being an intriguing choice for Jimmy to tackle.

"When I went back to Jamaica to do a recording, somebody shout at me on the streets, and when I looked around, it was Joe Higgs," says Jimmy of their reconnection. "Joe Higgs was somebody that I admired, and we went into Trench Town and started to talk, and he said he has a song he think I should sing. He asked me about my life, and I start telling him about my life, because we had never known each other personally before, only as artists, so he wrote the song 'Dear Mother' for me."

Unfortunately, the song's overall impact was slightly diluted by superfluous horn overdubs, though its ragtime piano melody was a nice touch, as were the backing vocals by the Wailing Souls.

Somewhat cryptic at first listen, "Wahjahka Man" was another infectious number that explored the heightened awareness of the citizens of the African diaspora, whose self-reliance and sagacious wisdom came as a consequence of the hardships faced for countless generations. In contrast, "Hypocrites" was another of the songs that spoke directly to "stinking" music industry thieves, while "The News" directly relayed the tale of Cliff's imprisonment in Nigeria, with plenty of percussion to bring home the message.

As had often been the case during this period, some tracks felt at odds with the rest of the material. For instance, the playful "Going Mad," also inspired by his Nigerian arrest, recast an old calypso melody, with a verse in Spanish no doubt aimed at Latin America. A bit of light relief, the song went against the grain of the disc's overall heaviness, though it worked well in a live setting; it later became popular in Brazil's northeast Maranhão state (perhaps partly because of its Latinesque rhythm), being one of the first Jamaican recordings to have an impact in the country (though Jimmy was unaware of it at the time). Another staple of the live sets of this period, "Remake the World" fell somewhere between reggae and pop, being a song that spoke out against the world's injustices, but rendered strangely upbeat by its poppy, optimistic chorus and bluesy guitar licks. The slow love ballad that closes the set, "You're the Only One," might have fitted better on *Another Cycle*, thanks to Van Dyke Parks's prominent electric piano and Dennis Coffey's wah-wah guitar.

Even more surprising was Jimmy's sensitive cover of Bob Marley's "No Woman No Cry," which also benefited from the Wailing Souls' harmony and tasteful guitar and keyboard overdubs. Since Cliff had conjured such wonderful material with the Wailers band on *Brave Warrior*, covering Marley's work seemed unnecessary, but Jimmy delivered his rendition with feeling. He also adapted its lyrics for his own purposes, mentioning "Brother Higgs" and shifting the scenario to Boys Town, to specifically give credit to Higgs's tutoring of the Wailers, which Jimmy felt was not properly acknowledged. As was true with the album generally, "No Woman No Cry" made little impact in Jamaica or North America, but it was another of his songs that proved popular in the developing world, especially in Africa and Brazil, territories where Jimmy's following would remain consistently strong in years to come.

In late October 1975, a new version of the Jamaican Experience hit North America in support of *Follow My Mind*. As the Soul Syndicate members had other commitments, the band now included drummer Sly Dunbar and his guitarist friend Bertram "Ranchie" McLean of Skin, Flesh and Bones, plus percussionist Sticky and an adventurous young rhythm guitarist from Trench Town, Philip White, of the supremely psychedelic Light Of Saba band, along with Santa, Bagga, Pablo Black and Joe Higgs. Mindful of the growing hunger for *The Harder They Come*, Higgs often opened the gigs with versions of the soundtrack's non-Cliff material, like the Slickers' "Johnny Too Bad" and the Melodians' "Rivers of Babylon"; he also sang recent songs of his own midway through the set. The tour was easily Cliff's most successful to date, with Jamaica's ambassador to the US, Alfred Rattray, coming backstage at Washington DC's Kisner Auditorium on 28 October to personally congratulate him. The capacity crowd at Toronto's Massey Hall gave the singer a standing ovation, while the audience at an Ann Arbor performance on 11 November showered him with praise. Television appearances on programs such as *Don Kirschner's Rock Concert* and *Saturday Night Live* also heightened awareness of the man's talents in this period.

However, the unfortunate reality of the belated release of *The Harder They Come* and its soundtrack in North America meant that audiences were less interested in Cliff's more recent material. Instead, their truest appreciation was shown for the soundtrack numbers and Jimmy's earlier hits.

Part of the problem was that the market was truly flooded with Jimmy Cliff albums, made up of both old and new material, which made it difficult for curious listeners to navigate his work. Indeed, in 1975 Island issued a double LP *Best Of* retrospective, while the following year, EMI cobbled together a compilation called *Oh Jamaica* and reissued *Unlimited* in Holland with the off-putting title *King Of Reggae*.

It was hard to tell whether Jimmy had taken one step forward or two steps backward since leaving Island, because *The Harder They Come* brought fame without proper economic recompense, and the belated success of its music overseas ultimately overshadowed more recent work. Faced with such a contradictory situation, Cliff knew that it was time to slow down, take stock, and contemplate his next move. There thus began a period of badly needed introspection, ultimately resulting in a different direction and a reconfigured sound.

9

Meeting in Africa: Journeys in the Motherland

During the mid-1970s, Jamaican politics entered a particularly volatile phase as the nation became ensnared in broader Cold War struggles. Michael Manley's instigation of 'Democratic Socialism' in September 1974, an ill-defined coupling of socialist values with free-market enterprise, drew the nation further Left, and overtures of friendship with Fidel Castro were viewed with trepidation by Washington. In December 1975, after Manley had voiced approval of the Cuban presence in Angola, whose Marxist MPLA government was fighting the CIA-backed South African army, American Secretary of State Henry Kissinger traveled to Jamaica to apply direct pressure on Manley, threatening to cancel a billion-dollar trade agreement unless Manley withdrew support.

As the export sector was affected and unemployment rose, politically motivated violence was also steadily increasing, and after JLP leader Edward Seaga began a dramatic offensive against Democratic Socialism, staging up to ten public meetings per day and mass rallies at night in the run-up to the approaching general election, the violence dramatically worsened. In January 1976 a partisan gunfight in Trench Town spiraled out of control, resulting in the firebombing of twenty homes. Then, public protests against an International Monetary Fund (IMF) convention in New Kingston turned into a politically sabotaged riot in which dozens lost their lives, including four policemen. In May, more firebombs were hurled into a West Kingston slum, rendering over five hundred homeless. By June, the annual murder count was already registering 163 bodies, including nineteen policemen, forcing Manley to call a State of Emergency.

The flagrant tension made Kingston something of a ghost town, its streets nearly empty much of the time, with routine roadblocks and the next violent flare-up only a breath away. Yet, despite all the chaos, Jimmy Cliff's career was coming into focus, both at home and abroad. Along with the core of Joe Higgs, Bagga, Santa and Sticky (occasionally augmented by young percussionist Christopher "Sky Juice" Blake), the Jamaican Experience now featured keyboardist Keith Sterling, a prominent member of club act the Boris Gardener Happening, and younger brother of saxophonist Lester Sterling; rhythm guitarist Noel "Sowell" Bailey, a Denham Town native who had played in the Rotations and Youth Professionals with Pablo Black; and, most importantly, lead guitarist Ernest Ranglin, whose masterful command of his instrument and musical arrangement of the band brought Jimmy's live sets to new heights.

During the spring of 1976 the group embarked on select tour dates that brought them to a whole new audience. On 3 May they appeared at Madison Square Garden for a benefit concert put together by Paul Simon for the New York Public Library, alongside versatile songstress Phoebe Snow and jazz-fusion wizards the Brecker Brothers. In the summer there was a notable appearance at the Schaeffer Music Festival in Central Park, and later performances were given as far afield as Marseilles, the band rubbing shoulders along the way with luminaries such as Elton John, Mick Jagger and Jimmy's old friend Joe Cocker.

Rehearsing at Lady Musgrove Road, 1976; bandleader Ernest Ranglin seated at left

Back in Jamaica, on 1 August, Jimmy was given pride of place at the second Carifesta, the Caribbean Festival of Arts, a grand showcase of the region's vibrant arts and folklore, his performance at the National Stadium being one of the true highlights of the eleven-day event, with new material such as the driving "Let's Turn the Table," which called for a negation of social inequalities, and the contemplative "Deal With Life" being as well received as his much-loved classics. Jimmy also gave a free concert in Montego Bay to demonstrate his appreciation for the people of his native St James.

"Let's Turn the Table" surfaced on a Sunpower single around this time, along with an excellent dub version, as did "Deal With Life," backed by the song "Pack Your Things." There were also two superb collaborations with Joe Higgs, namely "Sons of Garvey" and "Sound of the City." "Sons of Garvey" questioned why politicians were getting fatter while the people were starving, as Church and State preached about a love that was never imparted; naming the Jamaican people as the sons of Marcus Garvey, Higgs and Cliff declared that it was time for action. Similarly, the eerie "Sound of the City" warned of the perils of urban life, noting how easily a soul could lose focus and be crushed, instead of rising up to claim its rightful place and status. Both tracks were issued with splendid dub B-sides that heightened the tightness of the backing musicians. Although Higgs and Cliff were working on an album of similar material, nothing else has surfaced from the sessions.

In the aftermath of Carifesta, Africa became an increasingly important item on the agenda. A Senegalese businessman named Fall arranged several dates in the country, and, just as an offer came for Jimmy to perform in South Africa, a South African refugee became part of his band.

The singer, Aura Lewis, had recently arrived in Jamaica on a scholarship to study at the drama department of the Jamaica School of Arts. Born Aurelia Msimang Borman, she and her family had fled apartheid during the early 1960s, and after being chased out of Rhodesia by Ian Smith's racist government, they eventually settled in Sierra Leone, where Aura had sung with leading night-club act Sierra Success, the main rivals to Geraldo Pino's Heart-beats. In 1968 she traveled to New York on a scholarship to attend Hunter College, and married jazz drummer Art Lewis after becoming involved with Brooklyn's Caribbean American Repertory Theater. Before departing for Jamaica, Aura placed the couple's three-year-old son in the care of her father in Sierra Leone.

Soon after her arrival in Jamaica, Aura became friendly with fellow student Pamela Reid, a dancer and aspiring singer from South Carolina, with whom she was hoping to record. The concept was a vocal group called Full Experience, comprised of women from the African diaspora. As the pair made their way to college one morning, Aura spotted Jimmy on his veranda and went over to introduce herself.

"I told him who I am and where I'm from," Aura explains, "and he says, 'That's really a coincidence, because I've just been invited to go to South Africa.' And I said, 'I wouldn't suggest that you go, because of the cultural boycott.' We decided to meet after class and we told him that we were busy putting music together, that we wanted to do an album, shared this whole vision that we had with him, and he was excited about that. He says, 'Maybe I can use the two of you to back me, because I also will be going to West Africa.' Then, we used to go there every evening and he'd give us the music to listen to, like 'Follow My Mind,' 'Black Queen' and 'The Harder They Come.'"

Jimmy's latest band featured Sly, Ernest Ranglin, Sticky and Chinna, but as the rehearsal process was unduly slow, Pamela Reid returned to South Carolina during a term break, resulting in her replacement by another local singer. As the band began fine-tuning their set, in late 1976, Reprise issued *In Concert: The Best of Jimmy Cliff*, a live compilation album drawn from recent overseas dates, featuring seventy percent tried-and-true hits. Only "Under the Sun, Moon and Stars" was present from the Reprise studio albums, and the only truly new item was a poetic number called "Fountain of Life," which was not released in studio form. One unfortunate aspect of the disc, which was co-produced by former Rolling Stones manager Andrew "Loog" Oldham, is the obtrusive crowd noise that has been grafted onto the music to give the impression that the crowd never ceased roaring throughout every single song – a contrived device that was all too common, but which simply disrupts the listening experience.

Meanwhile, Jimmy and band flew to Senegal, where they had several engagements to fulfill. From the moment their flight touched down in Dakar, they were treated like long-lost heroes, perpetually receiving dramatic displays of reverence and affection.

"Traditional dancers and stilt-walkers met us at the airport," recalls Aura Lewis. "It was incredible. We had two stadium shows in Dakar, then one in a big bourgeois venue, then we went up into the countryside, and everywhere we rode, all these traditional drummers and schoolchildren would line the roadside, welcoming Jimmy. It was an incredible experience."

Being in Senegal provided a series of further revelations for Jimmy. The impressive opening act, Xalam, melded contemporary jazz with Wolof traditions; Aura says they had a sartorial edge, as they were always dressed in crisp traditional clothing, while Jimmy's band "looked like a rag-tag group."

In general, Jimmy was thrilled by the mbalax scene, which merged traditional Wolof expression with elements of rock, jazz, Afro-Cuban and Haitian styles. Sharing the stage with rising stars like Youssou N'Dour, he was mindful of the way Senegalese artists were trying to forge a new sound by blending disparate elements, as he had strived to do for much of his career. Jimmy also encountered an ancient rhythm called yela, which was used by the kings of old to summon the people. Similar to the sound made by women pounding grain in wooden mortars, some practitioners of yela placed emphasis on the third beat of every measure, which reminded Jimmy of the rhythmic bedrock that lies at the heart of reggae.

As news of Jimmy's presence spread along the coast, requests began pouring in from other territories, but Jimmy's musicians chose not to linger. As Aura recalls, "Mali wanted us, Gambia, Sierra Leone, all the way to Nigeria, but the musicians said they're not going there; I told Jimmy not to cancel, because in each of those countries, we could find an African band."

Still smarting from the mishaps of his previous visit, Jimmy decided to give Nigeria a wide berth, but accepted the other engagements. Xalam recommended a Banjul-based band called Farabundu for Gambia and Mali, while for Sierra Leone, percussionist Francis Fuster, a former member of the Heartbeats, who had lived in Lagos for a long period, assembled a band featuring members of Sierra Success. Thus, cassettes of Jimmy's Senegalese performances were dispatched and the groups given a few weeks to rehearse, allowing Jimmy to delve deeper into Senegal's music and culture.

Before leaving Senegal, Jimmy made a pilgrimage to the city of Touba, some 95 miles east of Dakar, for an audience with Sheik Mourtada Mbaké, the spiritual leader of the Baye Fall Mourides. The Baye Fall are disciples of Sheik Ahmadou Bamba Mbaké,

Mourtada's grandfather, an Islamic Sufi mystic and poet who was a key figure in the struggle against colonialism during the late nineteenth and early twentieth centuries. Founding the Mouride brotherhood in 1883, after a long period of exile, Bamba established a very African form of Islam in Senegal, in which traditional African values were not subsumed by Arab culture. Baye Fall devotees seek peace through prayer and work, their central tenet being, "Pray as if you will die tomorrow and work as if you will live for ever." Many are also instantly recognizable because they wear their hair in dreadlocks, following the example of Sheik Ibra Fall, who ceased cutting his hair after it had been touched by Bamba.

By the time Jimmy Cliff met Sheik Mourtada Mbaké, he had already become disillusioned with aspects of the Nation of Islam.

"When Elijah Muhammad's teaching was telling the people about themselves and their connection with Africa, it was something that attracted everyone," Jimmy says in *Moving On*, "but now that you are not telling them anything about their connection with Africa, they drift away. So it's something to consider about the growth of Islam in Jamaica, because it's evident that the people want to know about their culture, and not necessarily about religion."

Following a split among followers in Jamaica, Jimmy began to attend Temple Number 2, the second Nation of Islam temple in the Caribbean, established by Prince Buster at 47 Charles Street, but he continued to question aspects of its teachings. The Baye Fall experience was another step in his spiritual evolution; indeed, although he had been a Muslim for several years, he still traveled with copies of the Christian Bible, as well as the Koran, showing that, instead of merely abandoning one faith for another, he was drawing on key aspects of both, to better understand man's relationship with God. Discovering such an African form of Islam was highly inspiring, so much so that Jimmy left Senegal as a veritable cousin of the Baye Fall brotherhood, the patterned fez he had recently been wearing soon replaced by a knitted Baye Fall hat and patchwork clothing.

In Gambia, during the initial rehearsals with Farabundu, the musicians' competent handling of Jimmy's material was a pleasant surprise. "It was like the Jamaican band wasn't even gone," insists Aura, "this band playing his stuff note for note."

After the gigs in Gambia and Mali, Jimmy found that the musicians in Sierra Leone also got into his groove, though the atmosphere of Freetown was unsettling. The country was somewhat unstable, with growing opposition to the ruling All People's Congress sparking sporadic protests as the economy nosedived, the general tension resulting in deserted streets. He could not understand why the media was not giving exposure to the situation, which he found upsetting. Thus, when the concerts were over, Jimmy headed up to Lagos for a powwow with Fela Kuti, while Aura stayed behind with her family.

Reaching London together, the pair pitched up at Jimmy's Earls Court residence, where his biggest preoccupation was to make arrangements for recording a new album in Jamaica. He thus went down to the Fallout Shelter, the basement studio hidden beneath Island Records' Chiswick HQ, in search of Rebop Kwaku Baah, who was working on Steve Winwood's eponymous solo album, only to find Bob Marley and the Wailers recording a startling new creation with the eccentric Jamaican producer Lee "Scratch" Perry and Candy McKenzie, an aspiring local singer of Guyanese origin.

"When we got to Island Studios," Aura recalls, "Lee says to Jimmy, 'I'm doing something with Bob, and I've got Candy, but we're looking for another back-up vocalist.' And Jimmy says, 'Use Aura, she just came back from West Africa with me.' So I ended up spending four or five days recording 'Punky Reggae Party' and 'Keep On Moving' with them, whilst Jimmy was taking care of problems with his record label."

When Jimmy returned to Jamaica in early 1977, civil unrest was still simmering. Michael Manley had been returned to office in December 1976, but the atmosphere was generally unsettled, particularly in Kingston, where the threat of a gun battle or sniper fire was still very real. However, with plenty of new lyrics already written, Jimmy swiftly went into the studio to record "Material World," a superb slice of deep roots music, in which Jimmy decried the materialism and greed that was spoiling the planet. As with much of his material in this era, the song featured vibrant hand percussion and an eerie piano line; issued on Sunpower in late February, it was distributed in Jamaica by Tommy Cowan's Talent Corporation.

More engagements were mooted, such as a benefit concert at the Turntable club in aid of the cultural center run by the Mystic Revelation of Rastafari in east Kingston, and, later, an appearance at the annual International Festival of Arts in Nancy, France. But music was not the only thing on Jimmy's mind.

Greatly inspired by his travels in West Africa, which had helped him get in touch with aspects of his ancestry, and buoyed by his renewed links with Rebop, in July 1977, Jimmy traveled to Ghana to conduct further research. While exploring aspects of the nation and its culture, Jimmy met a pharmacist named Ernest Sampong Kofi-Badu, who established a local Jimmy Cliff fan club, as songs like "Struggling Man" had had a strong impact there. Within six months the club had over one thousand members, leading Kofi-Badu to travel to Jamaica as a guest at Lady Musgrave Road, where plans were made to establish a Jamaican club whose members could conduct cultural exchange programs with their Ghanaian counterparts.

Back in Jamaica, preparations for Jimmy's next album were long and complex, as no one from Reprise's parent label, Warner Brothers, wanted to risk traveling to Jamaica to execute the necessary contracts, eventually forcing Jimmy to fly to the Bahamas to complete the requisite paperwork.

Unfortunately, the Full Experience album project was gradually jeopardized, and following the disintegration of the group Aura Lewis eventually relocated to Miami. Confusingly, a mislabeled Full Experience single titled "Strictly Roots" surfaced on Sunpower, featuring instead an unrelated male harmony trio's rendition of the Drifters' "Up on the Roof"; Full Experience's album was never completed.

In any case, Jimmy had bigger fish to fry. There were important engagements to fulfill in foreign lands and, as he was seeking a different direction, he assembled a new band called Oneness, the robust core comprising Ernest Ranglin, Chinna Smith, Pablo Black, Sticky, and Rebop Kwaku Baah for overseas dates (with Studio One veteran Richard Ace sometimes handling additional keyboard duties). Along with Chinna's brother Leonard on rhythm guitar and percussion, there were also upcoming musicians from the countryside, such as drummer Ronald Murphy, who had played with singing sculptor Ras Karbi, and six-fingered bassist Leebert "Gibby" Morrison, who was introduced to Jimmy as a member of Noel Bailey's short-lived band Black Heat Incorporated (which Jimmy had contemplated using as a backing band shortly before forming Oneness).

In the spring of 1978, Jimmy and the band fulfilled several engagements in Japan, with Jimmy also reportedly traveling to the States, Britain, France, Russia and Egypt. Returning to Jamaica in late May, Jimmy Cliff and Oneness were recruited as the headlining act of the first Reggae Sunsplash, a week-long music festival held in Montego Bay. Also featuring Jacob Miller and Third World, the festival was estimated to have attracted more than one thousand foreign visitors to the island and was even attended by Andrew Young, the US ambassador to the United Nations.

Apart from Sunsplash, Oneness was chiefly occupied with the specifics of Jimmy's next studio album, *Give Thankx*, released by Warner Brothers toward the end of the year (with Jamaican Sunpower pressings distributed by new company Sonic Sounds, run by Byron Lee's brother, Neville). Titled in reference to the Rastafari concept of giving thanks and praises to the Most High for all things positive, the album pointed toward the growing influence of Rastafari on Jimmy's consciousness, a result of his long-term residence in Jamaica during a time when the movement was in ascendancy. In this period he was particularly close to figures such as Mortimer Planno, one of the movement's most respected leaders, and Kojo "Preacher" Brown in Montego Bay. Though he had avoided it during his years in London, Jimmy now started smoking ganja more frequently. He also allowed his hair and beard to grow, ate more of an "ital" vegetarian diet, and began wearing T-shirts emblazoned with the Lion of Judah, a potent symbol of Rasta iconography, or sometimes full military-style uniforms.

As had been the case since his days in London, Jimmy was still a voracious reader, using books in this period as a means to better understand the true history of the world and its people, knowledge he was motivated to share with the musicians of Oneness.

"Jimmy Cliff is a great teacher to me," says Gibby Morrison. "He had this big library at his house, and all of us used to sit down every night and read all kinds of books, like *Sufi Message* and *The African Origin of Civilization: Myth or Reality?* He had a wide view of the world and it shows in his music, which is universal."

Although *Give Thankx* was given finishing touches in the USA (with background vocals overdubbed at the New York Record Plant with singers such as Cheryl Lynn, Babi Floyd, Ken Williams and Janice Pendarvis), most of the album was recorded at the twenty-four-track Aquarius studio, one of Kingston's newest and most up-to-date facilities, with Mervyn Williams and Boris Gardiner as engineers, and Ansel Collins, Leslie Butler and Keith Sterling drafted to supply additional keyboard parts as necessary. Overseeing the project was co-producer Bob Johnston (noted for his work with Bob Dylan, Johnny Cash, Leonard Cohen and Simon and Garfunkel), who traveled to Jamaica with John Stronach, then a chief engineer at the California branches of the Record Plant.

"Jimmy Cliff is one of the nicest, most spiritual, talented and inspirational men I have ever met," reports Stronach. "He is a tremendous artist and I think underrated in the reggae world. Jimmy wanted to record in Jamaica with his friends and musicians from the small towns in the interior; I guess for years he had been a victim of having to go to New York or Miami to record, and this was a great idea on his part, because you can hear the authentic vibe from the players."

Give Thankx opens with a sterling new version of "Bongo Man," which slowly unfolds to reveal the exquisite percussion of leading niyabinghi collective Ras Michael and the Sons of Negus, whose African cadences gave greater emphasis to Jimmy's homage to the powerful Rasta icon that so influenced his youth. Backing vocals from the Meditations, one of the most impressive harmony trios of the era, plus the deep baritone of Watty Burnett from the Congos, also helped impart a dramatic atmosphere, reminiscent of a Rastafari groundation ceremony. Stronach says the track was recorded with a crowd of ganja-smoking friends in attendance.

"'Bongo Man' was recorded in a little studio near Trench Town, which was a very dangerous place in those days, due to a virtual race war caused by the near-collapse of the central government. Jimmy had brought probably twenty people, of all ages, along with his band; the view from the booth was just a series of silhouettes, passing a huge pipe made from a beanbag ashtray somehow connected to a large cardboard tube. When I first saw the twenty-four-track tape heads, I realized they were black with dirt and grease from never being wiped down... but when the music started, I was overwhelmed with the spirit of Jamaica – it was absolutely palpable. I think we ended up using the first or second take – pure magic which you can still hear on the recording today. I have never experienced anything that amazing, before or since, in a recording studio."

The rest of the album was equally inspiring. Issued as a single in January 1979, "Stand Up and Fight Back" was another of the album's most superb numbers, being a driving roots track concerned with self-determination, on which Jimmy reminds us that we are the only ones who can free ourselves, and that there is everything to be gained by fighting injustice; he also expounds on the interconnectedness of mankind, highlighting his concept of the "oneness" of the human race. In contrast, the single's B-side, "Footprints," is one of the album's more sentimental numbers, recounting the series of cycles that make up our lives.

"She Is a Woman," an ode to the restorative powers of the female half of a loving relationship, is the first track on the album

Military precision: the heights of live performance

slightly less locked into a reggae groove, with bluesy guitar licks and a percolating organ edging toward soul. Even farther from reggae is "You Left Me Standing by the Door," the only song on the album completely re-recorded with session players in California. According to John Stronach, the song was re-cut overseas because an engineer at Aquarius had placed an inferior take of the original recording on the album's unmixed master tape.

"When we got to the Sausalito Record Plant to do a marathon mix as we were behind schedule, that take just didn't hold up to the rest of the record, so we flew to LA for a few hours, just to record a better performance, using the great Jim Keltner on drums, and Will Lee, my favorite bass player. Although it was a great take and song, when I listened to the CD recently, you can tell that it doesn't have that intangible spirit that exists on the other tracks."

Side Two starts off in another direction entirely. "Meeting In Afrika" borrowed from various musical forms of the continent, its structure leaning heavily on South African township jive, but also echoing the highlife of Ghana and Nigeria and the intricate percussion of Senegalese mbalax. As Jimmy sang of the citizens of the black diaspora making an increasing dialogue with the African motherland, the backing music pointed to the new types of fusion that could result when Jamaica comes to Dakar, Los Angeles links with Lagos, and London is "talking to Johannesburg."

Heavily laden with African percussion, the spine-chilling "Lonely Streets" was inspired by the desolation Jimmy encountered in Sierra Leone, while "Wanted Man" was more firmly rooted in the classical reggae format, its lyrics depicting Jimmy as the kind of rebel outlaw he portrayed in *The Harder They Come*, seen as a threat to society simply for defending truth and rights.

Sounding slightly more rock-oriented, "Love I Need" expressed romantic frustration, while the lengthy closing track, "Universal Love (Beyond the Boundaries)," was another of the songs that came to him in the middle of the night during his sojourn in Sierra Leone – after he had seen a strange halo round the moon. Slowly building to a climax, Jimmy's intense intonation explored the very

Bongo power: reconnecting with Africa through the drum

concept of Oneness; namely that, beyond mental, tribal, social, spiritual, class and gender boundaries, we are all linked together by universal love, echoing ideas that stretch all the way from Rasta to Islam, from Confucian Buddhism to Krishna consciousness, from Christianity to Judaism, and back again.

In October 1978, Jimmy embarked on another extensive tour in support of *Give Thankx*, traversing North America, before heading on to further dates in Japan and Europe in early 1979. Everywhere the band played, the new material was well received, be it at Toronto's Massey Hall, where the mostly Caribbean crowd gave a standing ovation, or London's Hammersmith Odeon, where the white, middle-class fans were more sedate. *Give Thankx* itself garnered positive reviews, but spawned no hits, which is unfortunate, given the strength of the material. Perhaps part of the problem was that, as with all of Cliff's 1970s releases, the disc was not 100 percent reggae, despite being grounded in it. But even if the album did not achieve huge sales figures, it can still be seen as a return to form that places it above most of his other albums of the mid-1970s, evidence of the positive effect the African travels and Jamaican residency were having on his creative processes.

10

Roots Radical: Early 80s Rasta Resurgence

After *Give Thankx* had brought critical acclaim without the acco-
manying commercial success it deserved, Jimmy feared his career
was heading toward freefall. In order to get back on track, he en-
gaged the managerial services of Don Taylor, the controversial,
Jamaican-born artists' manager who had overseen Bob Marley's
career development since 1975.

Taylor, who revealed his links with organized-crime leaders in
Miami in his memoir, *Marley and Me*, instigated major changes
during the brief period he represented Jimmy Cliff. In 1979 he
purchased Jimmy's publishing, reportedly for US$40,000, and
clawed back £12,000 outstanding from Island, giving the singer
access to badly needed cash. Taylor also set about reshaping
Jimmy's sound, securing the involvement of figures from American
soul for Jimmy's next album project, *I Am the Living*, in an effort
to raise his popularity among black Americans.

Taylor was then dating Deniece Williams, a singer from Gary,

Indiana, whose soaring soprano had featured prominently on material by Stevie Wonder and Earth, Wind and Fire, helping her to launch a successful solo career. Taylor convinced Jimmy to take her on board as backing vocalist and co-writer, along with Alee Willis, a songwriter from Detroit, who had penned some of Earth, Wind and Fire's biggest hits. Noted producer Luther Dixon, who had worked with the Shirelles, Chuck Jackson and the Platters in the 1960s, was brought in to share production duties with record executive Chuck Tranel.

In the spring of 1980, Jimmy flew to Los Angeles to interact with Williams and Willis, quickly writing the album's title track and another number called "It's the Beginning of an End," which the team laid down as a demo. The bulk of the album was then recorded at Crimson Sound studios in Santa Monica with Tranel and Dixon, though the core of songs such as "All the Strength We Got" and the censorious "Satan's Kingdom" were laid in Jamaica with session players.

Jimmy had important live engagements coming up, so with the album unfinished, he quickly assembled a new touring band, flying a number of talented London-based players of Caribbean origin to rehearse at Lady Musgrave Road with bandleader Chinna Smith and percussionist Sidney Wolfe from the Sons of Negus. Along with old hand Trevor Starr on rhythm guitar, the imported players were Barbados-born guitarist Jimmy "Senyah" Haynes (a veteran of mixed pop act the Equals, who played guitar on Bob Marley's "So Jah Seh" but was here relegated to bass, as guitar parts were already covered); drummer Specs Bifirimbi of the Red Cloud band; and futuristic keyboard whizz Phil Ramacon, a young prodigy from Hackney and alumnus of Rico Rodriguez's band, who wound up being a key contributor to the new album, providing spectacular keyboard parts to "Satan's Kingdom" and the emotive "Love Again."

Released in the States in July on MCA through a licensing deal, *I Am the Living* was handled by Warner's WEA subsidiary in Europe. Although not as schizoid as some of his earlier albums, the disc still seemed almost divided in two, containing polished, pop-oriented works on Side One and ultramodern roots reggae on Side Two.

The most commercial songs were the collaborative numbers written with Williams and Willis, such as the buoyant title track. Framed by bright horn riffs and full vocal choruses, further embellished by complex percussion and synthesizer melodies, it was built on biblical imagery, its catchy refrain adapted from the Gospel of John, in which Jesus reveals his divine nature through the words, "I am the living bread, which came down from heaven. If any man eat of this bread, he shall live for ever." Far more subdued, "It's the Beginning of an End" was fully lodged at the soul end of the spectrum, its swirling orchestral arrangement verging on overkill and reminiscent of Peaches and Herb. "Another Summer" and "All the Strength We Got" were both issued as singles, and although they had much more reggae backbone, with the former driven by skanking guitar licks and the latter by vibrant conga beats, Deniece Williams's vocal gymnastics are all over the map, stretching each beyond the boundary of the reggae stratosphere.

Flip the disc to Side Two and the feeling is entirely different. The two tracks co-written by Phil Ramacon are particularly bubbling, "Love Again" being a heartfelt meditation on that emotion's universal and everlasting qualities, while "Satan's Kingdom" is a fiery reggae refutation of greed. Similarly, "Gone Clear" is a solid reggae groove with shades of funk in the bass, as Jimmy proclaims that Nature will prevail over nuclear weapons and other destructive elements of mankind, with the closing number, "Morning Train," edging ever nearer to the future shape of funk, its loping bass lines complementing a broad reggae beat.

Before the release of the album and "I Am the Living," "All the Strength We Got" and "Another Summer" as singles, a world tour was launched in support of the material, beginning with momentous dates in South Africa. The revamped Oneness band thus landed in Johannesburg on 11 May, traveling via Zimbabwe, along with tour manager Copeland Forbes (a former dancer who had

had a bit part in the film *The French Connection*), and Kojo Brown tagging along under the guise of "Spiritual Advisor."

Jimmy Cliff's performance at Soweto's 65,000-seat Orlando Stadium on 15 May was groundbreaking on many levels: not only was he the first reggae singer to perform in the country, but special permission had been granted for whites to attend the concert in what was otherwise an area designated for blacks, so long as they purchased advance tickets. Similarly, the few black foreign visitors to reach South Africa under apartheid were normally granted "honorary white" status, allowing them access to places where black people were ordinarily forbidden, but Jimmy was allowed to visit the country without this problematic designation.

The historic Soweto concert was simply incredible, the stadium's numbers swelled by thousands of poor township dwellers who gained access by crawling through holes in the fence. Here were black and white people together, all showing an outpouring of love and affinity with Jimmy's musical expression of oneness. Audiences at Durban's new Kingsmead Stadium and Cape Town's Hartleyvale Stadium were equally electric, but the concert in Soweto made the strongest impression, with members of the public appearing on stage, overcome with emotion.

The twelve days Jimmy spent in South Africa affected him deeply. In addition to being greeted as a hero by the nation's black majority, with ordinary folk thronging to him everywhere he went, he also met progressive whites who expressed their gratitude for his visit. One and all mentioned the strong effect his music had on the struggle against oppression, and none other than Nelson Mandela would later publicly confirm its importance in helping to dismantle apartheid. Jimmy also found the time to visit the countryside to meet herbalists and practitioners of traditional medicine, again helping to give context to his own cultural background. And while visiting Cape Town, the Oneness band conjured a spontaneous niyabinghi chant on Table Mountain, awed by the stunning landscape below. They saw their mission partly as a means to spread Rastafari theology, their travels in the region being an antidote to the recent African tour undertaken by Pope John Paul II.

Although *The Harder They Come* had been banned in South Africa, *Follow My Mind* had sold over one million copies on Warner Brothers' African subsidiary, WBA, so Jimmy was presented with a special granite rock, infused with South African gold, in place of an ordinary platinum record. However, not everything about the South African jaunt was positive. Indeed, one afternoon, while Jimmy was driving, police pulled him over and manhandled him, objecting partly to his military-styled garb.

Of course, Jimmy's South African journey was highly contentious. But Jimmy knew that his decision was the right one – particularly as the South African promoter behind the engagements was a black man – and has continually stated that he has no regrets about the experience.

"One of the most memorable concerts of my life was the concert in Soweto, and it was one of the most controversial things I have ever done in my life," he states. "[Anti-apartheid activists] really give me a hard time for going there, because they had this embargo

The Brazilian connection: with Gilberto Gil (right) and Liminha (left)

against artists going there, but the same thing they were fighting for, I was fighting for... only I did it my way."

When Oneness left South Africa, they headed straight for Brazil, where Jimmy had a handful of stadium gigs supporting Gilberto Gil. The week-long tour kicked off at Belo Horizonte's Mineirinho on 24 May, followed by dates in Salvador, Recife, São Paolo, and a return to Rio's Maracanãzinho.

As both artists were signed to Warner Brothers, it was easy for Jimmy's Brazilian representative to suggest the pairing to Gil, who readily agreed to the idea, and the concept made perfect sense, because Gil had been the first local artist to give reggae a major boost throughout the country. During the mid-1970s, reggae had begun making an impact in the northeastern Maranhão region (thanks in part to the popularity of Jimmy's local hit, "Going Mad"), as well as in Gil's native state of Bahia, home to Brazil's largest black population, but reggae did not achieve nationwide permeation until 1978, when Gil recorded the *Realce* album, featuring reggae-influenced originals and a massively successful cover version of "No Woman No Cry," based on Jimmy's reading of the tune.

"I was already under the impact of the song for three years or so before recording it," Gil clarifies. "I was on a beach one day in Maranhão, and the first time I heard it, I heard Jimmy's version, which was very popular there; the song was catchy and I was really moved. In '78, my version became a huge hit in Brazil and I started introducing the reggae taste in my own songs, and that helped the Brazilian general audience to come into the reggae thing a little more. Then, in 1980, an agent had the idea of putting together Jimmy and Gil in Brazil, so I said, 'Yeah!'"

"I met Gil and Caetano Veloso when they were in exile in England," adds Jimmy. "They were the first Brazilians to start experimenting with reggae. By the time he invited me to Brazil, Gil had become a full-fledged star. He said, 'Come, let's do a show together,' and in many ways, it was a special moment, the first kind of show like that in Brazil. They were very inspired by reggae music, and they played it on samba drums."

"He was into the whole cultural, new Jamaican thing," Gil continues. "He was vegetarian, with a close-to-Rasta kind of attitude, but not like Marley or other Rastas. The music was the upfront thing, and the whole Jamaican design, but the stage was one thing, while the private life was very isolated and insulated."

The performances were a resounding success, a particular highlight for the audiences being when Jimmy came back on stage during Gilberto Gil's set to join him for "No Woman No Cry." And as had been the case in Africa, Brazilian audiences showered Jimmy Cliff with love.

"He was like a king," Gil reminisces. "In Bahia, we had twenty thousand people at the airport receiving him, and at the stadium, we had eighty thousand people."

Back in Jamaica, Jimmy mourned for his father, who had died on 23 May 1980 at the age of seventy-two. His passing came as a hefty blow. In his youth, Jimmy learned so much from his father, who set about giving him the kind of unwavering support he really needed to succeed in life; indeed, the care, guidance and wisdom he imparted formed an unbreakable bond between the two, and although he initially disapproved of Jimmy's chosen career, he later acknowledged his son had achieved his goals (though he preferred to give the credit to God, rather than Jimmy). Despite seemingly insurmountable differences regarding matters of faith and lifestyles in general, Jimmy Cliff and his father remained exceptionally close throughout Lilbert's lifetime, and both Jimmy and Victor would hold their father in high regard long after his earthly passing.

But when Jimmy returned to Jamaica following the Brazil dates, there was truly time for little else other than rehearsals, as the European leg of the tour began in London at the Venue on 28 June. Aura Lewis was back in the band, as was Rebop Kwaku Baah, who was also facing a personal calamity, as his young son had recently died in a tragic accident.

During the *I Am the Living* tour, audiences were ecstatic in both West and East Germany, and Jimmy's appearance at the Montreux Jazz Festival on 6 July went down so well that a second festival date was hastily added. Then at Austria's Open Air Festival, on 8 July, Jimmy's electrifying performance compelled Mexican-American guitar wizard Carlos Santana to join him onstage for a blistering collaboration.

The following month saw performances in the US Virgin Islands, and then, coinciding with the Jamaican issue of *I Am the Living* on Sunpower, a free concert was held in Jimmy's hometown of Somerton, the intention being to give something back to the people. Thus, in preparation for the event, local volunteers helped build the stage that Jimmy had dreamed of in his youth.

As Oneness began rehearsing in earnest at Jimmy's Somerton home with backing vocalist Barbara Jones, Mortimer Planno introduced a dynamic new vocal element in the form of Mutabaruka, a young poet based in the neighboring district of Potosi who had already published a book of verse and collaborated with the National Dance Theater Company of Jamaica. Much of Muta's heavily Afrocentric work was concerned with liberation struggles and delivered in thick patois dialect. When he recited the poem "Every Time A Ear de Soun," an astounded Chinna Smith decided to set it to music, the end result being that the poet performed two songs at Reggae Sunsplash, backed by Jimmy's band, and began recording with the group in Kingston for Chinna's High Times label. The resulting album, *Check It*, is rightly regarded as a classic of the then-emerging genre of dub poetry.

Despite heavy rainfall delaying its start, twenty thousand people witnessed the Somerton concert, which became the centerpiece for *Bongo Man*, a concert film bio-pic made in collaboration with German director Stefan Paul, who had already achieved considerable success with a film of the 1979 Sunsplash concert. *Bongo Man* also featured portions of Jimmy's historic Soweto concert, and had incidental footage of Jimmy "reasoning" with Planno, Kojo and Muta, as well as people from various St James communities who had sought Jimmy's practical support.

Meanwhile, Jamaica was in the midst of horrendous civil unrest, particularly in urban areas, as the nation once again prepared to go to the polls. Facing growing opposition from Washington, Michael Manley's second term in office was marked by food shortages, power outages, strikes, hyperinflation and runaway unemployment. Though a short-lived peace treaty between partisan

Stamina: keeping fit at home

street gangs stopped bloodshed for a few months in 1978, the violence surrounding the 1980 election was akin to an undeclared civil war.

In April snipers fired on Manley as he campaigned in downtown Kingston, leading machine-gun-toting PNP activists to storm a JLP fundraising dance on Gold Street, killing five and injuring eleven. The following month, an armed coup was discovered and prevented by the army, leading Manley to fear a destabilization campaign waged by foreign interests; CIA operatives active in Jamaica were subsequently named in the American press. When the elections were held in late October, Edward Seaga and the JLP scored a resounding victory, but election-related violence was said to have been responsible for the loss of over a thousand lives, so it was probably just as well that Jimmy's live engagements kept him off the island for much of this period.

Shortly after the election, Jimmy and Oneness were back in North America for more engagements on the east coast, finishing in early December with another sold-out date at Toronto's Massey Hall with Third World. Unfortunately, the shocking news had surfaced that Bob Marley was receiving medical treatment at a New York hospital after being diagnosed with cancer of the lungs. Jimmy tried desperately to see him before the tour was through, but was denied access to the singer and could not glean concrete information about his health. The following May, after torturous further treatment at a controversial German clinic, Marley ultimately succumbed to the disease.

By then, Jimmy was back in the US with a revamped Oneness, now featuring Chinna, Dougie Bryan, Sticky, Ansel Collins, Phil Ramacon, drummer Mikey "Boo" Richards, and Ranchie McLean tackling bass duties. One of the more notable performances of the tour came at the Ritz in New York in late June, witnessed by Mick Jagger, Keith Richards and Charlie Watts of the Rolling Stones. Then, in early August, Jimmy delivered another phenomenal set as return headliner at Reggae Sunsplash, and at the end of the month he appeared at the Montreux Jazz Festival with Gilberto Gil.

In contrast to the slick overproduction of *I Am the Living*, Cliff's next studio album, *Give the People What They Want*, was a back-to-basics set of roots reggae. Released in the States by MCA in September, as well as on Jimmy's new Oneness label in Jamaica and later via WEA in Europe, it showed just how excellent his work could be when unencumbered by the trappings of commercialism.

The bulk of the album was cut at Channel One with the core of Oneness, augmented by superb musicians such as Augustus Pablo on keyboards, with brass provided by saxophonists Dean Fraser and "Deadly" Headley Bennett, trumpeters David Madden, Bobby Ellis and Arnold Breckenridge, and trombonist Nambo Robinson. Fine harmony vocals were supplied by Michael Rose and Duckie Simpson of Black Uhuru, along with the Tamlins, Barry Biggs and Pam Hall, while Senyah Haynes and Trevor Brown also put in their musical two cents' worth before heading back to the UK. Once most of the album had been completed in the spring, Jimmy and Ranchie brought the master tapes to Compass Point, the state-of-the-art studio Chris Blackwell had opened in the Bahamas.

Compass Point's house band featured Sly Dunbar, Robbie Shakespeare, Sticky Thompson and their guitarist friend Mikey Chung, as well as an English guitarist, Barry Reynolds, and Dahomey-born, Paris-based synth wizard Wally Badarou. Most of these players ended up embellishing Jimmy's album at Compass Point, while Jimmy laid vocal harmonies on Joe Cocker's "Sweet Little Woman" for the *Sheffield Steel* album (which also featured Cocker's cover of "Many Rivers To Cross").

"Jimmy came to Nassau to employ some of the Compass Point All Stars as we were in the midst of Grace Jones's *Nightclubbing* sessions," says Badarou. "That's how, Mikey and Barry excepted, we all ended up being involved."

Badarou's mastery of the Prophet 5 synthesizer and Sly's syndrum experiments gave Jimmy's songs a futuristic edge, the final mix-down executed by Ranchie and Jimmy heightening such elements. According to Badarou, the sessions were very relaxed,

Guitar guru: Oneness bandleader Earl "Chinna" Smith

thanks largely to Jimmy's warmth and openness.

"He was very easy-going, with an everlasting smile, and a positive soul, though I can't recall having had the luxury to tell him that he was my long-time hero, my first awareness of reggae, back in my African youth."

The album starts off firing on all cylinders and never really hits any weak spots. Opening number "Son of Man" adapts passages from the Bible's Book of Micah to remind us that doing justice, showing mercy and being humble is all that is required for mankind. Then comes the horns-driven title track, in which Jimmy proclaims that reggae, the music of liberation, is the key accompaniment to the food, clothes, shelter and clean air that the people truly need to survive. The militant "Majority Rule" is a brilliant fanfare celebrating African independence; as Jimmy points out that Zimbabwe, Zambia and Namibia are as free as Jamaica, America and Russia, and that majority rule exists all over the world, the inference is clear: the days of apartheid were numbered, as black Africans would soon rule South Africa. There were also powerful re-cuts of "Let's Turn the Table" and "Material World," the latter now augmented with the sound of a crying infant to better bring home its message.

In contrast, "Shelter of Your Love" was Jimmy at his most vulnerable, its restrained arrangement allowing a quiet expression of love's healing powers. A couple of numbers edged into funk territory without losing their overarching roots sensibility, the most overtly funky being "Experience," in which Jimmy expressed the view that our individual life journeys bring unique wisdom, while "World in Trap" employed a complex rhythm, embellished by Sly and Wally Badarou, to warn that foolhardy politicians and corrupt leaders are trying to ensnare the Earth. "What Are You Doing With Your Life" reminded that our time on earth is not a dress rehearsal, while closing number "My Philosophy" was a peculiar quasi-medley, issued as a single, in which Jimmy revisited the themes that ran through old and new material, all the while accompanied by bluegrass slide guitar.

Shortly after the album's release, Jimmy and Oneness headed north for a series of sold-out gigs with Peter Tosh in Montreal and Toronto. Then they made their way to Cuba, with Mutabaruka in tow, to participate in the Festival International de Varadero, where Jimmy's brief performance was so well received that the Ministry of Culture arranged for a special concert at Havana's National Theater the following night, to allow Jimmy ample time to express himself. The Havana concert, which was opened by Muta, lasted over two hours, its stage being swamped by the public at the end of the show. Sonny Okosun was also on the island, and when Jimmy caught his performance in Havana some days later, the Nigerian invited his Jamaican friend on stage for an impromptu collaboration.

Although Jimmy was making waves internationally and was often away from Jamaica, he continued to stimulate local talent. In addition to his encouragement of Mutabaruka, Jimmy was working on an album with Jackie Bernard, the expressive former lead singer of the Kingstonians. Only two singles surfaced on Oneness from the sessions, the first being a heavy roots track called "Remand," the other being the romantic ditty "I Need You Tomorrow," though neither made much impact.

Around the same time, Jimmy's nephew, Newton "Sipho" Merritt, brought an aspiring young singer called Ini Kamoze to his attention. Impressed by the youth's obvious vocal ability, Jimmy encouraged him to begin recording, even loaning his musicians to cut a debut single called "World Affairs," which refuted the notion that the Rasta movement was curtailed by the death of Marley. The song was issued on a label formed by Kamoze called Mogho Naba, and was followed swiftly by "Trainer's Choice" and the slang-laden "Murteller." Though sales of all were slim, Jimmy continued encouraging the singer and eventually helped him score a contract with Island by hooking him up with Sly and Robbie.

"Even though we got some airplay, it wasn't happening like we wanted it to happen, so I was at the point of giving up," Kamoze recounts, "but Jimmy Cliff was explaining that this is what he went through too. So due to the encouragement from Jimmy Cliff, I did six songs on a demo tape; he gave Sly the tape, and that was how that whole thing started."

Meanwhile, for Jimmy, 1982 brought plenty of significant changes, especially after Danny Sims got concretely involved in his career. Traveling regularly between New York, Miami and Kingston, Sims was negotiating a record deal for Peter Tosh, and was also working with American soul singer Betty Wright (who had married a Jamaican, Noel Williams, aka King Sporty, a veteran toaster and record producer). Sims ultimately brokered a new record deal with broadcasting giant CBS, designating future Jimmy Cliff material to the Columbia imprint stateside and CBS elsewhere. The album on which this deal hinged was *Special*, recorded with long-standing Rolling Stones associate Chris Kimsey in the producer's chair.

"My manager, Mim Scala, had a connection with Danny Sims," says Kimsey, "and Danny went to Jamaica with a view to signing as many people as he could, making records and trying to do deals. He started working with Jimmy, Peter Tosh and Betty Wright, so Mim said, 'Why don't you jump on a plane and see how you get on with everyone?' Danny met me at the airport and we went straight to Channel One studio, where I sat in the control room for three or four days, just grooving on the music that was going on, until I was invited to sit at the console."

Thankfully, Kimsey did not attempt to force Jimmy too far into rock territory on *Special*, allowing him and Oneness to stick to a roots reggae framework during a few weeks of sessions conducted at Channel One and Dynamics. However, as the team were hoping for an international hit, Kimsey flew in keyboard player Byron Allred of the Steve Miller Band, whose atmospheric ARP synthesizer parts were aimed at American radio.

In March, once the rhythm tracks had all been laid, Cliff, Kimsey and Channel One engineer Anthony "Crucial Bunny" Graham traveled to New York to lay vocals at the Hit Factory, where Stones guitarist Ron Wood also added tasteful overdubs to a couple of numbers. Then Kimsey set to work mixing the album, with Crucial Bunny providing abstract assistance.

"He'd be half-asleep, under the console," laughs Kimsey, "and I'd get to a point in the song, and he'd go, 'Turn up the bass, man! Turn up the bass!'"

When the album surfaced in the summer, the opening title track, issued as a Columbia single, set the tone, being a spongy reggae love song with bubbling synths and bright brass blasts. Similarly, "Love Heights" was a bouncing ode to a woman's appeal, framed by slick keyboard grooves, while "Love Is All I Have To Give" was an open love letter, delivered in a gentle falsetto, in which Jimmy reminds us that material things are completely immaterial in the face of a devoted relationship. The closing number, "Where There Is Love," also spoke of love's almighty power, this time against a slow and sentimental rhythm.

In the aftermath of Bob Marley's death, many in reggae were searching for the way forward, so some songs show the influence of the emerging dancehall style. The most notable was the Cliff-produced "Rub-A-Dub Partner," a percussion-laden dance number written by Ranchie McLean that references a style of close dancing then highly popular in Jamaica. Its Jamaican issue hit the island's Top 10 in February, prompting Jimmy to release an extended version, complete with a toast by deejay Errol Scorcher, while CBS timed their issue of the single to coincide with the album's release.

"Keep On Dancing" pointed toward a rock-pop direction, thanks partly to Ron Wood's guitar licks, but more in a roots vein was "Treat the Youths Right," a strong indictment of the way that society tends to ostracize its youth, often with dire consequences; the song's superb stereo arrangement highlighted the band's excellent musicianship. "Roots Radical" was also a forward-facing slice of roots, in which Jimmy again reveled in the persona of a roving rebel outlaw, defiant and righteous to the end. "Peace Officer" adapted a track that Chinna had worked on some years earlier with a Greenwich Farm singer called Earl Zero, asking why police and soldiers, in their alleged roles as peacekeepers, had to be so heavily armed; Jimmy's rendition was a drawn-out funky groove, peppered by rock guitar from Ron Wood. There was also the rootsy "Rock Children," written by Dougie Bryan, while at the extreme end of the roots spectrum was the autobiographical "Originator," in which Jimmy rebukes his critics against a stunning niyabinghi backdrop, subtly enhanced by kalimba notes from Jimmy's friend Wayne Jobson, leader of the Ocho Rios-based reggae-rock band Native, whom Kimsey was shortly to produce.

Though he would stay in Jamaica the better part of a year, working on Peter Tosh's *Mama Africa*, Kimsey says *Special* was the highlight of his Jamaican experience. "I still regularly pull that album out because it sounds incredible sonically. One of my most favorite parts of my history of recording is that experience with Jimmy, and what a wonderful man – just a heart of gold, and such an inspiration. Jimmy's voice, it was just like recording an angel. He's always remained quite innocent and childlike in his love and affection for music, and never let any of the business crap deter him; he's remained true to the music, which is hard to do."

Some weeks before the album was released, Jimmy and Oneness had engagements to fulfill in Zambia, though, unfortunately, Ansel Collins was unable to make the journey as he was recovering from gunshot wounds received when someone tried to rob him, so Tyrone Downey of the Wailers band traveled in his place. Arriving in Lusaka in May, they were greeted at the airport by hundreds of fans, who broke through security barriers to hoist Jimmy over their shoulders, carrying him to the VIP lounge. Later, the President, Dr Kenneth Kaunda, held a state banquet for Jimmy, honoring him with a tributary poem that named the singer as an African music maker who inspired Africa.

Shortly after his return to Jamaica, Jimmy received the Norman Manley Award for Excellence in the field of music at an emotional ceremony held at the Carib Cinema on 6 July. Collecting the award from Manley's widow Edna, with tears in his eyes, Cliff said it was encouragement for the Jamaican people to "cross the rivers that we have to cross as individuals, as a nation and as a people," before launching into an unaccompanied rendition of "Many Rivers To Cross," which gained a standing ovation. Rex Nettleford read the award's citation, while guest speaker Harry Belafonte took the opportunity to lambaste Ronald Reagan's policies toward persons of color, warning that Jamaica had become "the new pawn of the United States... used one way or another to illustrate the concept of domination." The resulting furore that erupted in the media sparked heated debates about freedom of expression, partisan politics, and Jamaica's relationship with the USA.

In August and September, Jimmy and Oneness were back on the road, touring the US in support of *Special* on a double-bill with Peter Tosh. In November, they gave a government-backed charity performance in independent Zimbabwe, with the proceeds donated to farming and youth employment projects, and immediately upon returning to Jamaica, performed at the opening night of the World Music Festival, a three-day event held at the newly constructed Bob Marley Memorial Center on a strip of wasteland in Montego Bay's Freeport. Arranged by Denver-based promoter Barry Fey, who was inspired to launch the event after visiting MoBay in September, it joined American soul and rock veterans with upcoming new wave acts, as well as the cream of Jamaica's contemporary artists. Officially opened by Edward Seaga and other local politicians, with a dedication to Bob given by widow Rita and mother, Cedella Booker, the festival attracted fifteen thousand people, many of them overseas visitors.

On 27 November, following performances by the I Threes, the Melody Makers, Toots and the Maytals, the B52s and Gladys Knight and the Pips, Jimmy took the stage around two o'clock in the morning to deliver a scorching set, his performance of "Peace Officer" being particularly pertinent, since machine-gun-wielding officers formed a menacing presence among the spliff-toking dreads and tourists in the audience. Psychedelic rock act the Grateful Dead then finished off the proceedings with a lengthy set that lasted to sunrise.

Then, on Christmas Day, four days after the death of his

beloved Aunt Vi, Jimmy took the stage at the National Stadium for the Youth Consciousness concert, held in Bob Marley's memory in conjunction with Peter Tosh and Bunny Wailer, the latter long absent from the Jamaican stage. Although affected by heavy rain, the half-full grassroots event was generally perceived as positive, with Jimmy joining Peter and Bunny for versions of "Keep On Moving" and "Get Up, Stand Up," as well as "No Woman No Cry," in which Judy Mowatt also participated.

Such events show that, at the start of the 1980s, Jimmy was able to reconsolidate his standing in Jamaica, while also making major inroads overseas; later in the decade, his international profile would increase dramatically.

11
American Sweet: Commercial Success Stateside

At the start of 1983 one of the first things that Jimmy did was to go into the newly built Music Mountain, a studio perched above Kingston in the tranquil confines of Stony Hill, to record the Oneness single "Under Pressure," a humanistic exploration of potential reactions to various forms of stress, opened and closed by snatches of backwards vocals. The title of the record was an apt one, for he continued to face public condemnation for his 1980 visit to South Africa.

In the spring, Jimmy gave a few performances in Trinidad, before staging a massive free concert in Negril on 12 March, billed as an "African Oneness Vibration," with rising roots singer Don Carlos as opening act, and an afternoon screening of *The Harder They Come*. However, just after Jimmy announced a five-day "African Oneness Liberation Festival" to be held in Somerton in May as a fundraising effort to help break apartheid, planned performances in Zimbabwe had to be abandoned, because of a travel ban imposed by the Organization of African Unity; he had also been placed on a UN blacklist, forbidding a return to South Africa.

The bans prompted discussions with figures from the African National Congress (ANC), who agreed that the restrictions should be lifted after Jimmy Cliff had issued a public statement that he would not return to South Africa until apartheid ended; the situation, and Cliff's prior visit, continued to be hotly debated in the local and international press.

The Somerton concerts, scheduled for 25–29 May, were to be staged in conjunction with the Royal Ethiopian Judah Coptic Church, one of the more radical branches of Rastafari, whose leader, Stendrick Whyte, had unsuccessfully petitioned Queen Elizabeth II for the repatriation of black Jamaicans to Africa. Although Stevie Wonder, Marvin Gaye, Earth, Wind and Fire and other leading stars were mooted for the events, along with the cream of local Rasta talent, the festival never came to fruition.

By the end of April, Cliff and Oneness were back on the road for a three-week tour of Europe in support of *Special.* They played to a sold-out house at London's Dominion Theater on 1 May, and at another packed venue in Birmingham, before heading to Holland, Belgium, France and Germany. During the summer, they also participated in the Nyon Folk Festival in Switzerland and appeared in Sweden with Nigerian juju star King Sunny Ade.

In Jamaica, Oneness were hard at work on Jimmy's next album, *The Power and the Glory,* the only change to the line-up being that Phil Ramacon was replaced by Mallory Williams, son of noted bandleader Luther Williams. The bulk of the sessions took place at Channel One with Crucial Bunny, with additional recordings made at Tuff Gong with Scientist, one of the island's most impressive dub engineers.

Jimmy was now making use of the managerial services of David Sonenberg, the noted New York music lawyer and artists' manager who had launched theatrical rocker Meat Loaf's career. At Sonenberg's suggestion, Jimmy brought his incomplete master tapes to the House of Music studio in West Orange, New Jersey, to begin collaborating with producer and musician Amir Bayyan (aka Kevin Bell), the youngest brother of Ronald "Kool" Bell and Khalis Bayyan (aka Richard Bell) of prolific funk act Kool and the Gang. The idea was to fashion new songs that would better help him crossover to American audiences, as well as to rework the Jamaican recordings in a mode better suited to American ears through backing vocals and overdubs provided by various Kool and the Gang associates.

Amir Bayyan was then working on La Toya Jackson's *Hearts Don't Lie* album, and a pop-dance track that the pair had written for it, called "Reggae Night," was removed from its roster and given to Jimmy instead. There was also a contemplative number, "We All Are One," co-written by Amir and peers Huey Harris, Raymond Harris and Joseph Williams. However, the basic tracks were only partly finished when Kool and the Gang set to work on their *In the Heart* album (next door in Studio B), while Amir was busy with La Toya and other projects, leading engineer/musician Rick Iantosca, a former staff writer at DeLite Records who had worked with white soul duo Hall and Oates, to become more concretely involved, putting finishing touches to the tracks that Amir had started, and helping Jimmy craft the optimistic new numbers "Sunshine in the Music" and "Love Solution."

Over a number of months Cliff and Iantosca worked closely together, trying to shape the album into a cohesive whole. Faced with the typical Cliff conundrum, where half of the tracks were roots reggae songs recorded in Jamaica on basic equipment, greatly contrasting with the pop-funk material cut in New Jersey on high-tech gear, Iantosca set about painstakingly rebuilding the Jamaican backing tracks through a complicated composite process. The most laborious part involved Mikey Boo's drums tracks, which were replaced by the sound of a Linn drum machine, triggered by his original beats.

"We had to make his drums sound the same as ours, to make the record contiguous," Iantosca explains. "So we triggered the drummer's drums into the Linn and used the Linn sound on all the songs, so that it sounded like it was the same drummer. To do this, we had to turn the tape upside down, which was tedious, ridiculously hard. Then we used Cynthia Huggins and two other backing singers and put them on all the songs, which made them even more contiguous."

Jimmy's Jamaican recordings now had sufficient overdubs to bring them into the realm of the New Jersey tracks. But the New Jersey recordings were totally devoid of any reggae feeling, since Oneness had made no contribution. Naturally, CBS was reluctant to fly Jimmy's entire band to New Jersey, so Iantosca settled for the next-best thing, sending master tapes of the New Jersey originals down to Jamaica, to allow Oneness to add additional instrumentation, which he worked into the overall mix when the augmented tape was returned.

"It was unheard of, but it made Jimmy really happy," says Iantosca. "I didn't know if it was going to work and it did. And Jimmy was thrilled, because the spirit of those guys was there."

Released in October 1983, *The Power and the Glory* had some of the most pop-oriented material Jimmy ever recorded, thanks to the New Jersey sessions. "Reggae Night" was the most blatant effort, but it yielded spectacular results. Aided by regular radio airplay and heavy promotion of the accompanying video (in which tourists are enchanted by exotic Jamaica), its irresistible hooks propelled it onto dance floors all over the world, leading to a gold record in France. Jamaican listeners also loved it, keeping it in the island's Top 10 for over three months, where it ultimately captured the number-one position.

Similarly, opening number "We All Are One" had a tight funk groove totally apart from standard reggae, but its lyrics fitted perfectly with Jimmy's concept of Oneness; issued as a single the following January, with reluctant roots groove "No Apology" on the flip, the song made its way onto US cable channel MTV via a colorful video, shot on a Rio beach. And although never issued as a single, the bright sing-along of "Sunshine in the Music" was also taken into pop territory through a call-and-response choral chant

Another trance: contemplation at the microphone

In the spirit, on stage, as usual

and synthesizer overdubs, while "Love Solution" was shaded by gentle funk tinges.

The rest of the album retained more of a Jamaican sensibility, dealing as it did with themes of equal rights and justice, black history, and Rastafari "livity." For instance, "Piece of the Pie" demanded an equal share by any means necessary, its spongy rhythm driven by Sidney Wolfe's tight conga beats, while closing track "Journey" spoke eloquently of the rootlessness black people face in the West as transplanted Africans removed from their homeland during slavery, and "Roots Woman" updated the "Black Queen" concept, seemingly more censorious, "American Dream" warned Jamaicans flocking north that the nation could prove a nightmare for the disempowered – a CBS executive even protested that one of its verses was potentially anti-American (according to Rick Iantosca, the song remained intact, despite the executive's insistence that the offending lines should be removed). Similarly, the powerful title track used the closing doxology of the Lord's Prayer to question the neo-imperialism and world domination of America and the Soviet Union, warning that God would ultimately unleash his wrath in the form of natural disasters. All of which was a far cry from the jolly fluff of "Reggae Night."

But even if the album, in typical Cliff fashion, seemed to point in more than one direction, it all held together nicely, the cross-Atlantic overdubs ultimately aiding its cohesion. In fact, the pop tracks made it Jimmy's biggest-selling album in the USA since *Wonderful World*, resulting in a nomination for the first reggae Grammy (eventually awarded to Black Uhuru's rock-oriented *Anthem*). Within six months of its initial release, *The Power and the Glory* had sold over 250,000 copies worldwide.

As Jimmy approached his fortieth year on the planet, the success of the album, and especially "Reggae Night," brought him back on the road for four months of touring in the spring and summer of 1984. Oneness now featured Stranger Cole's son Squidly on drums and Harold Butler as second keyboardist, with Crucial Bunny and Mervin Williams as live engineers. Jimmy was now being road managed by his brother, Victor, who had remained active in agriculture. Nephew Sipho Merritt was also on hand as a roadie, with Jimmy's friend Ray Watkins also present for some dates.

In April, during a brief lull, Jimmy had the pleasure of hanging out with Gilberto Gil at Tuff Gong, where Gil and his bass player and co-producer, Liminha, were recording with the Wailers band. Then Jimmy's massive tour began, with performances in Brazil in May, followed by forty-one European dates in June and July, as well as major television appearances. Highlights of the European tour included performances at the Lucerne Song Festival, Holland's Pink Pop, Denmark's Gentorre Rock Festival, and the Antibes Jazz Festival in France, while their Düsseldorf gig, shared with Jamaican band Chalice, was broadcast on German television. Then, at the personal invitation of President Thomas Sankara of Burkina Faso, they performed in Bobo-Dioullaso and Ouagadougo as part of celebrations to mark that country's year-old revolution, followed by a performance in Algeria near the Sahara Desert.

In June, while the tour was underway, Jimmy was named Most Outstanding Showman at the third annual International Reggae Music Arts Awards in Chicago. Then, in August, CBS issued a self-produced rub-a-dub dance track, "Reggae Movement," with "Treat the Youths Right" on the B-side, in place of the dub version that graced its Jamaican issue. In recent months, Jimmy and his peers had also been running the Oneness Record Shop and Culture Restaurant on Barnett Street in Montego Bay, and toward the end of the year plans were made to develop a major shopping center, Oneness Plaza, directly behind their premises, though it would take time to come to fruition, opening to the public the following June.

In the autumn of 1984, Cliff returned to New Jersey to work on *Cliff Hanger*, the follow-up to *The Power and the Glory*. The process was much the same as before, with Jimmy bringing up master tapes of initial tracks laid in Jamaica with Oneness (whose latest incarnation featured Chris Meredith on bass, now that Ranchie had replaced Dougie Bryan on rhythm guitar), while other tracks were built in New Jersey, based on demos Jimmy sent up on cassette.

About half the tracks were built with Amir Bayyan, who was operating out of another nearby studio with programmer Peter Dlugokencky; two numbers were again co-written by La Toya Jackson, one of which featured an intricate bass line from former Weather Report member Jaco Pastorius. The remainder was fashioned over several months with Rick Iantosca at House of Music, while Kool and the Gang were again next door (this time with former Compass Point engineer Kendal Stubbs, reworking the *Emergency* album); at one point, Sly and Robbie were brought in to enhance the rhythm of one of the new tracks.

In December, just as the *Los Angeles Times* named *The Harder They Come* as the third best rock film ever made, Parliamentary Secretary Olivia "Babsy" Grange chose "Wonderful World, Beautiful People" as the theme song for the International Youth Conference and Festival of Arts, to be held in Kingston in April as part of the United Nations-designated International Youth Year. Although Jimmy was very pleased with the song's nomination, he was becoming increasingly preoccupied with political developments in Africa, specifically in Ethiopia, where two separate famines raged.

After the 1974 deposal of Haile Selassie by the Derg, a dreaded Marxist military junta led by Mengitsu Haile Mariam, Ethiopia became a hard-line one-party state. The subsequent civil war between the Soviet-backed Mengitsu regime and US-backed insurgent groups in the north and southeast disrupted agricultural production, especially after the Derg introduced drastic punitive measures, and when the rains failed, famine affected up to eight million people. Thus, in late November 1984, Jimmy responded with the Africa Upliftment Fund, raising $1,500 for the cause within three weeks.

A number of other fundraising drives had been spearheaded in Jamaica by various civic, Rastafari and Christian groups, so Jimmy and Samuel Clayton of the Mystic Revelation of Rastafari approached Babsy Grange and Rastafarian Senator Barbara Blake-Hannah to request the government's assistance in forming a national committee that would ensure the collected funds reached the appropriate aid agencies in Ethiopia. The government's response was overwhelmingly positive, with Edward Seaga pledging to contribute an additional $50,000 to the appeal.

Jimmy recorded a heartfelt roots single, "De Youths Dem a Bawl (Beggar's Banquet)," the proceeds of which he donated to the fund, while Rita Marley instigated a charity EP, "Land of Africa," with contributions from her I Threes trio, Mutabaruka, and other notable vocalists.

Iconic American rocker Bruce Springsteen had been performing Jimmy's "Trapped" for a number of years and when "The Boss" covered it for the *We Are the World* charity album at the start of 1985, Jimmy donated his songwriter's royalty to the famine victims as well. Around the same time, Jimmy contributed to the "Sun City" anti-apartheid protest song, put together by Springsteen band member "Little" Steven Van Zandt and producer Arthur Baker, and recorded "You Don't Have To Cry," which Van Zandt had written in response to the recent riots that had broken out in Jamaica after a gasoline price hike, resulting in seven deaths. This Baker-produced track later surfaced on the soundtrack of

Jonathan Demme's comedy *Something Wild*, being selected for it by Talking Heads founder David Byrne.

After more concerted work on *Cliff Hanger* in February, Jimmy Cliff checked into the Marbella Club Hotel at Dragon Bay, a tranquil resort outside Port Antonio on the eastern edge of Jamaica's north coast, to write seven songs for the soundtrack of the comedic feature film *Club Paradise*, which he would shortly record with Oneness and Sly and Robbie.

Co-written and directed by Harold Ramis (who made *Animal House* and co-wrote the hit comedy *Ghostbusters*), *Club Paradise* cast Jimmy Cliff as Ernest Reed, a rebellious reggae singer and hotel hustler on the fictitious island of St Nicolas, playing opposite comic actor Robin Williams as a retired Chicago fireman who uses his injury settlement money to help Ernest revitalize his dilapidated beach club. Along with Peter O'Toole, who plays a jaded Governor General, Adolph Caesar as a corrupt Prime Minster, and ex-model Twiggy as Williams's love interest, the film featured guest appearances by Carl Bradshaw, comedian Charles Hyatt, folklorist Louise Bennett and numerous other notable Jamaicans, as well as Jimmy's band and brother Victor.

Following the success of *The Harder They Come*, Jimmy had been offered several film parts, but most cast him in roles he did not wish to portray, such as a womanizing stud or frivolous playboy. *Club Paradise*, on the other hand, allowed him to play a more sympathetic character, as well as to contribute to the soundtrack. Filming began on 22 April and was finished on 4 July.

Apart from *Club Paradise,* in the latter half of 1985, Cliff made a cameo on "Too Rude" (which was a loose interpretation of "Winsome" by rising Jamaican vocalist Half Pint); it was one of the most obviously reggae-influenced recordings the Rolling Stones ever made, though the album it appeared on, *Dirty Work*, was an unfortunately disjointed set that suffered from animosity between Mick Jagger and Keith Richards, following Jagger's successful solo album.

Perhaps more importantly, during the same period, Jimmy decided to cease smoking herb, due to the potentially negative effects it had on his voice. As Jimmy explained to *Beat* journalist Roger Steffens in 1986: "There was a time in the 70s when I stopped smoking herb and I found that my voice quality was much better, and then when I went back to Jamaica, I started smoking again, and I find I got hoarse easily... now I find breath control is easier, voice quality sounds better. That's my instrument, my voice, and I have to take care of that."

In addition to soothing his vocal cords, the absence of herb probably kept his mind more focused as well, making it easier to keep his career on track. But the biggest boost to his career, especially in the USA, was ultimately achieved via the release of *Cliff Hanger*. Because it had been subjected to a similar process as its predecessor, *Cliff Hanger* had the same aspect of continuity, despite being cut in disparate places with different producers and musicians. Opening number "Hitting with Music" set the tone with a crisp 80s drum sound augmented by sequenced drumbeats and soaring rock guitar; even though Jimmy sang in semi-patois, using biblical language as usual to decry the world's political mess, the overall sound was that of a light-hearted party, as opposed to anguished outrage. Similarly, the heavily sequenced "Dead and Awake" used symbolic language to relate the crippling effects of an earthquake, but the track was couched within a dance-floor groove, framed by bright notes from the Kool and the Gang horn section. "Arrival" also held a serious symbolic message, but rock guitars and squealing synths distracted from it. Only the closing number, "No Nuclear War," kept its serious message totally intact.

The most blatantly commercial tracks were those co-written by La Toya, namely the funk-rock groove "American Sweet" and the radio-friendly "Brown Eyes," which, without Jaco Pastorius's sterling bass solo, would have been real throwaway pop. "Reggae Street" also came across as pop-rock, its music somewhat at odds with Jimmy's lyrics, though Sly's syndrums and Robbie's loping bass helped retain its reggae sensibility, and the jaunty "Sunrise," punctuated by the crows of a cockerel, was also far from traditional reggae. Farther still was the sentimental "Now and Forever," the most dramatic of the tracks built from scratch at House of Music. But the track that proved most popular was "Hot Shot," a funky reworking of "Gone Clear" from *I Am the Living*, which was a hit in several territories, aided once more by an abstract beachside video. The song was issued as the album's lead single in July, backed by another Amir Bayyan co-production, "Modern World."

In February 1986, *Cliff Hanger* scored Jimmy Cliff a Grammy for best reggae album, despite being one of the most non-reggae albums he ever recorded, sounding far less reggae than competing entries from Burning Spear, the Melody Makers and Judy Mowatt. Nevertheless, as Cliff entered his forties, America was finally embracing him; it seemed the only way to go was up.

12
Rebel in Me: Breaking Free from the Majors

Upon winning the Grammy, Jimmy was summoned to King's House to receive official congratulations from Edward Seaga. Then, in addition to the usual round of live dates in Europe, Jimmy Cliff's spring 1986 tour took him to new African lands, including the former French colonies of Morocco, Madagascar and Reunion Island.

Before setting off for the tour, Jimmy made arrangements for a portion of the profits of the Mystic Revealers' debut single, "Mash Down Apartheid," to benefit the ANC; produced by Sipho Merritt and issued on Oneness, the song was a local hit, launching the Revealers as a respected roots outfit of integrity.

On 23 July, two weeks after its Hollywood debut, *Club Paradise* was given a gala Jamaican premiere at Port Antonio's Delmar Theater, with proceeds donated to the local hospital. The film received scathing reviews in America and fared poorly at the box office, the general consensus being that its characters were woefully two-dimensional, while the shambolic plot relied on cheap gags involving sun, sex and the inevitable ganja. The subplot of corrupt island politics was also poorly executed, making Ernest's spearheading of an armed revolt less than plausible, though many felt that Jimmy Cliff's presence was one of the most positive things about *Club Paradise*.

When the film's soundtrack surfaced on CBS, it held a few surprises, especially the standout single, "Seven Day Weekend," which Jimmy voiced as a duet with post-punk polymath Elvis Costello. The rollicking new wave track, produced by Nick Lowe, was recorded in London with Costello's Attractions band.

Cliff's other contributions were straightforward roots reggae, pointed toward the contemporary dancehall style by Sly Dunbar's modernistic drumming. Given the film's light-hearted nature, there were some startlingly serious messages in the music, especially on the critical "Third World People," which objected to the commonplace media depiction of the developing world. Pointing out that "life could not begin in a refrigerator," Cliff reminds us that Africa is the cradle of humankind, so its people should never be

Hot shot: the Club Paradise *cast cool off*

denigrated as "third." Unfortunately, the message was probably lost on the film's audience, because "Third World People" became the platform for a cheap sing-along gag, and in any case only short snatches of the soundtrack songs are actually present in the film itself. Nevertheless, "American Plan" described the problematic allure of the States for Jamaican sufferers, while "The Lion Awakes" was a spongy update of "King of Kings," featuring snatches of African language. Both "You Can't Keep a Good Man Down" and "Brightest Star" bridled with typical Cliff optimism, while the catchy title track neatly encapsulated the film's storyline.

Although the Grammy-nominated soundtrack was not exactly a Cliff classic, it still held noteworthy moments of particular appeal. By the time of its release, Cliff was already working on his next studio album, and any spare time was devoted to a couple of creative writing projects, the first being the script of a semi-autobiographical film, tentatively entitled *Rude Boys*, exploring the Jamaican influence on the British popular culture of the 1960s. The other prose vehicle was a book called *Reggae Feelings*, which was conceived as a first-hand account of the music's evolution, penned by one of its leading lights. Unfortunately, the many demands on Jimmy's time meant that neither project was completed.

In this period, Jimmy often hopped into his jeep at weekends to travel to Somerton, where he would engage in soccer matches with the team of the Oneness Youth Club, established to give guidance to local youngsters. Jimmy actively contributed to the welfare of many young folk in Somerton, typically paying for school fees, clothing and books. Although he was commanding higher wages on the live circuit, he never seemed to have much ready cash, since he was constantly spreading around what came in, but he was still able to upgrade the small demo studio that he had installed at the Lady Musgrave Road property a number of years earlier, to enable minimal productions aimed at the local market.

Due to the advent of computerization, Jamaican music production was undergoing dramatic changes. After Wayne Smith's totally digital "Under Mi Sleng Teng" became an unstoppable hit in 1985, roots producers like Prince Jammy and Winston Riley switched wholeheartedly to digital production, their island-wide successes prompting many new producers to rise overnight, using inexpensive keyboard synthesizers and drum machines as the basis for quickly made, durable dance tracks. For the moment, Jimmy Cliff avoided the digital mode for his own work, with singles such as "Step Aside (Roots Girl)" recorded in the traditional reggae format with the full Oneness band, but once the digital home-studio was fully operational, he decided to jump into the production fray with gusto, letting his Sunpower production team use the Oneness label as a launching pad for fresh talent, backed by tough digital beats. Indeed, the hilarious "Raggamuffin Selector" by deejay Chicken Chest was a hit on release in 1986, leading to further digital Sunpower productions the following year with fellow dancehall contenders Shaka Shamba, Shortie Ranks and Sister Maureen, as well as veterans such as Sugar Minott and Little John, though none of the releases made much impact.

Meanwhile, in the autumn of 1986, Cliff and Oneness were back on the road for an extensive North American tour. One of the highlights came early, on 7 September, when Jimmy appeared at the Saratoga Performing Arts Center in upstate New York as the special guest of his old friend Steve Winwood, then riding high with the chart smash "Higher Love." Later, once the American tour dates were out of the way, Oneness returned to the African continent for performances in the Ivory Coast, Cameroon and Zaire. In Cameroon, Jimmy collaborated with noted protest singer Lapiro de M'Banga, on a song aimed at corrupt government officials, called "No Make Erreur," which became a huge hit in the territory.

In Zaire, the final concert of the tour was held before an expectant audience at Kinshasa's massive Palais du Peuple. Oneness flew back to Jamaica directly after this performance, but Jimmy decided to remain in Kinshasa for an extended period. He felt the need to commune again with the people of the African motherland, and was inspired to take what he later called a long overdue "working holiday."

The local concert promoter, Tamukati Ndongala, installed Jimmy in a villa in the lively Binza district, on the western outskirts of the capital, where music was a constant feature. Jimmy spent a couple of months touring the capital's nightspots, taking in as much live music as he could, stupefied by the mesmerizing Congolese soukous, a guitar-based music, known as the "African rhumba," that had shades of Afro-Cuban styles hidden in its complex cadences. The groups that most impressed him were the "Tout Poissant" ("very hot") OK Jazz, led by the immortal Franco; Afrisa International, the excellent backing band of top-ranking singer Tabu Ley "Rochereau"; and Grand Zaïko Wawa, an offshoot of the esteemed Zaïko Langa Langa, led by innovative guitarist Pepe Felly.

In February 1987, with Tamukati's assistance, Jimmy took these three backing bands across the Congo River, into the Republic of the Congo, to record one song with each at IAD Studio, Brazzaville. He used Grand Zaïko for "Love Me, Love Me," which addressed universal love, rather than shallow romance; set to an intricate arrangement by Pepe Felly, the song had Zaïko's vocalists echoing Jimmy's choruses in Lingala and Swahili, while the band saluted Jimmy on behalf of the children of Africa, during the *sembene* instrumental break midway through. Afrisa International played on "Girls and Cars," which attacked the consumerist, sex-crazed obsessions that were distracting youth all over the world. The pick of the bunch though was "Shout for Freedom," a heartfelt hymn to self-determination, punctuated by the powerful brass and sterling guitar lines that have defined OK Jazz's best efforts.

Jimmy had been popular in the region for decades, so the musicians were thrilled to work with him. And even if they did not speak each other's language, the musical communication and comradeship was instantaneous.

"I knew his music from when I was a kid," says Pepe Felly. "For me, it was a really big thing. I always wanted to work with Jimmy Cliff one day, but I didn't expect to have Jimmy Cliff at my home in the evening, to speak, eat and drink with me. And I understood that this man is very humble."

Refreshed from his African sojourn, Jimmy returned to Jamaica with the Brazzaville master tapes in time to sing the national anthems of Jamaica and Brazil at the National Stadium in March, opening a friendly soccer match between a team from São Paolo and the Caribbean All Stars. A few months later he was back on the road, performing once again on the US west coast in the autumn. But the biggest focus was his upcoming album, *Hanging Fire*, the last he would record for CBS. In fact, it was reported that Jimmy had turned down a role in Australian action comedy *Crocodile Dundee II* while he was fashioning the album at Tuff Gong with Oneness. The band now featured bassist Glen Browne and drummer Tony "Ruption" Williams, former members of noted backing band Infinite Sensuality, with upcoming keyboardist Bowie McLaughlin and veteran rhythm guitarist Lloyd "Gitsy" Willis joining Ansel Collins and Dougie Bryan at the band's core.

As with his other CBS albums, *Hanging Fire* was built through a composite process, whereby skeletal tracks cut in Kingston were subsequently reworked at House of Music in New Jersey with Amir and Khalis Bayyan, this time with Kendal Stubbs as engineer. And to give the album an outstanding difference, two of the Brazzaville recordings were also brought into the mix.

Hanging Fire surfaced in March 1988, facing in different directions as usual. The most commercial tracks were placed on Side One, while Side Two was slightly more grounded in reggae.

"Love Me, Love Me" and "Girls and Cars" made the cut, with the former even issued as a single, but only their original vocals were intact; probably mindful of America's narrow tastes, the Bayyans completely transformed the rhythms into slick funk grooves, driven by big 1980s drum sounds, with a screeching fuzz-rock guitar tacked onto "Girls and Cars." The snippets of African vocals that remained from the initial sessions were intriguing, but the lack of relation to the rest of the music made them seem strangely isolated rather than a component of successful "world music" fusion (all three Brazzaville tracks would eventually surface on a clandestine maxi single, unfortunately marred by poor sound quality).

In contrast, the languorous funk recasting of Joe Higgs's "She Was the One" (re-titled "She Was So Right for Me") was a pleasant diversion, while the hard-edged title track, which symbolically examined the terrifyingly destructive power of nuclear weapons, had a solid reggae core hidden beneath rock guitar overdubs.

On Side Two, reggae was more in charge. Although the celebratory "It's Time" and optimistic "Soar Like an Eagle" were marked out by thumping pop beats, both were underscored by upfront reggae cadences, while the vengeful "Hold Tight (Eye for an Eye)" was reggae in content and form. The most straight-up reggae number of all was "Reggae Down Babylon," which highlighted the role of the music in putting pressure on apartheid.

Hanging Fire was nominated for a Grammy, but lost out to Ziggy Marley and the Melody Makers' *Conscious Party*. However, even if *Hanging Fire* did not quite scale the heights of popularity accorded its predecessors, on a coast-to-coast tour of the USA in support of it, Jimmy was playing to larger audiences, headlining the San Francisco Reggae Fest in August and opening for the Grateful Dead at an Oregon stadium gig.

But as Jimmy worked to consolidate his popularity on the international stage, it seems nature had more punishment in store for Jamaica. On the morning of 12 September, Hurricane Gilbert unleashed its full wrath on the island, killing more than forty people, destroying hundreds of homes and causing an estimated US $4 billion damage. Strong winds and flood rains had battered the eastern parishes the night before, and by the time the hurricane reached Jamaican soil, the southeast coast was being lashed by 40-foot waves and 125-mile-per-hour winds. Ninety-five percent of all buildings in St Thomas parish were affected, many of them totally destroyed. And instead of heading north, the eye of the hurricane went west, meaning that Gilbert's trail of annihilation passed across the entire length of Jamaica, before moving on to cause further destruction in the Cayman Islands, Mexico and Texas. Jamaica suffered the worst damage from Gilbert, with over 500,000 made homeless. The island's vital services were also affected, bringing power cuts and

JIMMY CLIFF: AN UNAUTHORIZED BIOGRAPHY 160

food shortages. Gilbert was the worst Jamaican storm since Hurricane Charlie in 1951, and the most intense hurricane to reach the Atlantic basin.

In October, when Jimmy's live tour reached the Hawaiian islands, he wasted no time in collecting charitable donations, presenting $10,000 to various Jamaican civic bodies on his return, such as the Cornwall Regional Hospital in Montego Bay, the Mona Rehabilitation Center, and the Islamic Council of Jamaica, whose South Camp Road mosque was where he currently worshipped, as well as to local residents of Somerton and Montego Bay. The following month Jimmy was one of the main acts at a gala relief show, "Give Thanks Jamaica," held at Madison Square Garden with Burning Spear, Third World, Rita Marley, Ziggy Marley and the Melody Makers, Mutabaruka, and soca stars David Rudder and Arrow.

By this time, Jimmy Cliff was reaping the benefits of a commercial endorsement of Shandy, a mildly alcoholic beverage that blended lager with Jamaican ginger: "Reggae pioneer and world-class superstar Jimmy Cliff is one of a kind, just like new Shandy," proclaimed local adverts. In Jamaica, Jimmy's profile remained generally high: at the start of the year, he had performed in Port Royal for an HBO reggae special, and had dropped by Chris Blackwell's Goldeneye residence for the launch party of the debut album by Foundation, who Blackwell was branding "the new Wailers." But Cliff never divorced himself from the everyday Jamaican public and continued to champion new talent, as seen by the release of the *Innocence* album, recorded with a pubescent deejay called Beenie Man at Cliff's Sunpower studio. The talented young toaster, who would later emerge as one of dancehall's biggest stars, had been brought to the studio by Sidney Wolfe (the brother of Beenie's stepfather, Solomon Wolfe), shortly before Sidney succumbed to emphysema.

Now that Jimmy was free from the constraints of a major label, he was able to concentrate on making music on his own terms. In early 1989 an anti-apartheid single surfaced that showed just how good Jimmy sounded in digital dancehall. "Pressure on Botha" was a hard-hitting blast that directly named the South African President as the enemy; calling for continued pressure to be applied to the apartheid regime, it incorporated a complementary toast from Josey Wales, one of dancehall's most stylish rappers. The track was recorded at Music Works, a downtown Kingston studio run by veteran producer Gussie Clarke, its captivating rhythm crafted by an ace set of studio musicians that included keyboardist Wycliffe "Steely" Johnson and bassist Cleveland "Clevie" Browne (one of Glen Browne's younger brothers), the rhythm builders then responsible for some of dancehall's most noteworthy backing tracks (another Browne brother, guitarist Dalton, also contributed). Split onto both sides of a twelve-inch single, "Pressure" was licensed to Greensleeves Records in the UK, where it made a considerable impact, stoking interest in Jimmy's output from the growing mass of overseas dancehall fans.

While at Music Works, Jimmy also voiced a duet with Gregory Isaacs called "Jealousy," which warned of the destructive perils of envy. The song featured on Gregory's album *IOU*, issued by Greensleeves in the UK and RAS Records in America.

All the while, Jimmy Cliff continued to maintain a hectic schedule, with trans-Atlantic flights being part and parcel of the monthly grind. Thus, on 18 March, Jimmy and Oneness gave a greatly anticipated performance at the Accra Sports Stadium in Ghana. As had always been the case with his African appearances, Jimmy was hailed as a legendary role model, to be feted during his time on African soil.

Back in Jamaica, Jimmy spent the following months working on a new album, called *Images*, which would be left free from major-label meddling. After the bulk of the album was on tape, he spent a few weeks in Miami reworking the material at Audio Vision Studios, founded by former Criteria main man Mack Emerman and Steve Alaimo of TK Records (home of disco-funk outfit KC and the Sunshine Band). The studio was recommended to Jimmy by King Sporty, whose wife, Betty Wright, was issuing material through Alaimo's independent distribution offshoot, Vision

Records. In addition to voicing much of *Images* at Audio Vision, adding an R&B flavor through harmony vocals provided by Wright and her peers, Jimmy decided to channel the album through Vision, forming Cliff Sounds and Films Incorporated as his own independent production company, free of record industry control, as well as a new publishing company, named Lilbert Music in honor of his father. Thus, the first Jimmy Cliff release handled by Vision in July was "Dance Reggae Dance," the anticipatory single that pointed toward the upcoming album.

Soon Jimmy was back on the road in support of *Images*, a live engagement in Tunisia being followed by more US west coast performances in August. In September, the tour continued through the Eastern Caribbean islands, and on to the US east coast, to roughly coincide with the album's release.

Although its form was not dictated by any major label, *Images* still aimed for the broadest audience possible, as heard on the spirited opening number, "Turning Point," which featured a searing sax from TK Records' session player Gerald Smith. Several songs also featured full female choruses from Betty Wright, Jeanette Wright-Black and Anita Faye Green, then working with hit pop dance act Miami Sound Machine.

In addition to a slightly altered "Pressure," which no longer mentioned Botha by name, the strongest tracks on *Images* were fashioned in Kingston with Steely and Clevie, and Browne brothers Glen, Danny and Dalton. "Save Our Planet Earth" was a brilliant dance-hall hymn to conservation, warning that humans were destroying the planet; "No Justice" was a hard-edged groove that railed against oppression, be it in the form of societal inequality or the stilted mechanics of the music industry. Sounding a bit looser, but still retaining an edge, "Image of the Beast" equated human greed with the Devil and decried the falseness of plastic surgery, while the gentle "Rebel in Me" spoke of the way a solid love can bring out the rebellious side of each half of a couple.

As the rest of the album featured the more traditional backing of the Oneness band, *Images* still held something of the typical

Cliff duplicity, though as he remained fully in control of the production, nothing sounded too far from its reggae origins. There was a dancehall update of the Slickers' "Johnny Too Bad" that worked fairly well, and a sample-heavy re-cut of "Trapped." In contrast, "First Love" drifted into sentimental ground, while the deeply personal "Everliving Love" had some appealing guitar work, but degenerated toward its ending, overburdened by keyboards, drum machines and a corny vocal chorus featuring Betty Wright's young offspring.

Images surfaced during the era when vinyl albums were giving way to the new Compact Disc format, and in order to entice audiences to make the switch, many CD releases had extra tracks not available on vinyl. Thus, when the *Images* CD was released in November 1989, it also featured the bonus tracks "Dance Reggae Dance" and an upbeat number full of typical Cliff optimism, "The Grass Is Greener."

The initial issue of *Images* did not achieve much in the way of sales, probably in part because it lacked major-label backing. But as had happened decades earlier with some of his most noteworthy material, in time, the disc would fully permeate other territories, the wonders of the silver screen ultimately aiding the exposure of some of the album's finer moments.

Following the *Images* tour, Jimmy Cliff was among the featured guests at Motown's "Soul By The Sea" thirtieth anniversary concert, staged on 30 November at a north coast beach resort at Tryall, some ten or so miles west of Montego Bay. During the grand finale of Stevie Wonder's performance, Jimmy took the stage with upcoming R&B acts Guy, the Boys and Wreckx-n-Effect, to join Stevie for an extended version of Bob Marley's "Waiting In Vain." The event was filmed for an American cable station, Black Entertainment Television (BET), and broadcast live on Frankie Crocker's influential New York radio show.

A week and a half later, on 9 December, Michael Manley was returned to office after a surprisingly peaceful election. This time round, Seaga and Manley agreed to a pre-election truce, ensuring their party supporters refrained from armed attacks, resulting in only minimal disturbances. As eight and a half years of "Seaganomics" had failed to stem the downward spiral of the Jamaican economy, Seaga's adoption of Ronald Reagan's "trickle-down" policy proving an abject failure, the PNP won the election by a sizeable majority, but it was a cowed and less idealistic Manley that came to power, mindful of the need for Washington's approval, as well as Cuba's waning regional influence. Although he reversed several of Seaga's most punitive policies, Manley surprised many loyal supporters by implementing conservative fiscal policies, as well as market-liberalizing reforms. Almost immediately, he negotiated another major IMF loan, though economic planning was already severely constrained by debt servicing.

As the new decade dawned, it was not entirely clear which way Jamaica was heading. Although the lack of election unrest and Manley's measured policies suggested stability, the threat of violence had certainly not evaporated. During Seaga's reign, Jamaica had become a place of strategic importance in the international cocaine trade, with the island used as a way-station for Colombian and Peruvian coke bound for North America and Europe; as the cold war faded and use of the smokable crack cocaine accelerated, those same gunmen who had previously been in charge of "enforcing" party loyalty in Jamaica became major players in the illicit trade, with street gangs formed along partisan lines evolving into rival drug "posses," all of which worked to make Jamaica more violent, with overseas Jamaican communities also blighted by the drug's corrosive influence. The 1980s were bloody times in Jamaica, and everyone hoped the 1990s would be more peaceful.

Jimmy welcomed in the new decade at Montego Bay's Club Inferno, taking in the Superstar Extravaganza, headlined by Frankie Paul. He was also filmed at the Hedonism II resort in Negril for a Fox television special, along with the Jamaican bobsleigh team. He started working on a script for a planned sequel to *The Harder They Come* and was touted to star in the screen adaptation of Anthony Winkler's *The Painted Canoe*, but neither project came to fruition. However, when summoned to Los Angeles by 20th Century Fox and presented with a film script, tentatively entitled *Screwface*, about Jamaican crack dealers wreaking havoc in a small American town, Jimmy agreed to write a song for the film, in which he was to briefly appear through a live performance cameo with Oneness. The film was a vehicle for martial arts expert Steven Seagal and, unbeknownst to Jimmy at the time, the script was later to be significantly rewritten and the film ultimately retitled *Marked For Death*.

Back in Jamaica, Jimmy fasted for the Ramadan holiday in April, celebrating Eid at the mosque on South Camp Road. In June, he was back in Miami, performing with Santana and UB40, returning to Jamaica just in time to catch the stage play *Black Heroes in the Hall of Fame* at the Carib Theater. Then, at the end of the month, he flew up to New York to reconnect with Fela Kuti, sharing an excellent double-bill at the Ritz that was greatly appreciated by the packed audience. He also reconnected with guitarist Philip White, who had moved to New Jersey after breaking up the Light of Saba; before rejoining Jimmy's band, White had worked for DeLite Records, Atlantic and a number of other labels in various capacities.

In August there was a quick day's filming for *Marked For Death*, as well as a four-date tour of Hawaii, followed by performances in Japan and Australia. Bassist Glen Browne had been replaced by Richard Barr, another alumnus of Cedric Brooks's jazz group, while percussion was handled by Loris Lawrence. Meanwhile, despite not achieving much in the USA, *Images* was gradually building interest closer to home. Although "Trapped" had been tipped as locally hit-bound in the spring, it had somehow evaded the Jamaican charts. The surprise success turned out to be "Rebel in Me," which took flight throughout the Caribbean during the summer, holding the number-one spot in the Jamaica *Star* chart for three weeks – as well as topping the charts in Brazil – leading Dynamic Sounds to relaunch *Images* in Jamaica in September, while a licensing deal brokered with Musidisc in France saw the album issued there in October under the alternative title *Save Our Planet Earth*, just as *Marked For Death* became a box-office smash.

A resolutely bloody film, directed by Dwight H. Little (who made splatter-fest *Halloween 4*), *Marked For Death* sought to portray the ruthlessness of Jamaican drug posses and their increasingly problematic presence on American soil. However, its implausible voodoo subplot, wherein dreadlocked Rasta gang members were adherents of Abaqua, an Akan-derived secret society of Cuba, seemed ham-fisted and over the top. Jimmy and Oneness appeared in one of the few scenes shot in Jamaica in an effort to provide "local color," performing the eerie "John Crow," a plot-summarizing track that Jimmy wrote especially for the film, at a packed nightclub. "No Justice" also featured in the soundtrack (as did a brief snippet of "Rebel in Me"), and although the song worked perfectly when set to scenes of deprivation on Orange Street, there was a deep irony in it also being used for a scene in which crack cocaine was weighed up by dreadlocked villains in a Chicago suburb.

When the credits rolled, a brief disclaimer explained that "the posse phenomenon is estimated to be less than a fraction of one percent of the Jamaican population," which did little to assuage objections from the Jamaican-American Rasta community. Jimmy even voiced criticism of the film himself, since he never got a chance to view it before it was released, but he really had little to do with the production, and his contributions to the soundtrack were only present as bonus tracks on its CD release. However, there was no disputing the film's overarching success.

Meanwhile, the belated popularity of "Rebel in Me" brought an extensive Brazilian tour, organized by producer Béco Dranoff, opening in Rio on 22 November. Some weeks earlier, via CBS's global network, Jimmy had been approached on behalf of an upcoming Brazilian reggae band, Cidade Negra (Black City), who hoped to secure his participation on their debut album, *Luta Para Viver* (*Struggle To Survive*), recorded for the Epic subsidiary. The band hailed from the badlands of Belford Roxo, a rough town of dirt streets located about twenty miles outside Rio, in the neglected

lowland plains known as Baixada Fulminese. When Jimmy
checked out the cassette he was sent, he liked the band's style, and
appreciated that its members hailed from the ghetto. He thus flew
to Rio a few days before the tour began to nip into Polygram's studio with the band and their perceptive producer/manager Nelson
Meirelles, one of the driving forces behind reggae in Rio. The resultant Cliff guest spot on the song "Mensagem" ("Messages")
boosted the band's popularity, assisting their emergence as the
most important reggae act in the land.

Jimmy Cliff played to adoring audiences in nine different cities
in Brazil, a particular highlight being the performance on 23 November before 100,000 people, in the reggae heartland of São Luis
do Maranhão, to mark the election of Governor Edison Lobão.

"I will never forget, as long as I live, our days in São Luis with
Jimmy and the band," says Béco Dranoff. "Before our plane
landed, we could see that the airport terminal was taken over by
fans – it was literally like God had landed. I had never seen anything like that before: there were thousands of people screaming
and waving at Jimmy, so we were rushed from the plane ahead of
all other passengers to a secure internal room and then through a
side door to the tour bus; the luggage and gear was delivered to
the hotel later, as we just had to get out of that airport very fast!
We could feel the terminal vibrating with excitement and noise,
like what the Beatles must have felt. The show was to be held at
this huge parking lot, so a large metallic pipe stage was built spe-
cially for the occasion; sound-check went smoothly the next afternoon but when we returned to the stage that night, Jimmy and
the group were surprised by the sheer number of people already
there – a humongous audience, as this was a free concert, the first
time a major international reggae star was performing there.

"Everyone came out that night, so we had to have extra police
and security all over the stage; the band was amazing and all was
going great, Jimmy and the crowd were in heaven. At some point,
I remember seeing a light tower slowly tumbling onto the audience
in slow motion, but there were so many people that they were able

to hold the tower before it hit the ground, and slowly make it stand up again! At another point, the crowd started climbing onto the huge pile of PA speakers next to the stage, so the police stopped the concert until everyone got off the speakers. After a very long and slamming performance, Jimmy and the band were exhausted, but the crowd wanted more. Backstage, we were surrounded by a sea of people, and when they realized it was Jimmy inside the car, they went nuts, banging on the hood and windows; police and security could not contain the crowd, but after a few tense minutes, we were able to slowly leave. I also remember the hotel manager telling me that fans were trying to break into the hotel to greet Jimmy, so we should lock our doors. Everyone was amazed by the grandeur of that gig, and the vibe, the excitement and the size of the show in São Luis do Maranhão is etched in my memory forever."

The performance at Salvador's massive soccer stadium on 1 December was another highlight for Jimmy, not only because Brazil's black population showed their obvious identification with the man and his music, but also because the concert again featured Gilberto Gil, as well as local reggae singer Lazzo Matumbi and versatile pop chanteuse Margareth Menezes, a recent Island Records signee and David Byrne collaborator, who drew heavily on reggae, soca and funk.

The Brazilian dates drew to a close on 15 December, but Jimmy and the band were soon back for more, playing to another 100,000 spectators at Rio's Maracanã stadium on 18 January, on the opening night of the second Rock In Rio festival. The week before, Jimmy spent time in Salvador with noted impresario Daniel Rodrigues, manager of Gilberto Gil, who proposed that Jimmy begin working with local artists, including the cultural group Ara Ketu, whose leader, bassist Zéu Góes, had mastered various forms of African rhythm. Jimmy also agreed to produce Lazzo Matumbi's next album. Although that disc never surfaced, Lazzo and Jimmy wound up sharing guest vocals on Margareth Menezes's version of Lazzo's "Me Abraça e Me Beija" ("Hug Me and Kiss Me"), a

Samba reggae: with João Jorge of Olodum

samba-reggae hybrid on her *Kindala* album, that proved to be her biggest-ever hit, while Lazzo became a long-standing member of Jimmy's live touring band.

Additionally, having been introduced to the group by a Senegalese engineer called Daoud, Jimmy was soon collaborating with Olodum, the politically active Afro-Bloco Carnival drum troupe and leading samba-reggae progenitors, whose cultural activist wing was educating the youth of Salvador about their civil rights and the importance of their African cultural heritage.

"When he performed with Gilberto Gil at this big concert, the first song was 'Bongo Man,' a very emblematic song," recalls João Jorge, leader of Olodum. "The concert was very important for the black community in Salvador, because we were raising our black consciousness and the presence of Jimmy Cliff reinforced that."

Jimmy participated in Olodum's 1991 Carnival parade, being the first international artist to do so. He also helped their theater group compose a song called "Summer Reggae" and then went into WR Studios with Olodum to record "Reggae Odoya" (a hymn to the Orisha Yemanjá, Goddess of the Sea, venerated in the local Yoruba-derived religion of Cambomblé), for which Jimmy spontaneously composed lyrics highlighting black communities around the world, as well as figures like Marcus Garvey, Malcolm X, Martin Luther King and Elijah Muhammad.

"His presence in Salvador is very important for Bahian music," continues João Jorge. "When Bob Marley and Peter Tosh died, he became a reference for the Afro-Bloco groups, a nice reference for us, because he is still a reggae man, alive, in Brazil, doing the work."

During this period, Jimmy Cliff felt very at ease in Brazil. When he passed through the Baixada Fulminese for a photo shoot with Cidade Negra, he played soccer with the locals and toured around on a bicycle. Many aspects of life were familiar there, despite the language difference, and in the coastal cities of the northeast, Jimmy felt an even greater affinity, most especially in Afrocentric Salvador. In fact, the more time he spent there, the more it felt like home.

13
Samba Reggae: The Salvador Phase

Jimmy's extended stay in Salvador was particularly productive. He recorded a number of tracks for the forthcoming *Breakout* album at the Tapwin and Propago Som studios with Ara Ketu, Lazzo Matumbi, producer Cesar Napoli and Guyanese backing singer Ricky Husbands, a former member of the Surinam-based Duehsmo Syndicate, who later became a regular member of Jimmy's live touring band. From March 1991 these musicians backed Jimmy on performances throughout the country, with bassist Zéu Góes of Ara Ketu acting as bandleader. But Cliff had other working commitments that soon drew him away from Brazil, so, with the album as yet unfinished, he and Oneness conducted another US tour during the summer of 1991 that included well-received festival dates on the west coast.

Jimmy then put some finishing touches to *Breakout* at a Los Angeles studio with guitarist Philip White, who introduced Jimmy and his brother Victor to former United Artists label boss Artie Mogul and his associate Joe Isgro, then running the independent JRS Records, the short-lived home of Kool and the Gang and rock super-group Asia (Isgro had recently been prosecuted on payola charges, though the case was dismissed; he would plead guilty to unrelated extortion charges in May 2000 and be sentenced to fifty months' imprisonment). JRS thus ultimately became the American home of *Breakout*, though it was issued first in Brazil on Som Livre, a division of the massive Globo network.

As the album had been recorded in Salvador, Kingston and Brazzaville, *Breakout* was another Cliff stew that delved into different genres, but despite its disparate origins the disc held together well, helped along by an up-to-the-minute modernity and supported by superb musicianship. Opening the album was "I'm a Winner," a blazing blast of upbeat reggae rock; cut with Cesar Napoli, Lazzo and Ricky Husbands, the track was an optimistic proclamation of self-belief that had Jimmy trying out his skill as a rapper. He also rapped on the equally upbeat title track, recorded with Ara Ketu, which saluted love's liberating powers. Retaining a hard-rocking edge through a fuzz-box guitar lead, "Oneness" was another modernistic number, which highlighted Jimmy's belief in the need for universal love. Zéu Góes's arrangement of the poignant "War a Africa" really brought to life the fantastic Afro-Brazilian percussion that lay at Ara Ketu's heart, giving a dramatic underpinning to Jimmy's reading of the destructive conflicts that blighted the African continent and the terrible developments in the Middle East that had resulted in the first Gulf War, working in a phrase from an old mento number to highlight the human flaws of religious leaders. The other most obviously Brazilian track was Jimmy's adaptation of Olodum's "Samba Reggae," again tastefully supported by Ara Ketu.

The rest of the album was a real mixed bag of old and new, but with plenty of noteworthy moments along the way. "Roll On Rolling Stone" was a particularly compelling roots track, cut around the time of *Give Thankx* with Chinna, Gibby Morrison and Reebop, while "Shout For Freedom" from the Brazzaville sessions was another inclusion from the archive (unfortunately presented here with gratuitous keyboard overdubs). Several other tracks were cut at Music Works with Steely and Clevie (and various Browne brothers), including "Jimmy Jimmy," which recounted the delights of Mr Cliff's trip to Ghana, plus a driving dancehall update of the Willows' "Baby Let Me Feel It" and a digital adaptation of an old rock steady number, "Be Ready." Another full-on digital number, "True Story," used a tough Danny Browne beat as the platform for a challenge to the distorted history lessons that typically denigrated the black experience, resulting in alienation and a poor sense of self for black youth; using Rastafari language to decry corrupt ideology, the song also referenced a Nation of Islam concept that traced the African presence in the western hemisphere to a forgotten Moorish empire that extended from Africa to Central America via the lost oceanic continent of Mu-Atlantis (first explored by Moorish Science Temple founder Noble Drew Ali, a contemporary of Marcus Garvey, and later adapted and espoused by Elijah Muhammad). There was also a bright re-casting of "Sitting in Limbo" as the far more confident "Stepping Out of Limbo," completed by a full horn section, but the song Jimmy believed had the greatest chance of chart success was the captivating "Peace," a quietly emotive track warning that war would always rage if injustice prevailed. Similar in theme to Peter Tosh's "Equal Rights," it was delivered with far more pain and sorrow, though its schmaltzy keyboard overdubs placed it more in the mode of soft-rock AOR, rather than firebrand roots reggae.

Like *Images* before it, the Grammy-nominated *Breakout* remains an underrated album of the period, one of Jimmy Cliff's few last gasps before his studio output slowed. Despite aiding his popularity in Brazil, the album made less of an impact elsewhere, though it was later repackaged in France on more than one occasion.

"We thought 'Peace' might have been a hit in America, cause it got great reviews there," Jimmy laments, "but I didn't have such a good label, so it didn't get anywhere."

Through his current Jamaican manager, Norman Reid, Jimmy

had been in discussions with Texan businessman Brady Oman about making a sequel to *The Harder They Come*, but the project quickly stalled. Then, in the spring of 1992, Cliff was back in Brazil, promoting *Breakout* via more live performances with Ara Ketu. Invited to participate as a Spiritual Advisor at the United Nations Conference on Environment and Development, aka the Earth Summit, held in Rio over eleven days in June, Jimmy delivered a number of songs to the delegation, including a new number called "Higher and Deeper Love," in which he proclaimed that the remedy for the planet's untenable situation was a divine love that embraced the earth and all of its living creatures equally; religious leaders and politicians were not doing their jobs properly, Jimmy explained, so it was up to humankind to make the change.

Then came the 1992 "World Beat" tour, headlined by Jimmy throughout North America in July and August, featuring Burning Spear and Nigerian reggae star Majek Fashek also on the bill. Among the most notable engagements were a spot at the Reggae on the River festival in California, a stadium gig in Boise, Idaho, and a return to New York's Ritz, as well as a gala event at Berkeley's Greek Theater with the reformed Skatalites, Montserratian soca star Arrow, and rising Cameroonian band Les Têtes Brûlées.

Intoxicated by his successes in Brazil, Jimmy was now dividing his time between Jamaica and Salvador (when not traveling elsewhere for live engagements), spending between one third and half of the year on Brazilian soil, his growing popularity even resulting in a Brazilian branch of Sunpower.

In December 1992, shortly before his appearance on the *Arsenio Hall Show*, Jimmy contributed to a new version of Bob Marley's "One Love," put together in Kingston by Chinna Smith and Ziggy Marley and the Melody Makers, to benefit the establishment of a Bob Marley Community Center in Trench Town. Issued on Ziggy's Ghetto Youths United label in February 1993 to coincide with Marley Senior's birthday, the track also featured members of Black Uhuru, Steel Pulse and Third World, plus Dennis Brown, Freddie McGregor and Beres Hammond.

In the New Year, Jimmy and Ernest Ranglin were honored at the Jamaican Music Industry (JAMI) Awards, the Jamaican equivalent of the Grammys. It was another tense time on the island, as violence escalated in the run-up to the 1993 general election, which the PNP won by a decisive majority. PJ Patterson, a Somerton native who had become Prime Minister a few months earlier, following Michael Manley's health-related retirement, remained in power as a center-left leader who would ultimately stimulate investment in tourism and end Jamaica's reliance on IMF loans.

In mid-1993, Jimmy began working with inventive producer Clive Hunt, who roped in quality veterans, such as guitarist Wayne Armond and drummer Wayne Clarke of the Chalice band, and keyboardist Tyrone Downie of the Wailers, plus upcoming musicians such as keyboardist/programmer "Computer Paul" Henton. Hunt had a long and varied involvement in Jamaican music, having worked with the Abyssinians and Max Romeo during the roots era, before moving to New York and recording for producer Lloyd "Bullwackie" Barnes. Unfortunately, the stateside switch led to an eleven-year crack cocaine habit and eventual deportation to Jamaica, but even crack addiction could not stop Hunt from creating hits. In fact he had engineered Beres Hammond's "Putting Up Resistance," a remix of which became one of the biggest successes of 1992, shortly after Hunt came out of rehab. Thus, after Hunt was officially drug-free, Jimmy Cliff sought to make use of his services in sessions conducted at Mixing Lab and Tuff Gong studios.

Together with Computer Paul, Hunt co-produced Cliff's pop-styled reworking of Johnny Nash's 1972 hit "I Can See Clearly Now," for the soundtrack of the Disney film *Cool Runnings*, a family-oriented comedy based on the exploits of the Jamaican bobsleigh team at the 1988 Winter Olympics. On its release in October 1993, the film was spectacularly successful, its popularity rapidly bringing Jimmy's soundtrack single into the charts in several territories (handled by Sony's Chaos offshoot in the US and Columbia internationally). Early in 1994, the single peaked at number 18 on the *Billboard* Top 100, being Cliff's first US Top

20 entry since "Vietnam" some twenty-five years earlier. It also reached number 23 in the UK pop charts, hit the Top 20 in Australia, and reached number one in New Zealand and France, where the song went silver, selling over 125,000 copies.

During this time, Maxine Stowe, niece of Clement "Sir Coxsone" Dodd and wife of popular vocalist Sugar Minott, was in charge of the Jamaican acts on Chaos. She signed numerous high-profile dancehall acts to the label, such as Super Cat, Tony Rebel and Tiger, and was breaking Jamaican music into the American mainstream by promoting artists who blended dancehall with hip-hop and R&B, such as Diana King and Worl-A-Girl; all these artists featured on the film soundtrack, along with Jimmy and fellow veterans the Wailing Souls. As the *Cool Runnings* film gathered steam, Stowe thus arranged a "Cool Runnings" tour to hit US stages in the autumn of 1993, showcasing the acts that featured on its soundtrack, along with guests such as singer Carla Marshall, a gala at Madison Square Garden being one of its most notable engagements.

The year had been a grueling one for touring, taking Jimmy to Brazil and Argentina, twice through Europe, over to Japan, Guam, Australia and New Zealand, before finishing up in the States with the Cool Runnings dates in late November.

When that tour was over, Jimmy was back at Mixing Lab with Clive Hunt, cutting tracks related to a corny basketball comedy, *The Air Up There*, in which an African tribesman is recruited for an American college team. Neither Jimmy's up-tempo version of Jackie Wilson's chart smash "(Your Love Keeps Lifting Me) Higher and Higher," nor his English-language version of the Swahili song "Watch Me Fly" actually appeared in the film, being reserved instead for the companion album, *Music from and Inspired by The Air Up There*, which is probably just as well, since the film itself flopped on release, due to its insensitive portrayal of racial and cultural differences.

Cliff's follow-up to *Breakout* was reportedly finished around the same time, but the material was inexplicably shelved for an extended period. On a more personal level, further appreciation was shown for the man in February 1994, when Jimmy received an award for his ongoing contributions to the development of his alma mater, Kingston Tech. Then, just after celebrating his fiftieth birthday, on 14 August, he led an "All Star Reggae Jam" as the closing act at the revived Woodstock Festival, held in honor of the twenty-fifth anniversary of the original upstate New York hippie event; Cliff's section also featuring Rita Marley, Toots and the Maytals, Worl-A-Girl, Diana King, stylistic sing-jay Eek-A-Mouse, and top-ranking dancehall star Shabba Ranks. Back in Jamaica, at the end of the year, Cliff also received a Hall of Fame Award for Excellence from the Caribbean Development for Arts and Culture organization (CDAC).

In February 1995, as the shine from *Cool Runnings* began to diminish, Jimmy Cliff scored another hit with a song related to a film soundtrack. The animated Disney feature *The Lion King*, which drew on elements of *Hamlet* and featured songs written by Elton John and Tim Rice, had been a tremendous box-office success, but the soundtrack songs were delivered in clownish cartoon voices by its cast. In order to make the material more appealing to music fans, South African actor and singer Lebo M conjured pop adaptations of the songs for an album called *Rhythm of the Pride Lands – Music Inspired by The Lion King*, on which Jimmy Cliff contributed "Hakuna Matata," the title being a Swahili term meaning "no worries for the rest of your days." Cut primarily in Jamaica with keyboardist Fabian Cooke, the "Rass Brass" horn section of Dean Fraser, Chico Chin and Nambo Robinson, plus Toots's daughter Leba on backing vocals (with additional vocals overdubbed in the US), the song quickly became a hit in Europe and was also popular on the African continent.

Then, in May 1995, Jimmy went back on the road as part of the "Natural Mystic" tour, held in honor of what would have been Bob Marley's fiftieth birthday and featuring Ziggy Marley and the Melody Makers, the I Threes, the Wailers Band (with original members Al Anderson and Tyrone Downie), and British toaster

More dramatic communication on stage

Pato Banton. The fifteen-date European tour, arranged by Marley's associate Neville Garrick, also featured engagements in Israel.

Later in the year, Jimmy helped link Olodum with Michael Jackson, after being approached on Jackson's behalf by film director Spike Lee. Shot by Lee behind Jackson in the sprawling Rio favela of Dona Marta, Olodum were thus featured in the music video of Jackson's "They Don't Care About Us," giving the Salvador Afro-Bloco the maximum worldwide exposure possible.

That Jimmy could link Lee and Jackson with Olodum said a lot about his standing in the music and film worlds, as well as attesting to his strong presence in Salvador. However, Jimmy's time in Brazil was drawing to a close. Despite the great popularity he held there, Jimmy's wandering spirit ultimately pointed him in another direction, partly due to new-found fans in a European territory.

14
Higher and Higher: The French Connection

Toward the end of 1995, Jimmy Cliff's status in France began climbing to another level. At a Clive Hunt-produced session recorded at Tuff Gong with Sticky and the Rass Brass, Jimmy provided guest vocals on "Melody Tempo Harmony," a reggae-rock hybrid by versatile French rocker Bernard Lavilliers, which quickly went gold in France. In October, Cliff and Lavilliers performed the song live on French television, and as Jimmy's fame continued to grow in the land, he found himself spending increasing periods there.

The following year, as his Gallic status continued to rise, French journalist Hélène Lee and director François Bergeron made a television documentary profile of Jimmy Cliff called *Moving On*. The sympathetic portrait, filmed in Jamaica, had Jimmy recounting tales of his early life, expounding on motives and spiritual philosophies, and voicing a general antipathy toward religion, including disappointment with the shortcomings of Christianity and the Nation of Islam. Like *Bongo Man* before it, the film made clear that Jimmy was still deeply connected to the downtrodden Jamaican public, and also showed him preparing for overseas tour dates with the latest version of his backing band, now featuring guitarist Wayne Armond and drummer Wayne Clarke of Chalice, plus Berklee graduate bassist Benjy Myers of the Rhythm Kings and keyboardist Jimmy Peart of the Skool Band.

In the summer of 1996, the inevitable overseas concerts included spots at San Francisco's Maritime Hall and a headlining appearance at Colorado's Reggae on the Rocks festival, while at the end of the year, Jimmy's latest album, *Higher and Higher*, gave him an even greater boost in France.

The album surfaced on Island Jamaica, the sub-label launched by Chris Blackwell to specifically showcase contemporary Jamaican product, now run by Maxine Stowe, who rapidly rose in the label's ranks following her departure from Sony. Stowe specifically aimed *Higher and Higher* at French audiences, choosing to forgo an American issue of the disc, and the strategy proved an astute one, for the album quickly sold seventy thousand copies in France, reaching the Top 10 album charts and ultimately bagging a gold record in the territory.

Produced in conjunction with Clive Hunt, Computer Paul, Sly and Robbie, and keyboardist Handel Tucker, most of the album was thoroughly commercial, although recent collaborations with inventive French-Canadian producer and multi-instrumentalist Daniel Lanois and Jamaican-American re-mixer Pete Rock were somehow left off. Along with the film hits "I Can See Clearly Now" and "Higher and Higher," there was "Melody Tempo Harmony" (replaced on some reissues of the album by the original studio version of "The Harder They Come"), plus decent updates of Cliff classics such as "Wonderful World," "You Can Get It If You Really Want," and a live version of "Many Rivers To Cross" featuring the Sounds of Blackness gospel group, as well as "Rebel in Me" and "Save Our Planet Earth." Though the funk slush of "Soul Mate" was somewhat overproduced, other tracks were more positively challenging: "Ashe Music" explored the jazz-based, Afro-Bloco-derived form of Bahian pop known as Axé, and "Bob Yu Did Yu Job" saluted "brother Bob Marley" in fine reggae style, while the hard-hitting "Crime" reminded that there was not necessarily any difference between police and thieves or preachers and sinners, and that gun manufacturers are ultimately more responsible for death than those that wield firearms. (The Japanese edition issued by Polygram also featured the bonus track "True Revolutionary," an excellent political diatribe, also issued as a Oneness single, based on a re-cut of the "Mean Girl" rhythm built by Sly and Robbie and Handel Tucker). But despite such noteworthy material, the album was almost totally overlooked outside France.

Jamaican music was then finding many new fans in the region, and Jimmy helped spearhead its dissemination by appearing before ten thousand people in Cannes at the opening of the International Market of Records and Musical Editions (MIDEM) convention in January 1997, being part of a grand Jamaican delegation that featured dancehall artists like Shaggy, Papa San, Chakademus and Pliers, and Everton Blender, as well as reggae veterans such as Ken Boothe, Freddy McGregor, Ernest Ranglin, Chalice, and the Mystic Revealers. He also appeared live on French television performing "Melody Tempo Harmony" with Raï star Khaled.

In early March, Jimmy was back in Brazil for a special live collaboration with São Paolo-based rock act Titãs (Titans), performing a semi-acoustic version of "The Harder They Come" with the group at Rio's João Caetano Theater as part of MTV's *Unplugged* series. One of the most impressive of the "new Brazilian rock" groups to emerge in the early 1980s, Titãs adapted "The Harder They Come" as "Querem Meu Sangue" ("They Want My Blood") for their 1984 debut album, but the song did not hit until it was reissued with Jimmy's participation on a live companion DVD, culled from the *Unplugged* performances.

Returning to Jamaica directly after, Jimmy Cliff headlined the closing night of the Negril Music Festival, delivering a stunning performance before seven thousand spectators at the Samsara

Dr. Cliff: receiving his honorary doctorate from the University of the West Indies

Hotel on 15 March, just days after the passing of Michael Manley signaled the end of an era in Jamaican politics. The Negril show, highlights of which were broadcast on MTV, was Jimmy's first proper Jamaican concert for a number of years, the dramatic energy he imparted being highly appreciated by local and foreign concertgoers alike.

During this time, and for a few years to come, there were further plans to make a sequel to *The Harder They Come*, with Wyclef Jean, of reggae-influenced hip-hop act the Fugees, reportedly cast as Ivan's son, though the project itself was very slow to progress and Perry Henzell not always pleased with the concept.

Jimmy's 1997 return to Nigeria was tinged with sadness, for although he was received with open arms by the usual adoring public at his stage show, his friend Fela Kuti had been seriously ill for some time, eventually dying of AIDS on 2 August, after refusing conventional medical treatment. On a more positive note, toward the end of the year Jimmy was feted in his own land when awarded an honorary Doctor of Letters (D.Litt) degree from the University of the West Indies on 14 November, during a ceremony in which Chris Blackwell was also made an honorary Doctor of Laws

(LLD). Immediately after the ceremony, Drs Cliff and Blackwell headed to the offices of Island Jamaica in New Kingston for a gala celebration that also served as the launch party for the belated local release of *Higher and Higher*.

Then, on 16 November, at the National Stadium, Jimmy sang the national anthem at the crucial soccer match between Mexico and Jamaica which saw the "Reggae Boyz" qualifying for the 1998 World Cup. Thus, in June 1998, Jimmy and fellow artists Diana King, Ernie Smith, Tony Rebel, Buju Banton, Julian and Damian Marley, plus the Stone Love and Bodyguard sound systems, traveled to France for complimentary performances held around the matches, during which Jamaica was eliminated after losing two out of three games. Further European tour dates followed for Jimmy, including headlining spots at the Spring Vibration festival in Austria in June and the Köln Summerjam in July.

In September, Island Jamaica issued Jimmy's latest album, *Journey of a Lifetime*, another largely overlooked set, marketed primarily in France. Unlike *Higher and Higher*, *Journey* had no cover tunes and maintained a thoroughly modern grounding, aided in part by a hip-hop element on a few tracks, including a collaboration with young French-British rap duo Squeegee.

Two of the album's strongest numbers, the determined "Looking Forward" and the defiant "Burden Bearer," were produced with Clive Hunt. "Democracy Don't Work" was critical of Western political systems that only really benefited the rich, while "Change" and "Where Will U Be" noted that the world was on the cusp of another era, as the new millennium approached. "Street Vibes" spoke of urban hardship atop a tough hip-hop groove, the rap portions bringing the message home with greater clarity, contrasting a ragamuffin dancehall sensibility with American east coast b-boy twang. Similarly, the jauntily defiant "Rubber Ball," which spoke of resilience in the face of adversity, was given its defining contours by a stylish rap segment. Conversely, the sentimental "Daddy" was a heartfelt tribute to Jimmy's cherished father, which also cleverly acknowledged the nature of fatherhood in general.

As well as brief between-song interludes, in which Jimmy waxes lyrically in patois about various philosophical concepts, there was plenty of other message music on the disc. "Let It Go" spoke of ways to avoid being paralyzed through doubts and fears, while "Learn To Love" declared that love is the way by which humanity can progress. "Super Bad" furthered a concept explored on Jimmy's re-cut of "Johnny Too Bad," namely that there will always be someone "badder" than whoever thinks they are the "baddest," leading to an endless cycle of self-destruction, while "Higher and Deeper Love" was resurrected from the Rio Earth Summit, delivered here as a slow funk groove. A few numbers were unfortunately overly laden with string synthesizers, which pushed them over the edge of shlock sentimentality; the worst offenders were the sappy "All For Love" and the easy-listening title track. In contrast, the catchy closing number, "Simple Truth," was another reggae/hip-hop hybrid, with Squeegee here providing the bilingual rap highlights that indicated the album was primarily aimed at France.

A few weeks after the release of *Journey of a Lifetime*, Jimmy was honored at the inaugural Doctor Bird Awards, held in Kingston by filmmaker Lennie Little-White, director of the 1979 film *Children of Babylon* and the son of Robertha White, the teacher who had given Jimmy so much motherly guidance during his youth. During the joyous occasion, other award winners joined Cliff for a spontaneous chorus of "The Harder They Come."

Jimmy's final album of the century, *Humanitarian*, was issued in June 1999 on the Los Angeles-based independent, Eureka Records, surfacing in France on the Globe Music label, its front cover showing a bald-headed Jimmy splashing in a swimming pool. Largely comprised of further collaborative work with Clive Hunt, Handel Tucker, Computer Paul, and Sly and Robbie, some of which was recorded during the *Higher and Higher* sessions, the album featured Jimmy's regular touring unit, supplanted by guests such as Tyrone Downie and Family Man Barrett of the Wailers band, Cat Coore from Third World, and digital rhythm kings Steely and Clevie, as well as Daniel Lanois and Pete Rock. Perhaps the most cohesive of his late 1990s releases (with the exception of a couple of regrettable cover tunes), *Humanitarian* had the political relevance and emotional resonance that fans have always expected from a Jimmy Cliff album.

The title track, which was present as an opening ska and reprised in a slower, more spacious form, had Jimmy proclaiming himself a humanitarian, noting that his musical mission has always been one that aimed to unite and uplift humanity as a whole. More in the dancehall mode, "Rise Up" implored the public to shake off uninterested inertia and rebel against a fraudulent system, taking better control of its destiny by becoming involved; similarly, "Giants" asked the "sleeping giants" in our midst to awake from their slumber and seize the time, while "How Long" used a complex hip-hop beat to refute the need for war, and the bubbling "Let's Jam" called for songs of freedom in an increasingly troubled era.

Various other musical forms and themes filled out the rest of the disc. Thanks to the Wailers band (with Tyrone Downie blowing a mean harmonica), "Drifters" had the wonderful hallmark of classic roots reggae, while the pop shadings of "I Walk with Love" held a tight reggae groove at its core; in contrast, the funk-driven "Keep the Family" highlighted that family unity was the key to a progressive society, despite the media's fixation on the familial-destroying vices of sex and violence, and the sensual "Come Up to My Love" rode a complex dancehall hybrid of electronic hip-hop beats, peppered by Indian elements and bubbling reggae organ. More oblique in terms of message, "The Hill" also carried a feeling of defiance, while the gentle bounce of "I'm in All" attempted to relate the cosmic consciousness of universal spirituality. Somewhat strangely, the disc closed with a salsa-dancehall remake of the Beatles' "Ob-La-Di Ob-La-Da" and a lackluster cut of Carole King's "You've Got a Friend."

Touring the world in support of *Humanitarian*, Jimmy went as far east as Japan and as far south as Madagascar, as well as playing throughout North America in the summer months, headlining festivals such as Colorado's Reggae on the Rocks and San Francisco's One Festival with Burning Spear and Maceo Parker. He also appeared as the opening act for the Dave Matthews Band on nine dates in the States, with the South-African-born singer-songwriter, a huge Cliff fan, personally introducing him on stage at each performance.

After the tour, Jimmy was honored in Kingston at the Hall of Fame Awards for his outstanding contribution to and achievements in arts and culture. Then, after an official meeting with PJ Patterson, Cliff agreed to take part in Telefood 99, a charitable concert to be held on James Bond Beach, near Oracabessa, to benefit the United Nations' Food and Agriculture Organization. He thus traveled to New York at the end of October to collaborate on a theme song with Wyclef Jean and other participants.

On 20 November, Jimmy Cliff, Perry Henzell and Trevor Rhone were feted at the Jamerican Film and Music Festival, held at the Wyndham Rose Hall Hotel, St James, just as Cliff and Henzell were again in protracted negotiations about the planned sequel of *The Harder They Come.* The following week, Jimmy appeared at the Telefood concert with Miriam Makeba, Hugh Masakela, Gilberto Gil, Maxi Priest, Shaggy, and the Sounds of Blackness, whom Jimmy joined on stage for "Many Rivers To Cross."

One week later, Jimmy was part of the stellar cast that performed at James Bond Beach for the Bob Marley One Love All Star Tribute Concert, filmed for cable channel TNT's *Master* series. Backed by Ziggy Marley's band, featuring Chinna Smith and Family Man, Jimmy joined Chrissie Hynde, former lead singer with the Pretenders, for a version of "Jammin'," and nu-soul diva Erykah Badu for a heartfelt "No Woman No Cry," playing bongos at various other points and kicking off the messy grand finale of "One Love." And, as part of the festivities, Jimmy even had a hotel suite named after him at the San Souci resort, which hosted many of the concert's performers.

The rest of the year passed tranquilly and, although he received several live engagement offers, Jimmy chose to spend millennium eve off-duty, welcoming in the new era away from the limelight.

15

Black Magic: Furthering the Journey in the New Millennium

At the start of the new millennium, although his schedule was not as hectic as before, Jimmy Cliff continued to promote his music through a handful of notable performances across North America with the latest incarnation of Oneness (now with several new members, since Wayne Armond and Wayne Clarke were focusing on the reformed Chalice). After appearances on the US east coast in May, Jimmy gave a riveting performance at WOMAD Seattle in June. At the end of the following month, he braved the looming specter of Hurricane Debby to headline the closing night of Carifesta in St Kitts, sharing the bill with dancehall crooner Sanchez. Thing were relatively quieter for much of the following year, though in February he again sang at the National Stadium during a Reggae Boyz soccer match, this time against Trinidad.

In December 2001, just three months after Islamic extremists used hijacked commercial airliners to attack the World Trade Center and the Pentagon, Jimmy Cliff gave a few more live performances on the US east coast, most notably joining the Harlem Gospel Choir for the Sounds of Hope charity concert, held at Riverside Church to benefit AIDS orphans in South Africa. Although the city was still reeling from the September 11th attacks, Riverside was far enough uptown to be spared the chaos surrounding lower Manhattan's "ground zero."

At one of the US concerts, Jimmy met his old friend Wayne Jobson of Native, now a program director at XM satellite radio in Washington DC. Wayne's brother Brian had sent a message from Jamaica saying that the English singer and producer Dave Stewart was on the island, seeking to make Jimmy's acquaintance. Best known as half of the Eurythmics, one of the biggest pop-rock acts of the 1980s, Stewart is a creative maverick who counts Bob Dylan, Mick Jagger, Paul McCartney and Ringo Starr among his close friends. Since the demise of the Eurythmics, Stewart had been involved in various solo projects and recorded a number of film soundtracks. More recently, he had delved into other media arenas with mixed results: in the year 2000 he launched a New Age self-help cable television channel in Europe called Innergy, broadcasting "transformational TV," and made his directorial debut with the film *Honest*, reviews of which were largely negative.

As a result of his long and varied musical experience, Stewart had become greatly disillusioned with the exploitative workings of the music business, and was thus in the process of setting up Artist Network, an independent company that pledged to give the artists on its roster greater creative freedom and higher royalty rates, to stimulate more meaningful output. There would be associated film, television and book publishing wings, and artists active in different media would be encouraged to work with each other. As contracts would have overall transparency and not be weighted against the artist, Artist Network aimed to turn the accepted in-dustry model on its head, while more realistic sales projections would generate higher profits during an age when CD sales were greatly affected by unauthorized Internet file-sharing. Dipping into his own reserves and gaining further investment from a former asset manager of Deutsche Bank, as well as the founders of alternative cosmetics firm the Body Shop, Artist Network reportedly had $10M of start-up funding.

As Dave Stewart had owned a holiday home in the Jamaican countryside for a number of years, he spent considerable time on the island, and when Brian Jobson brought Jimmy Cliff to his residence, Cliff found Stewart in the company of Sly Dunbar, which instantly put him at ease; in any case, Cliff had been impressed by the Eurythmics' "Sweet Dreams," and was thus already motivated to meet its co-composer. Stewart told Cliff about Artist Network, and Jimmy was impressed by his intentions; their rapport was fairly instantaneous, so a few days later they went into a studio in Ocho Rios to bat some ideas around, quickly building the shell of a song called "Jamaica Time."

"He told me what his concept of Artist Network was, and it sounded really good to me, like when I was recording with Beverley's, and the business side of it is a lot more fair than anything I've been with before," Jimmy explains. "And he has this imaginative mind, this brilliant creative mind. We just make things happen, and it works."

Over the next few months, Cliff and Stewart met frequently in different locations, fleshing out ideas for further material. First, Jimmy spent a few days at Stewart's home in leafy Surrey, where the pair quickly penned three more songs. In March they were back in Jamaica, trading ideas in Port Antonio and in the tranquil confines of Strawberry Hill, Chris Blackwell's exclusive hotel complex overlooking Kingston. Later, there were recording and voicing sessions at Stewart's Church Studios in north London, and at another facility in the British countryside. Sometimes they would meet up informally in Paris as well, where Jimmy was becoming a long-term resident.

Fantastic Plastic People, the album Jimmy recorded with Dave

Stewart, featured a number of notable guest artists. Most noteworthy were the duets Jimmy voiced with Stewart's former counterpart Annie Lennox, former Clash leader Joe Strummer, and Sting of the Police, plus a Jamaican rapper called Nadz (aka Nadirah X), who Stewart had discovered at the Caribbean Music Expo in March (where an absent Jimmy was granted a lifetime achievement award). The backing band featured Gary "Mudbone" Cooper of Funkadelic, keyboardist and television presenter Jools Holland from Squeeze, and Fela's drummer, Tony Allen, on a couple of tracks, along with Brian Jobson on bass. The result was a lush, pop-oriented album with a slight urban flavor that held little reggae in its contours.

As the album received its finishing touches, Jimmy's profile continued to receive momentary boosts. In early June, the Jamaican premiere of Desmond Gumbs's low-budget crime flick *Rude Boy: The Jamaican Don*, revealed a surprise cameo by Jimmy, playing an elder called Wise Man, but the film's hammy acting, visual gore and paper-thin plot brought poor reviews. More positively, Jimmy made an important contribution to the BBC's three-part television series *Reggae: The Story of Jamaican Music*, broadcast in August to tie-in with the fortieth anniversary of Jamaican independence. But Dave Stewart really helped bring Jimmy Cliff back into the limelight through a number of other notable collaborations. Their joint pop single, "Peace One Day," recorded with Mudbone and Nadz, was cut in support of filmmaker Jeremy Gilley's campaign to designate 21 September as an annual day of worldwide ceasefire. Cliff and Stewart also performed at the closing ceremony of the 2002 Commonwealth Games in Manchester on 4 August, and Stewart arranged for Cliff to give a performance on 12 September to a full house at the revamped Marquee club, now located in Islington and largely owned by Stewart.

On 1 October, shortly before the release of his new album, Jimmy performed at the Music of Black Origin (MOBO) awards in London, where he received a lifetime achievement award. To stimulate anticipation of the album's issue, and to counter the corrosive effects of illegal file-sharing, Artist Network placed tracks from *Fantastic Plastic People* on Internet peer-to-peer sites a few weeks before its official release. When the album surfaced as the first full-length Artist Network CD – with a goofy cover showing Cliff with glittering stars pasted all over his head – its production style felt a bit overloaded in places, but there was still plenty of Cliff pertinence in the lyrics. The opening title track was one of the strongest, decrying society's superficiality over a tight hip-hop groove, while "The City" was a haunting song that described the lure and pitfalls of urban life. The most overtly political numbers were also particularly noteworthy, especially the hard-hitting "War in Jerusalem" and "Terror," the latter Jimmy's response to September 11th, in which he points out that every action brings a reaction, cautioning the powers that be to look at their own misdeeds before pointing the finger of blame. The defiant "People" used a complex arrangement that featured bass and vocals from Sting and a chorus from the London Community Gospel Choir, while rocky dirge "Over the Border" was a terse duet with Joe Strummer (which Strummer had begun independently, but brought to Jimmy after picturing his voice on the track).

In contrast, "No Problems Only Solutions" and "I Want I Do I Get" were brightly optimistic pop tracks that once again saluted self-determination, as did hip-hop number "Positive Mind (The World Is Yours)" and the acoustic closer, "Dreams." The most blatantly pop-oriented track was the fully orchestrated "Love Comes," featuring Annie Lennox, while the closest thing to reggae was "Jamaica Time," the song Cliff and Stewart first developed in Jamaica.

Though the album received mixed reviews, there is no doubting the boost it afforded Jimmy's profile, especially after Artist Network's concerted publicity campaign. It also led to a fully orchestrated ska version of "Dreams," included on Jools Holland's *More Friends* album, and a guest performance of the track by Cliff at Holland's Royal Albert Hall performance on 28 November, as well as a Cliff guest spot on Holland's *Hootenanny* program on New Year's Eve.

Honors list: receiving the Order of Merit, with fellow honor recipient Derrick Morgan

Stewart, meanwhile, helped Jimmy and Perry Henzell to reconcile some differences, putting the sequel to *The Harder They Come* back on the menu, this time with Henzell allocated the role of co-writer. There were also plans for Jimmy to issue an autobiographical video and publish a book of interview material culled from conversations with journalists, as well as the history of reggae he had planned decades earlier. Stewart additionally secured Cliff's involvement in the 46664 project, named from Nelson Mandela's old prison number, which Joe Strummer used as the basis of a charity single to combat the spread of AIDS in South Africa (composing and voicing the song shortly before succumbing to a fatal heart attack in December 2002); a benefit concert on Robben Island was initially scheduled for February 2003, but postponed due to funding issues.

On 1 February, Jimmy made a surprise guest appearance during Dave Stewart's set at the Air Jamaica Jazz and Blues Festival in Montego Bay, performing "City" from the new album. In March, he began several months of extensive touring in support of *Fantastic Plastic People*, kicking off with a six-date stretch in the UK and Ireland, followed by a week in Angola in April. In July, the European wing of the tour saw headlining spots at Germany's Summerjam and Rototom Sunsplash in Italy, as well as a return to the Nyon Festival. Then he went across to the USA for further prominent festival dates in August and September, including California's Reggae on the River and WOMAD in New York's Central Park. From here onwards, backing was provided by the Skool Band, one of Jamaica's most noteworthy live groups, featuring drummer/bandleader Desmond Jones, bassist Dale Haslam and keyboardist Christopher McDonald.

Unfortunately, by the summer of 2003, Artist Network was already experiencing financial difficulties, after the Marquee relaunch brought insurmountable cash-flow problems and pledged funding failed to materialise. The company entered into a Company Voluntary Arrangement in June, and was soon to be wound up completely.

Back in Jamaica, things were more positive: on 9 October, Jimmy Cliff received the Vice Chancellor's Award for Excellence, along with a number of academics based at the University of the West Indies' Mona campus. Then, on 20 October, he was granted the Order of Merit, Jamaica's third-highest national honor, for his outstanding contribution to the island's film and music industries, receiving the award from Governor General Sir Howard Cooke in a public ceremony at King's House.

Meanwhile, as Artist Network was no longer active, and because *Fantastic Plastic People* was geared toward a British rock audience, Jimmy decided to re-fashion the album for his core reggae fans with input from leading dancehall practitioners such as Steely and Clevie, Glen Browne and his son Shams, and Mixing Lab mainstay Colin "Bulby" York. Together with the remixers, Jimmy stripped down the rhythms to make them more in tune with the predominant dancehall style, embellishing the tracks with additional contributions from dancehall deejays, and adding new duets with black pop stars. He also cut an alternative pop remix of the album with the French market in mind, and thus returned to Paris the day after gratefully receiving his OM to record a duet with Yannick Noah, the professional tennis player of part-Cameroonian origin, who had launched a successful career as a pop singer during the early 1990s.

At the end of November, Jimmy flew to Cape Town to join the Eurythmics, U2, Bob Geldof, Peter Gabriel, Beyoncé, Queen, Cat Stevens (now known as Yusuf Islam), Baaba Maal, Youssou N'Dour, Angelique Kidjo and other stars for the delayed 46664 benefit concert, held before forty thousand people and an Internet audience of millions. A highlight of Jimmy's performance came when he was joined on stage by Johnny Clegg, founder of the first racially mixed South African band, for a rousing version of "People."

The following February, Cliff continued his civic activities by auctioning an *a capella* performance of "Rebel in Me" and "Many Rivers To Cross" at the Farewell Fundraiser, an annual event held during Chinese New Year by staunch PNP supporters Monica Chen and Mavis "Pinky" Bowers, in conjunction with Prime Minister PJ Patterson, to raise funds for various charitable causes. The songs in this instance netted JA$250,000 for Somerton All-Age School, the alma mater of both Cliff and Patterson.

In April 2004, Warner Brothers issued Jimmy's pop repackaging of *Fantastic Plastic People* in France under the title *Black Magic*.

This French edition had the entire *Fantastic Plastic People* album (except for the song "Dreams") given a pop-oriented mix-down less weighted toward rock and roll. In addition, there were three new pop songs, the most obviously hit-bound being "(Ooh La La La) Let's Go Dancin'," a fresh collaboration with Kool and the Gang that employed a pleasant steel-pan refrain. There was also the eerie title track, about a mysterious woman's dangerous romantic charms, as well as the carefree "Dance," featuring a toast from Wyclef Jean about how music helped him overcome his experiences of childhood deprivation (the toast also included the line, "Shoot the sequel to *The Harder They Come*, we'll leave you in the dirt," referencing a new rap remake of the film that was to be directed by Stephen Williams and scripted by *Basketball Diaries* screenwriter Bryan Goluboff with rapper Mos Def in the lead role, but when Def opted for *16 Blocks* with Bruce Willis instead, the project was quashed, and subsequent versions starring rapper Eve and Lauryn Hill also failed to reach fruition).

In contrast, the restructured dancehall format of *Black Magic*'s re-sequenced American issue, which surfaced on the independent Artemis label in the summer, placed the same material in the realm of contemporary Jamaican reggae: "People" now had a sing-along toast from Tony Rebel; "Love Comes" had rapping embellishments from deejay Hawkeye; "I Want I Do I Get" featured female toaster Spice; and "The World Is Yours" had contributions from Tessane Chin, an upcoming vocalist who had backed Jimmy during his recent Angola tour. There was also "Good Life," based on a looped sample from John Holt's "Stealing Stealing," while "(Ooh La La La) Let's Go Dancin" here featured a stylish toast from Bounty Killer, one of Jamaica's most popular rappers. Generally garnering more praise than *Fantastic Plastic People*, the US version of *Black Magic* fared strongly enough in the States to be nominated for a Grammy, while the French version briefly skirted the Top 150 album charts.

Approaching his sixtieth birthday, in the summer of 2004, Jimmy was back on the road in support of *Black Magic*. In early

June, with Youssou N'Dour, French-African rapper MC Solaar, and French-Algerian rocker Rachid Taha, he took part in an AIDS awareness benefit held on Gorée Island, Senegal, the site from which millions of slaves were shipped across the Atlantic. A few weeks later, he appeared at a two-hundred-year-old castle on the slopes of Mount Liban in Lebanon for the Byblos International Festival, hitting Manchester's Move festival, Ireland's Oxygen and Guildford's Stoke Fest in July. Then, after performing at the inaugural Reggae Music Fest in New York in November, Jimmy was presented with the Marcus Garvey Lifetime Achievement Award at the Caribbean American Heritage Awards in Washington DC, receiving the award from Gordon Shirley, Jamaica's ambassador to the USA.

Returning to Jamaica at the start of 2005, Jimmy Cliff was given a hero's welcome at his homecoming concert on 15 January, held in rural St Elizabeth as the crowning glory of Tony Rebel's annual Rebel Salute festival. In a performance that lasted well over two hours, Cliff was given the audience's undivided attention as he sang through the highlights of his career, playing guitar and keyboards at key intervals, deejaying at one point, and even doing the splits, still possessing the magical energy that had always powered his live appearances. And during songs like "Save Our Planet Earth," Jimmy managed to link the global to the local, referencing victims of the Asian tsunami that had struck a few weeks earlier, as well as those affected by Hurricane Ivan, which had caused widespread destruction throughout the Caribbean region the previous September.

Three days later, Jimmy addressed a full house at UWI to launch *Black Magic* in Jamaica, introduced by Rex Nettleford, Mortimer Planno and Ibo Cooper of Third World. The following week, he found time to visit a cluster of UWI students, and then appeared at a fundraising concert for the Institute of Caribbean Studies (dubbed "Black Magic: Cliff on Campus"), at UWI's Oriental Gardens on 4 February, taking part in another Chinese New Year fundraising event for Somerton All-Age School shortly afterwards.

Meeting of minds: Jimmy with the late Rex Nettleford.

The pace seldom slowed in the months to follow. On 23 May he was in Stockholm, reading the official tribute to his friend Gilberto Gil, who was presented with the Polar Prize by the King of Sweden; four days later, Jimmy attended a JLP banquet thrown at the Pegasus Hotel in honor of Edward Seaga, who had stood down as leader of the opposition in January after forty-five years in politics. Held the day before Seaga's seventy-fifth birthday, and hosted by Grenada's right-wing Prime Minister, Keith Mitchell, the former JLP leader received a number of tributes, but was most visibly moved when Jimmy Cliff presented him with the guitar he had used to compose "Rebel in Me" and other works. Meanwhile, down at the Calabash Literary Festival, held in St Elizabeth by Perry Henzell's daughter Justine, Jimmy's lyrics were explored by Wayne Armond, Billy Mystic of the Mystic Revealers and Peter Tosh's former rhythm guitarist, Steve Golding.

In October, Jimmy was back on the stage at James Bond Beach for the Caribbean Rising festival, which marked the launch of MTV's Caribbean channel, Tempo. Although the crowd took a drenching from tropical storm Wilma during his performance, Jimmy's mastery of popular dance moves like the Willie Bounce and Chaka Chaka helped keep their rapt appreciation in focus. The following February, at the Prime Minister's annual Chinese New Year fundraiser, PJ Patterson announced that a Jimmy Cliff Center For Excellence was to be developed at Somerton All-Age School, which seems entirely fitting, considering Jimmy's continual support of local youth.

Throughout it all, Jimmy Cliff continued to perform at high-profile events, devoting considerable energy to charitable causes. In March 2006, he appeared at La Bal De La Rose, Monaco's prestigious charity event, followed by a prominent place at WOMAD in Adelaide, Australia, performing to seventy thousand people, and a spot at the Summer of Sound festival in Brooklands, New Zealand. At WOMADelaide, Jimmy was struck by the appearance of the Golden Pride Children's Choir of Tanzania, touring to raise funds for a village school, and thus invited the choir to join him at select European summer festival dates.

In April, Jimmy was back in London, attending the launch of the stage version of *The Harder They Come* at the Theater Royal Stratford East, along with an ailing Perry Henzell, who had adapted the storyline for the stage, but who was now seriously ill, having been battling cancer for a number of years. Fans of the movie doubted whether its magic could transfer to the non-celluloid setting of a stage musical, but the opening night drew a frenzied standing ovation that saw Jimmy spontaneously join the house band for an impromptu finale of the theme song. After months of sold-out performances, the play later transferred to West End theaters and eventually opened in Toronto, its overall success ultimately sparking renewed interest in Jimmy Cliff, leading to an increase in live bookings and a general reappraisal of his career.

In June 2006, after singing the Jamaican national anthem at a friendly Reggae Boyz match against England at Manchester's Old Trafford stadium, and an appearance at a Frankfurt gala concert for the Soccer World Cup opening, Jimmy kicked off another summer of extensive touring. In addition to sixteen European dates in July and August, there was an appearance at the Timitar Festival in Morocco (where Jimmy was the only non-local act), plus performances at Yokohama Sunsplash and WOMAD Singapore. Then, in mid-November, there was a week's worth of engagements in the UK, Ireland, Italy and Reunion Island, the tour closing shortly before Perry Henzell finally lost his battle with cancer on 30 November.

The following year began with another accolade, as Jimmy was granted the University of the West Indies Bob Marley Award from the American Foundation for the University of the West Indies (AFUWI) in New York, for his outstanding achievements in arts and culture. On 11 March he performed in Trelawny at the opening ceremony for the Cricket World Cup, assisted by Tony Rebel; two weeks later, he attended a tribute to Perry Henzell, held by Brian St Juste, president of the Video and Film Producer's Association, and son of Franklyn St Juste, cinematographer of *The Harder They Come*. Then, in the summer, Jimmy was back on the road for nineteen dates during the European festival season, playing the Montreux Jazz Festival and Tunisia's El Jem in July, followed by an open-air gig in the Swiss Alps and Holland's Reggae Sundance in August.

In October, Jimmy received an unexpected surprise when a band member informed him that "You Can Get It If You Really Want" had been adopted by the British Conservative Party as the theme song for their annual conference. A bemused Cliff quickly informed the UK press that he did not support party leader David Cameron, nor any other politician; always a supporter of the lower classes, who simply believed in right and wrong, he knew the electoral system of Western democracies was such a fraud that he had never voted in his life, nor did he intend to. Of course, it was not the first time the song had been appropriated by politicians, as it had notably been co-opted by the Nicaraguan Sandinista National Liberation Front for their unsuccessful 1990 re-election campaign – though at least the Sandinistas were more generally in tune with Cliff's revolutionary ideals.

There were a handful of European live dates in April 2008, before Jimmy headed to the south of France for a badly needed holiday. As usual, the summer brought another extensive European tour, with twenty-six dates taking him through a dozen different nations in June and July, though afterwards, there was time for more relaxation in Crete.

In March 2009, Jimmy continued his charitable works by appearing at a gala benefit staged for the National Council of Ghanaian Associations in New York. The event, which was held in Manhattan as part of celebrations to mark Ghana's fifty-second year of independence, served to raise scholarship funds for academically gifted Ghanaian youngsters seeking to further their education in the USA.

After his typically busy schedule saw Jimmy traveling between Paris, New York and Jamaica, the year ended with another significant accolade, as it was officially announced in December that Jimmy Cliff was to be inducted into the Rock and Roll Hall of Fame. At the ceremony, held on 15 May 2010 at New York's Waldorf Astoria hotel (and aired live over the Fuse music television network), Jimmy was presented with the award by Wyclef Jean, who spoke of the importance of Jimmy's music during his own formative years, as well as their first collaborative work, at a time when the Fugees were still to achieve a major breakthrough. During an emotional acceptance speech, Jimmy saluted his family, giving special mention to his grandmother, and spoke of the impact legendary figures such as Sam Cooke, Ray Charles, Fats Domino and Jimi Hendrix had on his work, as well as the importance of the working relationships he established with Leslie Kong and Chris Blackwell. Then, as the Bee Gees, Maroon 5, Jackson Browne and his old friend Bruce Springsteen looked on, Jimmy stole the show with powerful performances of "You Can Get It If You Really Want," "Many Rivers To Cross" and "The Harder They Come," the last delivered as a duet with Wyclef. Exiting the stage, he was personally congratulated by Phil Collins for the excellence of his delivery.

In the whirlwind of press coverage surrounding the event, it emerged that Jimmy had been working on a new concept album, titled *Existence*, during the last two years, putting many of the finishing touches to the album at the recording studio he had established a number of years earlier, a few streets away from his old Lady Musgrave Road headquarters; he was also in the process of building a brand-new, state-of-the-art recording facility, whose official opening was planned to tie in with the album's release. Rebellion, love and global warming are just a few of the themes covered on the disc, the backing band said to be largely comprised of young, upcoming musicians. Pre-release reports have stated that thirteen of the album's fifteen songs are newly composed, with a Joe Higgs track and an adapted "All For Love" being the only revisited material.

In support of the as yet unreleased album, a twenty-date North American summer tour was scheduled, including appearances at Tennessee's Bonnaroo Festival and the Atlantic City House of Blues in June, plus appearances at Central Park's Summerstage, the Ottawa Blues Fest, the Winnipeg Folk Festival and the Hollywood Bowl in July, as well as Connecticut's Gathering of the Vibes Festival and Denver's Mile High Fest in August.

Jimmy's work thus continues to take him all over the globe, and his music remains something that young and old still identify with. And although he has hobnobbed with world leaders on several continents, he has never cut himself off from ordinary people, particularly in his native Jamaica. But having been active as a professional musician for over fifty years, what else is next for Jimmy Cliff? He has reached the age when most bosses would expect an employee to retire, yet Cliff insists the word is not in his vocabulary. Instead, he looks set to continue his illustrious career as a singer, songwriter, humanitarian and actor, for, at the time of writing, reports have surfaced that Jimmy has been working on a new film project, based on the life of Woppi King, another original Jamaican rude boy, so it seems we have another venture on the silver screen to look forward to.

Jimmy Cliff has never been one to let his life be ruled by accepted conventions, preferring instead to simply follow his own path, and it seems unlikely that he will change tack any time soon. He has often described his role in the music as akin to that of a shepherd's, as he was present from the very beginnings of the Jamaican music industry, and continues to be an active force in it today. Remaining very much a master of his own destiny, as long as he has life and breath, he will surely continue to deliver his message through music, using his faith and wisdom to find the way to cross whichever rivers are still to come.

Select Discography

Singles

1961
I'm Sorry (Hi Tone/Blue Beat)

1962
Hurricane Hattie (Beverley's/Island)
Dearest Beverley (Beverley's/Island)
Miss Jamaica (Beverley's/Island)
Gold Digger (Beverley's/Island)
Since Lately (Beverley's/Island)
I'm Free (Beverley's/Island)

1963
One Eyed Jacks (Beverley's/Island)
My Lucky Day (Beverley's/Island)
Don't Play the Fool (Beverley's/Island)
King of Kings (Beverley's/Island)
Miss Universe (Beverley's/Island)
The Prodigal (Beverley's/Island)
The Man (aka Trust No Man – Beverley's/Black Swan)
Never Too Old To Learn (aka You Are Never Too Old – Beverley's/Black Swan)

1964
One Eyed Jacks (alternative version – Stateside)
King of Kings (alternative version – Stateside)

1966
Call On Me (Fontana)
Pride and Passion (Fontana)

1967
Give and Take (Island)
Aim and Ambition (Island)
I Got a Feeling (and I Can't Stop) (Island)
Hard Road To Travel (slow version – Island)
That's the Way Life Goes (Beverley's/Island/Fontana)
Thank You (Beverley's/Island/Fontana)

1968
Set Me Free (Jackie Edwards and Jimmy Cliff – Steady/Island/ Federal)
Here I Come (Jackie Edwards and Jimmy Cliff – Steady/Island/ Federal)
Waterfall (Island/A&M)
The Reward (Island)

1969
Wonderful World, Beautiful People (Beverley's/Trojan/A&M/Fontana/Philips)
Hard Road To Travel (fast version – Beverley's/Trojan)
El Bello Mundo de la Bella Gente (Wonderful World, in Spanish – Fontana/Philips)

1970
Vietnam (Beverley's/Trojan/A&M/Ariola)
She Does It Right (Beverley's/Trojan)
Suffering in the Land (Beverley's/Trojan)
Come Into My Life (Beverley's/Trojan/A&M)
You Can Get It If You Really Want (Trojan/Ariola)
Wild World (Beverley's/Island/A&M/Phonodor)
Be Aware (Trojan & Island/A&M/Phonodor)
Synthetic World (Island)
I Go To Pieces (Island)
Better Days Are Coming (Beverley's)

1971
Bongo Man (Beverley's/Summit)
Goodbye Yesterday (Beverley's/Island/A&M)
Breakdown (Beverley's/Island)
Let's Seize the Time (Island/A&M)
Sitting in Limbo (Island)
The Bigger They Come, The Harder They Fall (Island)
Going Back West (Beverley's)
Those Good, Good Old Days (Trojan)
Pack Up, Hang Ups (Trojan)
Take a Good Look At Yourself (Beverley's)
Oh How I Miss You (Beverley's)
My World Is Blue (Beverley's/RTB)
Where Did It Go (Beverley's/RTB)

1972
Trapped (Island)
Struggling Man (Island)
The Harder They Come (Island/Mango)
Many Rivers To Cross (Island/Mango)

1973
Black Queen (Reprise)
Born To Win (Reprise/Stateside)
Poor Slave (Stateside)
Rip Off (Stateside)
On My Life (EMI)
Oh Jamaica (EMI)
Fundamental Reggae (EMI)
Money Won't Save You (EMI)
Under the Sun, Moon and Stars (Stateside/EMI)
The Price of Peace (EMI)

1974
Music Maker (EMI/Reprise)
Look What You Done To My Life, Devil Woman (EMI)
I've Been Dead 400 Years (EMI)
Money Won't Save You (EMI)
You Can't Be Wrong and Get Right (EMI/Reprise)
Action Speaks Louder than Words (EMI)
Don't Let It Die (EMI)
Music Maker (EMI/Reprise)

1975
Brave Warrior (EMI)
Every Tub (EMI)
Oh Jamaica (EMI)
A Million Teardrops (EMI)

1976
Dear Mother (Reprise)
Remake the World (Reprise)
Look At the Mountains (Reprise)
No Woman No Cry (Reprise)
The Harder They Come (live version – Reprise)
Vietnam (live version – Reprise)
Let's Turn the Table (Sunpower)
Deal With Life (Sunpower)
Pack Your Things (Sunpower)
Sons of Garvey (Joe Higgs and Jimmy Cliff – Sunpower)
Sound of the City (Joe Higgs and Jimmy Cliff – Sunpower)

1977
Material World (Sunpower)
7X7 (Seven Times To Rise, Seven Times To Fall) (Sunpower)

1979
Stand Up and Fight Back (Sunpower/Warner Brothers)
Bongo Man (Warner Brothers)
Footprints (Warner Brothers)
You Left Me Standing by the Door (Sunpower)

1980
All the Strength We Got (WEA)
Love Again (WEA/MCA)
It's the Beginning of an End (MCA)
Another Summer (WEA/MCA)
Satan's Kingdom (Sunpower/WEA)
Standing Up for Love (Sunpower)

1981
I Am the Living (MCA)
My Philosophy (WEA)
Shelter of Your Love (WEA)
Give the People What They Want (Oneness/WEA)
Son of Man (WEA)

1982
Treat the Youths Right (Oneness/CBS)
Originator (Oneness)
Roots Radical (CBS)
Rub A Dub Partner (Oneness/CBS)
Special (CBS/Columbia)
Keep On Dancing (Dub) (CBS)
Peace Officer (Dub) (CBS/Columbia)
Midnight Rockers (Oneness)

1983
Love Is All (CBS)
Originator (Oneness/CBS)
Reggae Night (Oneness/CBS/Columbia)

Love Heights (Oneness/CBS)
Under Pressure (Oneness)
We All Are One (Oneness/CBS/Columbia)
No Apology (Oneness/CBS)

1984
Piece of the Pie (CBS)
Roots Woman (Columbia)
Reggae Movements (CBS/Columbia)
De Youths Dem a Bawl (Beggar's Banquet) (Oneness)
Black Bess (Oneness)

1985
Hot Shot (CBS/Columbia)
Modern World (CBS)
American Sweet (CBS/Columbia)

1986
7 Day Weekend (Jimmy Cliff, Elvis Costello & the Attractions –
Columbia)
Brightest Star (Columbia)
Club Paradise (Columbia)
Third World People (Columbia)
The Lion Awakes (Oneness)
Brown Eyes (Oneness)

1987
Hanging Fire (Columbia)
Step Aside (Roots Girl) (Oneness)

1988
Love Me Love Me (Columbia)
Sunshine in the Music (Columbia)
Reggae Down Babylon (Oneness)

1989
Pressure (aka Pressure on Botha) (Oneness/Greensleeves)
Dance Reggae Dance (Vision)

1990
Rebel in Me (Oneness)
True Story (Oneness)
First Love (Oneness)

1991
Peace (Cliff Sound)

1994
I Can See Clearly Now (Chaos/Sony/Jet Star)

1995
Hakuna Matata (Jimmy Cliff and Lebo M – Polydor)
Positive Energy (Island Jamaica)

1996
Crime (Island Jamaica)
True Revolutionary (Oneness)

1998
Rise Up (Cliff Sound)
Higher and Deeper (Cliff Sound)

2001
Harder than a Rock (Oneness)

2002
Humanitarian (Jimmy Cliff, Capleton & Bounty KiIller – Oneness)

Albums

The Real Jamaican Ska (Epic, 1964; includes "Ska All Over the World," "Trust No Man")

Ska At The Jamaica Playboy Club (Island, 1966; includes "Hey Boy, Hey Girl" [with Millie Small] and "King of Kings")

Hard Road To Travel (Island, 1967, reissued on Beverley's/Trojan)

Can't Get Enough of It (Veep, 1968)

Jimmy Cliff in Brazil (Philips, 1968)

Jimmy Cliff / Wonderful World, Beautiful People (Trojan, 1969; A&M, 1970)

Two Worlds (Beverley's, 1970)

Another Cycle (Island, 1971)

Goodbye Yesterday (Island/Ariola Benelux, 1971)

Wild World (Island, 1972)

Unlimited (EMI/Reprise, 1973)

Struggling Man (Island/Mango, 1973)

House of Exile/Music Maker (EMI/Reprise, 1974)

Brave Warrior (EMI, 1975)

Follow My Mind (Reprise, 1975)

In Concert: The Best of Jimmy Cliff (Reprise, 1976)

Give Thankx (Sunpower/Warner Brothers, 1978)

I Am the Living (Sunpower/WEA/MCA, 1980)

Give the People What They Want (Oneness/WEA/MCA, 1981)

Special (Oneness/CBS/Columbia, 1982)

The Power and the Glory (Oneness/CBS/Columbia, 1983)

Cliff Hanger (Oneness/CBS/Columbia, 1985)

Hanging Fire (Oneness/CBS/Columbia, 1988)

Images / Save Our Planet Earth (Vision, 1989; Musidisc, 1990)

Breakout (Som Livre, 1991; JRS, 1992)

Higher and Higher (Island Jamaica, 1996)

Journey of a Lifetime (Island Jamaica, 1998)

Humanitarian (Eureka/Globe Music, 1999)

Fantastic Plastic People (Artist Network, 2002)

Black Magic (Warner Strategic Marketing/Artemis, 2004)

Existence (forthcoming)

Original contributions to film soundtracks

The Harder They Come Soundtrack (Island/Mango, 1972; includes "The Harder They Come," "Sitting in Limbo," "You Can Get It If You Really Want")

Club Paradise Soundtrack (Columbia, 1986; includes 8 exclusive Jimmy Cliff songs)

Something Wild: Music from the Motion Picture Soundtrack (MCA, 1986; includes "You Don't Have To Cry")

Marked For Death Soundtrack (Delicious Vinyl, 1990; includes "John Crow," "No Justice," "Rebel in Me")

Cool Runnings Soundtrack (Disney, 1993; includes "I Can See Clearly Now")

Music from and Inspired by The Air Up There (Interscope, 1994; includes "[Your Love Keeps Lifting Me] Higher and Higher," "Watch Me Fly")

Rhythm of the Pride Lands – Music Inspired by The Lion King (Disney, 1995; includes "Hakuna Matata," with Lebo M)

Unique collaborations

Jimmy James and the Vagabonds: *The New Religion* (Piccadilly, 1966; Jimmy on backing vocals)

Joe Cocker: *Sheffield Steel* (Island, 1982; includes "Sweet Little Woman")

Sun City: *Artists United Against Apartheid* (Manhattan/EMI, 1985; Jimmy on vocals)

Rolling Stones: *Dirty Work* (CBS, 1986; includes "Too Rude")

Lapiro de Mbanga: *No Make Erreur* (Tshi/Sonodisc, 1986)

Gregory Isaacs: *IOU* (Greensleeves/Ras, 1989; includes "Jealousy")

Cidade Negra: *Lute Para Viver* (Epic, 1990; includes "Mensagem")

Margareth Menezes: *Kindala* (Polygram/Mango, 1991; includes "Me Abraça e Me Beija")

Olodum: *Revolution in Motion* (World Circuit, 1992; includes "Reggae Odoya")

Titãs: *Dose Dupla Vip – Acústico MTV* (Warner Music, 2002 [recorded 1997]; includes "Querem Meu Sangre")

Jools Holland & His Rhythm and Blues Orchestra: *More Friends* (WEA, 2002; includes "Dreams")
Various: *46664 Part II: Long Walk to Freedom* (Warner Records, 2004; includes "People" with Johnny Clegg)

Recommended compilations
Jimmy Cliff Anthology (Universal Music Enterprises, 2003)
Better Days Are Coming: The A&M Years 1969–1971 (Hip-O Select, 2006)
The EMI Years: 1973–1975 (EMI International, 2004)
Many Rivers To Cross: The Best of Jimmy Cliff (Trojan, 2003)
The Harder They Come: The Definitive Collection (Trojan, 2005)
The Ultimate Collection (Hip-O, 1999)
Jimmy Cliff (expanded edition) (Trojan, 2002)
The Harder They Come Soundtrack (deluxe edition) (Hip-O, 2003)

Select Bibliography

Books

Ali, Arif, ed. *West Indians in Britain.* London: Hansib, 1979.
Alleyne, Mervyn. *Roots of Jamaican Culture.* London: Pluto, 1989.
Barrett, Leonard. *The Rastafarians* (second edition). Boston: Beacon, 1988.
Barrow, Steve, and Peter Dalton. *The Rough Guide To Reggae* (second edition). London: Rough Guides, 2001.
Bradley, Lloyd. *Bass Culture: When Reggae Was King.* London: Viking, 2000.
Chang, Kevin O'Brien, and Wayne Chen. *Reggae Routes.* Philadelphia: Temple University Press, 1998.
Chevannes, Barry. *Rastafari Roots and Ideology.* Syracuse: Syracuse University Press, 1994.
Clarke, Sebastian. *Jah Music.* London: Heinemann, 1980.
Clifford, Mike, ed. *The Illustrated Encyclopaedia of Black Music.* New York: Harmony, 1982.
Collins, John. *Music Makers of West Africa.* Washington, DC: Three

Continents Press, 1985.

Dannen, Fredric. *Hit Men: Power Brokers and Fast Money Inside the Music Business.* New York: Vintage, 1991.

Davis, Stephen, and Peter Simon. *Reggae Bloodlines,* New York: Anchor, 1977.

Davis, Stephen, and Peter Simon, eds. *Reggae International.* New York: R&B, 1982.

Davis, Stephen. *Bob Marley: Conquering Lion of Reggae.* London: Arthur Baker, 1983.

Diop, Cheikh Anta. *The African Origin of Civilization: Myth or Reality.* Chicago: Lawrence Hill, 1974.

Faristzaddi, Millard. *Itations of Jamaica and Rastafari – The Second Itation.* Miami: Judah Anbesa, 1991.

Foster, Chuck. *Roots Rock Reggae,* New York: Billboard, 1999.

Haley, Alex. *The Autobiography of Malcolm X.* New York: Grove, 1965.

Henzell, Perry. *Power Game.* Oxford: Macmillan, 2009.

Johnson, Howard, and Jim Pines. *Reggae: Deep Roots Music.* London: Proteus, 1982.

Katz, David. *Solid Foundation: An Oral History of Reggae.* London: Bloomsbury, 2003.

Katz, David. *People Funny Boy: The Genius of Lee 'Scratch' Perry* (revised edition). London: Omnibus, 2006.

Larkin, Colin, ed. *The Virgin Encyclopedia of Reggae.* London: Virgin, 1998.

Lee, Hélène. *The First Rasta.* Chicago: Lawrence Hill, 2003.

Manley, Michael. *Jamaica: Struggle in the Periphery.* London: Third World Media, 1982.

Marre, Jeremy. *Beats of the Heart.* London: Pluto, 1985.

Murrell, Nathaniel, William Spencer, and Adrian McFarlane, eds. *Chanting Down Babylon: The Rastafari Reader.* Kingston: Ian Randle, 1998.

Owens, Joseph. *Dread.* Kingston: Sangster's, 1976.

Potash, Chris, ed. *Reggae, Rasta, Revolution.* New York: Schirmer, 1997.

Salewicz, Chris, and Adrian Boot. *Songs of Freedom*. London: Bloomsbury, 1995.

Salewicz, Chris, and Adrian Boot. *Reggae Explosion: The Story of Jamaican Music*. London: Virgin, 2001.

Small, Geoff. *Ruthless: The Global Rise of the Yardies*. London: Warner, 1995.

Steckles, Garry. *Bob Marley. A Life*. Northampton, MA: Interlink Books, 2009.

Steffens, Roger, and Peter Simon. *Reggae Scrapbook*. San Rafael, CA: Insight Editions, 2007.

Strong, Martin Charles. *The Great Rock Discography*. Edinburgh: Canongate, 2004.

Taylor, Don, and Mike Henry. *Marley and Me*. New York: Barricade, 1995.

Thelwell, Michael. *The Harder They Come*. New York: Grove Weidenfeld, 1980.

Thomas, Michael, and Adrian Boot. *Jah Revenge*. London: Eel Pie, 1982.

Thomas, Polly, and Adam Vaitilingam. *The Rough Guide To Jamaica* (second edition). London: Penguin, 2000.

Turner, Michael, and Robert Schoenfeld. *Roots Knotty Roots: The Collector's Guide To Jamaican Music*. Maryland Heights, MO: Nighthawk, 2001.

Wallis, Roger, and Krister Malm. *Big Sounds from Small Peoples*. London: Constable, 1984.

White, Timothy. *Catch a Fire* (definitive edition). New York: Owl Books, 1998.

Whitney, Malika Lee, and Dermott Hussey. *Bob Marley: Reggae King of the World*. Kingston: Kingston Publishers Limited, 1984.

Newspapers, magazines, websites, archives

Although sources used are too numerous to list fully here, I am particularly indebted to writers such as Arthur Kitchin, Barbara Ellington, Carmen Patterson and Mel Cooke in the *Gleaner*, Roger

Steffens in the *Beat*, Jon Pareles in the *New York Times*, Charlie Gillett in *Let It Rock* and *Rolling Stone*, Vivien Goldman and Rob Partridge in *Melody Maker*, Penny Reel in *NME*, Lloyd Bradley and Pat Gilbert in *Mojo*, Nick Hasted and Pierre Perone in the *Independent*, Lee Wohlfert-Wihlborg in *People*, Tom Lanham in *Wave*, Josh Chamberlain in New Hampshire's the *Wire* and Graham Reid in *Absolute Elsewhere*. I have also made use of Jimmy Cliff's excellent website, www.jimmycliff.com.

Select Videography

Bongo Man. Directed by Stefan Paul. Arsenal Films/Sunpower Prod., 1980. Films International/Castle Hendring Video, 1981.

Club Paradise. Directed by Harold Ramis. Warner Bros., 1986. Warner Home Video, 2006, DVD.

Deep Roots Music. Directed by Howard Johnson. Channel Four television series, 1982. MVD Visual, 2007, DVD.

A Hard Road To Travel: The Story of The Harder They Come. Directed by Chris Browne. The Official Film Company; BMG, 2001, DVD.

The Harder They Come. Produced and directed by Perry Henzell. Jamaica: International Films Inc., 1972. Criterion 2000/BMG 2001, DVD.

Jimmy Cliff: Moving On. Directed by François Bergeron. Morgan Production/La Sept Arte television broadcast, 1996. Quantum Leap, 2003/Shanachie, 2004, DVD.

Marked For Death. Directed by Dwight H. Little. 20th Century Fox, 1990.

Reggae: The Story of Jamaican Music. Directed by Mike Connelly. BBC2 television/Bravo 3-part series, 2002.

Roots Rock Reggae: Inside the Jamaican Music Scene. Directed by Jeremy Marre. 1977. BBC television broadcast, 1977. Shanachie, 2000, DVD.

Rude Boy: The Jamaican Don. Directed by Desmond Gumbs. 3G Films, 2002. Amsell Entertainment, 2003, DVD.

This is Ska. ITV, 1964. Island Visual Arts, 1989, VHS.

Index

*Photos are indicated by **bold** page numbers.*

"A Million Teardrops" 96
Ackee Walk camp (Edwards) 19
"Actions Speak Louder Than Words" 95
Africa
  political developments in Ethiopia 148–9
  Senegal and West Africa visit 108–11
  tours 93–5, 153, 156–7, 162, 185
  working holiday in Zaire and Congo 156–7
  See also individual countries
African Oneness Liberation Festival (planned) 141–2
African Oneness Vibration 141
"Aim and Ambition" 56
Air Up There, The (film) 176
Aitken, Laurel 15–17, 49
"Album of My Life" (Dean) 97
Albums. *See* discography
Ali, Muhammad 39
"All for Love" 184
"All Star Reggae Jam," Woodstock Festival 177
"All Star Spectacular" revue 34
"All the Strength We Got" 122, 123
Allen, Terry (Verden Allen) 53, 54–5, 58
ambition, early 7–9
America, performances in 38–9, 102, 120, 130, 156, 174, 185–6, 187, 201
"American Dream" 146
"American Plan" 155

"American Sweet" 151
"Andança (Me Leva Amour)" 64
Anderson, Esther 73
Another Cycle (album) 75–7, 86
"Another Summer" 123
Ara Ketu band 168, 171, 172, 174
Argentina 65, 75, 76, 176
Armond, Wayne 175, 180, 187, 197
"Arrival" 151
Artist Network 188–9, 191, 193, 194
"Ashe Music" 181
atlas, J.'s early fascination with 11
Audio Vision Studios 161–2
awards
  for contribution to development of Kingston Tech 177
  Doctor Bird Award 184
  Doctor of Letters (D.Litt) degree 182
  Hall of Fame, Kingston 186
  Jamaican Music Industry (JAMI) Awards 175
  Marcus Garvey Lifetime Achievement Award 196
  Most Outstanding Showman 147
  Music of Black Origin (MOBO) award 190
  Norman Manley Award for Excellence 137–8
  Order of Distinction 83, 90
  Order of Merit **192**, 193–4
  Rock and Roll Hall of Fame 200
  University of the West Indies Bob Marley Award 199
  Vice Chancellor's Award for Excellence 193

"Baby Let Me Feel It" (The Willows) 97, 173
Back-O-Wall community 18–19, 23
Badarou, Wally 131, 133

Bailey, Noel 106, 114
"Bandwagon" 95
Barrett, Aston "Family Man" 95,
    184, 186
Barrett, Carlton "Carly" 95, 96
Baye Fall Mourides 110–11
Bayyan, Amir (aka Kevin Bell) 143,
    148, 152, 158
Bayyan, Khalis (aka Richard Bell)
    143, 158
"Be Aware" 69
"Be Ready" 173
"Be True" 87
Beenie Man 160
Belafonte, Harry 30, 138
Bernard, Jackie 134
Beverley's
    Desmond Dekker 32
    development of skills at 27–9
    experience earned at 34–6
    J.'s first approach to 24–5
    recordings at 27, 31–2, 35–6
Beverley's All Stars 66, 90
"Bigger They Come, the Harder
    They Fall, The" 77
birthplace 3–4, **4**
Black Magic (album) 194–6
Black Uhuru 131, 147, 174
Blackwell, Chris 37, 40, 41–2, 45,
    48, 49, 50, 56, 60, 66, 75, 83,
    84, 86, 180, 182–3, 200
Blues Busters 30, 31, 44, 45
Bob Marley One Love All Star
    Tribute Concert 186
"Bob Yu Did Yu Job" 181
"Bongo Man" 74, 116, 169
Bongo Man (film) 128
"Born To Win" 87
Bounty Killer 195
Brave Warrior (album) 95–6, 101
Brazil
    collaboration with Titãs 181

impact of first trip on J. 62
increased time spent in (1990s)
    174
International Song Festival 62
J. extends early stay in 62–4
J.'s arrival in 61–2
recordings in (1968) 62–4
time in ends (1990s) 178
tour 166–70
"Waterfall" as hit in 62
during world tour 126–7
Brazzaville recordings 157, 158,
    172, 173
Breakout (album) 171–4
"Brightest Star" 155
Bright-Plummer, Guillermo (Guilly
    Bright) 75, 76, 77
Britain
    disappointment in 56, 59–60
    live performances 58–9
    northern clubs 51
    opening for the Steampacket in
        London 50
    recording debut 51–2
    ska, reaction to in 42–3
    tours 51–4, 90
"Brother" 91
"Brown Eyes" 151
Brown, Kojo "Preacher" 114, 124,
    128
Brown, Trevor "Starr" 92, 95, 122
Browne, Cleveland "Clevie" 161,
    162, 173, 184, 194
Browne, Glen 158, 161, 162, 165,
    194
Bryan, Radcliffe "Dougie" 66, 90,
    100, 130, 137, 148, 158
"Burden Bearer" 183
Burning Spear 152, 160, 174, 186
Bustamante, Alexander 2–3, 15, 31
Buzar, Nonato 63–4, **63**

Calabash Literary Festival 197
"Call On Me" 51
Can't Get Enough of It (album)
    57–8, 64
Caribbean Rising festival 197–8
Carifesta 107, 108, 187
Carnegie Hall 1974 93
Carvalho, Beth 64
CBS 135–6, 144, 146, 147–8, 154,
    158
Chalice (band) 147, 175, 180, 181,
    187
Chambers, Christine (mother) 4
Chambers, James Ezekiel. *See* Cliff,
    Jimmy
Chambers, Lilbert (father) 3, 5, 12,
    23, 127, 162
Chambers, Victor (brother) 5, 11,
    127, 147, 150, 172
"Change" 183
Channel One (studio) 99, 131,
    135, 142
charitable works
    46664 project 193, 194
    Africa Upliftment Fund 149
    after Hurricane Gilbert 160
    fundraiser for Somerton All-Age
        School 194, 196
    Institute of Caribbean Studies
        196
    National Council of Ghanaian
        Associations benefit concert
        200
    Telefood 99 186
Check It (Mutabaruka) 128
childhood 5–7
Chile 65
Chin, Tony 99
Christianity, J.'s rejection of 79–80
church during childhood 5
Cidade Negra 166, 170
"City" 191, 193

Clarke, Wayne 175, 180, 187
Clegg, Johnny 194
Cliff, Jimmy
    accolade 1974 92
    ambition of 52–3
    birthplace 3–4, **4**
    bow-tie look **88**
    childhood 5–7
    choice of name 10
    as disciplined and spiritual 99
    documentary on 179–80
    education 7–9
    embracing Islam 40, 79–80, 86,
        87, 91, 97, 111, 160, 173
    fundraising for Ethiopia 148–9
    Grammy for *Cliff Hanger* 152,
        153
    grandmother's influence 6–7
    help given to upcoming talents
        34, 44–5, 166–7
    influence of Rastafari on 19–20,
        35, 74, 91, 116, 124–5,
        146, 149, 173
    as perfectionist 52
    photos **58, 78, 88, 98, 107,
        117, 119, 125, 129, 145,
        146, 154, 169, 178, 182,
        192, 197**
    Shandy, endorsement of 160
    as voracious reader 115
    See also albums; awards; discogra-
        phy; films; live performances;
        tours
Cliff Hanger (album) 148, 150,
    151, 152
Cliff Sounds and Films Incorporated
    162
Club Paradise (film) 150, 153, 154
    154
cocaine trade in Jamaica 164
Cocker, Joe 59, 106, 131
Cole, Squidly 147

Cole, Stranger 42, 98, 147
collaborations discography 211–12
Collins, Ansel 92, 115, 130, 137,
   158
color prejudice 6–7, 48–9
"Come Into My Life" 68
"Come Up to My Love" 185
"Commercialization" 89
compilations 103, 109, 212
concerts. *See* live performances
Cool Runnings (film) 175–6
Count Boysie the Monarch 20–1
countryside life 3
"Crime" 181
Cuba 134

"Daddy" 183
"Dance" 195
"Dance Reggae Dance" 162, 163
Dansak Band 92
Davis, Carlton "Santa" 99, 102,
   106
"De Youths Dem a Bawl (Beggar's
   Banquet)" 149
"Dead and Awake" 151
"Deal With Life" 107
Dean, Nora 86, 97
"Dear Mother" 100
"Dearest Beverley" 24, 25, 26, 27
Dekker, Desmond 32, 66, 69, 74,
   82
"Democracy Don't Work" 183
digitization of music 156
discography
   albums 210
   collaborations 211–12
   compilations 212
   singles 203–9
   soundtracks 211
Dixon, Luther 122
Doctor Bird Award 184
Doctor of Letters (D.Litt) degree 182

documentary on J. 179–80
"Don't Let It Die" 96
"Don't Stay Out Late" 42
Downie, Tyrone 137, 175, 177,
   184, 185
Dragonaires 29, 37, 38, 42, 43, 45
Dranoff, Béco 166–7
"Dreams" 191, 195
"Drifters" 185
Dunbar, Sly 99, 102, 109, 131,
   133, 134, 135, 148, 150, 151,
   154, 180, 181, 184, 189

Earth Summit 174
education 7–9
Edwards, Jackie 41, 49, 56, 60, 90
elections in Jamaica 3, 105–6, 130,
   163–4, 175
EMI 43, 50, 83, 85, 87, 89, 90, 95,
   96, 102
Ethiopia, fundraising for 148–9
European tours 127–8, 147, 178,
   183, 193, 198–9, 200
"Everliving Love" 163
"Every Tub" 96
Existence (album) 201
"Experience" 133

Fantastic Plastic People (album)
   189–90, 191–5
father. *See* Chambers, Lilbert
Felly, Pepe 157
Festival International de Varadero,
   Cuba 134
films
   Air Up There, The 176
   Bongo Man 128
   Club Paradise 150, 153, 154,
      154
   Cool Runnings 175–6
   Harder They Come, The **72,** 73–
      4, **78**, 80, 81–4, 86, 89,

102, 125, 141, 148, 164,
174, 182, 185, 192, 195, 198
Lion King, The 177
Marked for Death 165
Rude Boy: The Jamaican Don 190
videography 215
"First Love" 163
folk music, early influences 8
Follow My Mind (album) 99–100,
102, 125
"Footprints" 116
4-H Club 9–10
46664 project 193, 194
France
early gigs in 55–6
J's later status in 179, 180
Full Experience (planned album)
113
"Fundamental Reggay" 87

Gambia visit 112
Ghana fan club 113
Ghana performance 161
"Giants" 185
Gil, Gilberto 61, **125**, 126–7, 130,
147, 168–9, 186, 197
"Girls and Cars" 157, 158
"Give and Take" 55, 56, 57, 59
"Give Thanks Jamaica" 160
Give Thankx (album) 116–20, 172
"Give the People What They Want"
133
Give the People What They Want
(album) 131–4
Gleaner and *Star* newspapers, J's
selling of 11
Góes, Zéu 168, 171, 172
"Going Back West" 74, 77, 89
"Going Mad" 101, 126
"Gold Digger" 32
"Good Life" 195
Goodbye Yesterday (album) 78

Graham, Anthony "Crucial Bunny"
135, 136, 142, 147
Grammy for *Cliff Hanger* 152, 153
Grand Zaïko Wawa 157
grandmother 6–7
"Grass Is Greener, The" 163
Green, Courtney 35

"Hakuna Matata" 177
Hall of Fame Awards, Kingston 186
"Hanging Fire" 159
Hanging Fire (album) 158–9
"Hard Road to Travel" 56–7, 68
Hard Road to Travel (album) 57
"Harder They Come, The" 77, 82,
83
Harder They Come, The (film) **72**,
73–4, **78**, 80, 81–2, 83–4, 86,
89, 99, 102, 125, 148
plans for sequel 164–5, 174,
182, 186, 192
stage version 198
Haynes, Jimmy "Senyah" 122, 131
Hendrix, Jimi 55, 200
Henton, "Computer" Paul 175,
180, 184
Henzell, Perry 71–2, 77, 82–3,
182, 186, 192, 198–9
"Hey Boy, Hey Girl" 52
"Hey Mister Yesterday" 64
Higgs, Joe 97–8, 100, 102, 106,
107, 159, 201
"Higher and Deeper Love" 174,
184
"Higher and Higher" 180
Higher and Higher (album) 180–1,
183
"Hill, The" 185
"Hitting with Music" 151
"Hold Tight (Eye for an Eye)" 159
homecoming concert 2005 196
"Honey Hush" (Small) 74

"Hot Shot" 152
"House of Exile" 91, 93
House of Exile (album) 90–2
"How Long" 185
"Humanitarian" 185
Humanitarian (album) 184–5
Hunt, Clive 175, 176, 179, 180,
    183, 184
Hurricane Charlie 6, 160
Hurricane Gilbert 159–60
"Hurricane Hattie" (song) 26, 27
"Hypocrites" 101

"I Am the Living" 123
I Am the Living (album) 121, 122–3
"I Can See Clearly Now" 175, 180
"I See the Light" 88
"I Walk with Love" 185
"I Want I Do I Get" 191, 195
"I Want To Know" 91
Iantosca, Rick 143–4, 146, 148
"I'll Go Wooing" 9, 20
"I'm a Winner" 172
"I'm Free" 32
"I'm Gonna Live, I'm Gonna Love"
    100
"I'm in All" 185
"I'm Sorry" 22
"Image of the Beast" 162
Images (album) 161–3, 173
In Concert: The Best of Jimmy Cliff
    (album) 109
independence, Jamaican
    festivities 30–1
    links with music 14–15, 30–1
Independence Jump Up tour 31
industrialization in Jamaica 3
"Inside Out, Upside Down" 76
International Festival of Pop Music
    58
International Market of Records and
    Musical Editions (MIDEM)

convention 181
International Song Festival, Brazil 62
Isaacs, Gregory 161
Islam 40, 79–80, 88, 91, 111, 120,
    173, 179–80
Island Records, J. leaves 84
I Threes 95, 138, 149, 177
"It's the Beginning of an End" 122,
    123
"It's Time" 159
"I've Been Dead 400 Years" 91
"I've Got a Feeling (and I Can't
    Stop)" 56

Jackson, La Toya 143, 148, 151
Jackson, Michael 178
Jagger, Mick 106, 130, 150, 188
Jamaica
    cocaine trade 164
    countryside life 3
    elections 3, 105–6, 130, 163–4,
        175
    industrialization 3
    J. returns to in 1969 65
    J. returns to in 1975 97–9
    labor disputes of 1930s 2–3
    Negril performances 141, 181–2
    political situation mid-1970s
        105–6, 112–13
    Reggae Sunsplash 114, 128, 130
    Second World War 1–2
    violence during 1980 election
        130
    World Music Festival 138
    Youth Consciousness concert 139
"Jamaica Time" 189, 191
Jamaican Experience band 99, 102,
    106, 137
Jamaican Music Industry (JAMI)
    Awards 175
Jamerican Film and Music Festival
    186

James, Jimmy 52, 53, 59
"Jammin'" 186
"Jealousy" 161
Jean, Wyclef 182, 186, 195, 200
Jimmy Cliff (album) 64
Jimmy Cliff Center for Excellence
    198
Jimmy Cliff in Brazil (album) 62–4
Jimmy Cliff Extravaganza, The 92
"Jimmy Jimmy" 173
jobs, early 11–12
Jobson, Brian 189–90
Jobson, Wayne 137, 188
"John Crow" 166
"Johnny Too Bad" 82, 102, 163, 184
Johnson, Wycliffe "Steely" 161, 162,
    173, 184, 194
Jorge, João 169–70, **169**
"Journey" 146
Journey of a Lifetime (album) 183–4

Kamoze, Ini 134
"Keep On Dancing" 136
"Keep On Running" (Edwards) 49
"Keep the Family" 185
Kimsey, Chris 135–7
"King of Kings" 35, 41, 43, 52, 155
Kingston
    accommodation in 13–14, 17–18
    arrival in 13–14
    music scene in 15–17
Kingston Technical School 11, 14,
    177
Kofi-Badu, Ernest Sampong 113
Kong, Leslie **24**, 24–5, 26–7, 33,
    36, 41, 65–6, 77, 200
Kool and the Gang 143, 148, 151,
    172, 195
Kuti, Fela 94, 112, 165, 182

labor disputes of 1930s 2–3
Lady Musgrave Road 97, 99, 113,
122, 155, 201
Lagos, Nigeria 93–4, 112
Lance, Major 42
"Learn To Love" 184
Lee, Byron 28–30, 34–5, 37, 38–9,
    40, 42–5, 66
Lennox, Annie 190, 191
"Let It Go" 184
"Let Your Yeah Be Yeah" (Pioneers)
    74
"Let's Jam" 185
"Let's Turn the Table" 107, 131
Lewis, Aura 108–9, 110, 112, 113,
    127
"Lion Awakes, The" 155
Lion King, The (film) 177
live performances
    1962–3 34–5
    "All Star Reggae Jam" 177
    America 38–9, 102, 120, 130,
        156, 185–6, 187, 201
    Bob Marley One Love All Star
        Tribute Concert 186
    Caribbean Rising festival 197–8
    Carifesta 107, 108, 187
    Carnegie Hall 1974 93
    in church as a child 5
    Cuba 134
    Earth Summit 174
    4-H club 9–10
    Ghana 161
    "Give Thanks Jamaica" 160
    Grand Cayman 1964 44
    homecoming concert 2005 196
    independence festivities 30–1
    International Festival of Pop
        Music 58
    International Market of Records
        and Musical Editions
        (MIDEM) convention 181
    Jamaica 1964 43–4
    Jamaica 1971 73–4

Montreal and Toronto 1980 134
Montreux Jazz Festival 127–8,
    130, 199
Motown's "Soul by the Sea" 30th
    anniversary concert 163
National Achievement Day 1959
    10–11
Negril 1983 141
Negril Music Festival 181–2
New York World's Fair 38, 39
opening for the Steampacket in
    London 50
Reggae Sunsplash 114, 128, 130
Ritz, New York 130, 165, 174
in school 7
at soccer matches 158, 183, 187,
    198
Somerton free concert 128
Soweto's Orlando Stadium 124
Split 70 Light Music Festival,
    Yugoslavia 69
"Stars on Parade" show 34
talent contests 16–17
Telefood 99 186
Trinidad 76, 93, 141
"Twisting To Independence"
    revue 31
UK 54, 55, 58–9, 60, 67, 90, 92
World Music Festival 138
Youth Consciousness concert 139
Zambia 133, 137
Zimbabwe 138
See also tours
London
    arrival in 1965 47–9
    Jimmy Cliff Extravaganza, The
        92
    music scene 1965 49–50
    opening for the Steampacket in
        50
"Lonely Streets" 118
"Long Time No See" 91

"Look At the Mountains" 100
"Look What You Done To My Life,
    Devil Woman" 92
"Looking Forward" 183
"Love Again" 122
"Love Comes" 191, 195
"Love Heights" 136
"Love I Need" 118–20
"Love Is All I Have To Give" 136
"Love Me, Love Me" 157, 158
"Love Solution" 143, 146

"Majority Rule" 133
"Man, The" 36
Manley, Michael 81, 83, 105, 112,
    129–30, 163–4, 175, 182
Manley, Norman Washington 2
"Many Rivers to Cross" 68, 75, 82,
    92, 131, 138, 180, 186, 194,
    200
maps, J.'s early fascination with 11
Marcus Garvey Lifetime Achieve-
    ment Award 196
marijuana, J. starts smoking 19
marijuana, J. stops smoking 150–1
Marked for Death (film) 165
Marley, Bob 32–4, 73, 84, 93, 95–6,
    112, 121, 130, 136, 138, 139,
    170, 174, 177, 181
Marley, Rita 86, 95, 138, 149, 160,
    177
Marley, Ziggy 159, 160, 174, 177,
    186
Maroons 4
"Mash Down Apartheid" (Mystic
    Revealers) 153
"Material World" 113, 133
Matthews, Dave 186
Matumbi, Lazzo 168–9, 171
Mayfield, Curtis 42
Maytals 43, 44, 66, 82, 138, 177
mbalax scene 110

McCook, Tommy 43, 65, 86, 90, 96
McIntosh, Jeremiah. *See* Count
      Boysie the Monarch
McKay, Freddy 97
McLean, Ranchie 102, 130–1, 136,
      148
"Meeting in Afrika" 118
Melody Makers 138, 152, 159,
      160, 175, 177
"Melody Tempo Harmony" 179,
      180, 181
mento 8, 30, 91
Merritt, Newton "Sipho" 135, 147,
      153
Miller, Jimmy 51, 55, 56
"Miss Jamaica" 31, 36, 41
"Miss Universe" 36
"Money Won't Save You" 91
Montreux Jazz Festival 127–8, 130,
      199
Morgan, Derrick 20, **21**, 25, 26,
      27, 28, 30, 32, **33**, 34–5, 43,
      49, **192**
"Morning Train" 123
Morris, Eric "Monty" 20, 26, 27,
      32, 38, 43
Morrison, Gibby 115, 172
Most Outstanding Showman award
      147
Motowns's "Soul by the Sea" 30th
      anniversary concert 163
Moving On (television documentary
      on J.) 179–80
Mowatt, Judy 86, 96, 139, 152
Muscle Shoals studio 67, 69, 70,
      75–6, 89
music
      in Back-O-Wall 18–19
      development of skills at Beverley's
          27–9
      digitization 156
      early influences 8–9

and independence movement in
      Jamaica 14–15, 30–1
See also albums; films; singles
"Music Maker" 91
Music Maker (album) 90–2
Music of Black Origin (MOBO)
      award 190
Mutabaruka 128, 134, 149, 160
"My Ancestors" 68
"My Boy Lollipop" 37
"My Friend's Wife" 76
"My Love Is Solid as a Rock" 91
"My Lucky Day" 32
"My People" 96
"My Philosophy" 133
"My World Is Blue" 74
Mystic Revealers (band) 153, 181,
      197

Nation of Islam. *See* Islam
National Achievement Day 1959
      10–11
National Council of Ghanaian Asso-
      ciations benefit concert 200
"Natural Mystic" tour 177–8
Negril Music Festival 181–2
Negril performance 1983 141
Nettleford, Rex 196, **197**
New York World's Fair 38, 39
"News, The" 101
Nigerian performances 93–4, 182
"No. 1 Rip-Off Man" 91–2
"No Apology" 144
"No Justice" 162, 166
"No Make Erreur" (M'Banga) 156
"No Nuclear War" 151
"No One" 42
"No Problems Only Solutions" 191
"No Woman No Cry" 101, 126,
      127, 139, 186
Norman Manley Award for
      Excellence 137–8

northern clubs of Britain 51
"Now and Forever" 151–2

"Ob-La-Di Ob-La-Da" 185
"Oh, How I Miss You" 76
"Oh Jamaica" 87
Okosun, Sonny 94, 134
Olodum 169–70, 172, 178
"On My Life" 87, 92
"One Eyed Jacks" 36, 43
"One Love" 174, 186
"Oneness" 172
Oneness band 114–15, 123–4, 126, 128, 130, 134, 135, 137–8, 141–2, 144, 147, 148, 150, 156, 158, 161, 162, 166, 171, 187
Oneness label 131, 134, 153, 156, 181
Oneness Plaza 148
"(Ooh La La La) Let's Go Dancin'" 195
"Opportunity Hour" talent contest 16–17
"Opportunity Only Knocks Once" 76
Order of Distinction 83, 90
Order of Merit **192**, 193–4
"Originator" 137
Orlando Stadium, Soweto 124
"Our Thing Is Over" 76
"Over the Border" 191

"Pack Up Hang Ups" 74
"Pack Your Things" 108
Paris residency 54
"Peace" 173
"Peace Officer" 136–7, 138
"Peace One Day" 190
"People" 191, 194
Phil Wainman Band 49–50
"Piece of the Pie" 146

Pioneers 74, 92
Planno, Mortimer 114, 128, 196
"Please Tell Me Why" 76
"Poor Slave" 88–9
"Positive Mind (The World Is Yours)" 191
"Power and the Glory, The" 146
Power and the Glory, The (album) 142, 144–7
prejudice, color 6–7, 48–9
"Pressure" (aka "Pressure on Botha") 160–1, 162
"Price of Peace, The" 88
"Pride and Passion" 51
Prince Buster 35–6, 37, 38–40, **39**, 49, 81, 111
"Prodigal, The" 36

racism 6–7, 48–9
Rainbow Theater, London 92
Ramacon, Phil 122, 123, 130, 142
Ranglin, Ernest 37, 92, 106, **107**, 109, 114, 175, 181
Rastafari movement 19–20, 114
Real Jamaican Ska, The 42
"Rebel in Me" 162, 165, 166, 180, 194, 197
recordings
    early attempts at 17, 20–2
    See also albums; discography; films
reggae, beginnings of 65
Reggae: The Story of Jamaican Music (BBC series) 190
Reggae Feelings (book) (planned) 155
"Reggae Movement" 147
"Reggae Night" 143, 144, 146, 147
"Reggae Odoya" 170
"Reggae Street" 151
Reggae Sunsplash 114, 128, 130
"Remake the World" 101
Reprise 85, 87, 89, 90, 95, 99, 109, 113

rhythm and blues as early influence
      8
Richards, Keith 130, 150
Richards, Mikey "Boo" 130
"Rip Off" 87–8
"Rise Up" 185
Ritz, New York 130, 165, 174
Rock and Roll Hall of Fame 200
"Rock Children" 137
rock steady 65
Rodrigues, Daniel 168
Rolling Stones 55, 56, 68, 74, 109,
      130, 135, 150
"Roll On Rolling Stone" 172–3
"Roots Radical" 136
"Roots Woman" 146
"Rub-A-Dub Partner" 136
"Rubber Ball" 183
Rude Boy: The Jamaican Don (film)
      190
Rude Boys (film) (planned) 155

"Samba Reggae" 172
Santana, Carlos 128, 165
"Satan's Kingdom" 122, 123
"Save a Little Loving" 96
"Save Our Planet Earth" 162, 180,
      196
Save Our Planet Earth (album) 166
Screwface (film) 165
Seaga, Edward 28–30, 38, 105,
      130, 138, 149, 153, 197
Second World War 1–2
Senegal 109–11, 196
"Serenou" 64
"Seven Day Weekend" 154
Shakedown Sound (band) 53–5,
      57–9, 58
Shakespeare, Robbie 100, 131, 134,
      148, 150, 151, 180, 181, 184
Shandy, J's endorsement of 160
"She Is a Woman" 116–18

"She Was So Right for Me" 159
"She Was the One" (Higgs) 159
"Shelter of Your Love" 133
Shirley, Roy 45
"Shout for Freedom" 157, 173
Sierra Leone visit 108, 110, 112
"Simple Truth" 183
Sims, Danny 30, 135
"Since Lately" 32
Singles. See discography
Sir Cavalier 22
"Sitting in Limbo" 76
ska 25–6, 29–30, 37, 38, 40, 42–3,
      65
"Ska All Over the World" 42
Skatalites 65, 174
Skool Band 180, 193
Sly and Robbie 134, 148, 150, 151,
      180, 181, 184
Small, Millie 37, 40, 43, 51, 74, 92
Smith, Earl "Chinna" 99, 109, 114,
      122, 128, 130, **132**, 136, 172,
      174, 186
Smith (Swift), Keith 22
"Soar Like an Eagle" 159
soccer matches, performances at
      158, 183, 187, 198
Somerton
      African Oneness Liberation
            Festival (planned) 141–2
      birthplace 3–4, **4**
      free concert in 128
      fundraiser for Somerton All-Age
            School 194, 196
      Jimmy Cliff Center for Excellence
            198
      J.'s contribution to youth welfare
            155
      venue at, J's dream of 11
Somerton All-Age School 194, 196,
      198
"Son of Man" 133

Sonenberg, David 142–3
"Song We Used to Sing, The"
    (Dekker) 69, 74
songwriting, early attempt at 9
"Sons of Garvey" 107
"Soul by the Sea" concert 163
"Soul Mate" 180
"Sound of the City" 107–8
sound systems
    in Back-O-Wall 18–19
    early use of in Jamaica 8
Sounds of Blackness 180, 186
soundtracks, film. *See* films
South Africa
    during world tour 123–6
    travel ban 142
South America
    J's travels in 65
    See also Argentina, Brazil, Chile
Soweto's Orlando Stadium 124
Special (album) 135–7
Spencer Davis Group 49, 50, 51,
    52, 54, 57
Split 70 Light Music Festival,
    Yugoslavia 69
Springsteen, Bruce 149, 200
"Stand Up and Fight Back" 116
"Stars on Parade" show 34
Steely and Clevie 162, 173, 184,
    194
"Step Aside (Roots Girl)" 156
"Stepping Out of Limbo" 173
Stevens, Cat 68, 69, 78–9, 194
Stewart, Dave 188–90, 193
Stowe, Maxine 176, 180
"Street Vibes" 183
Stronach, John 115, 118
"Struggling Man" 79
Struggling Man (album) 89
"Suffering in the Land" 68
"Summer Reggae" 170
"Sun City" 149

Sunpower Productions 97, 156
"Sunrise" 151
"Sunshine in the Music" 143
"Super Bad" 184
Supersonics 65–6
Swampers 66–7
Swift, Keith. *See* Smith, Keith
"Synthetic World" 70

"Take a Look At Yourself" 75
talent contest 16–17
Taylor, Don 121–2
Telefood 99 186
television programs 179–80, 190
"Terror" 191
"That's the Way Life Goes" 58
Third World (band) 114, 130, 160,
    174, 184, 196
"Third World People" 154–5
Thompson, Sticky 95, 102, 106,
    109, 114, 130, 131, 179
"Those Good, Good Old Days" 74
"Time Will Tell" 68
Titãs 181
"Too Rude" 150
Tosh, Peter 334, 95, 134, 135, 137,
    138, 139, 170, 173
Total Sounds 85
Touba, J's pilgrimage to 110–11
tours
    1978 114, 120
    Africa 93–5, 153, 156–7, 162,
        185
    America 120, 130, 156, 174,
        185–6
    Black Magic album 195–6
    Brazil 126–7
    Britain 51–4, 90
    Caribbean 76, 162
    Europe 127–8, 147, 178, 183,
        193, 198–9, 200
    Give Thankx album 120

Humanitarian album 185–6
Images support 162
Independence Jump Up 31
Jamaica 1962 30
"Natural Mystic" 177–8
Nigeria 93–5
Paris 55
Senegal and West Africa 108–11
Virgin Islands 76, 99, 128
"World Beat" 174
world tour 1980 123–8
See also live performances
Traffic (band) 58, 59, 89
"Trapped" 79, 149, 163, 165
"Treat the Youths Right" 136, 147–8
Trinidad 15, 30, 76, 93, 141, 187
"True Revolutionary" 181
"True Story" 173
"Trust No Man" 42
Tucker, Handel 180, 181, 184
"Turning Point" 162
"Twisting To Independence" revue
    31
Two Worlds (album) 77

"Under Pressure" 141
"Under the Sun, Moon and Stars"
    87, 93, 109
University of the West Indies, J's
    visit to 196
University of the West Indies Bob
    Marley Award 199
Unlimited (album) 85–9
"Use What I Got" 68

Vagabonds 31, 34–5, 43, 49, 52,
    53
"Vesti Azul" 64
Vice Chancellor's Award for Excel-
    lence 193
videography 215
"Vietnam" 68

Virgin Islands tours 76, 99, 128
vocal talent, early recognition of
    10–11

"Wahjahka Man" 100–1
Wailer, Bunny 34, 86, 139
Wailers (band) 34, 84, 90, 95, 101,
    112, 147, 160, 177, 185
Wailing Souls 98, 100, 101, 176
Wainman, Phil 49–51, 52–3
Walker, Errol "Bagga" 99, 102, 106
"Wanted Man" 118
"War a Africa" 172
"War in Jerusalem" 191
"Waterfall" 60, 62–4
"We All Are One" 143, 144
Weaver, Mick 59
West Kingston, J. moves to 18
"What Are You Doing With Your
    Life" 133
"Where There Is Love" 136
"Where Will U Be" 183
White, Philip 102, 165, 171
White, Robertha 7, 11, 184
"Who Feels It (Knows It)" 100
"Wild World" 69, 71
Wild World (album) 78
Williams, Deniece 121–2
Willis, Alee 122
Winwood, Muff 49, 58, 60
Winwood, Steve 49, 112, 156
"With You, Without You" 64
Wolfe, Sidney 122, 146, 160
"Wonderful World, Beautiful People"
    67, 148
Wonderful World, Beautiful People
    (album) 67–70, 75
Wood, Ron 135–7
Woodstock Festival 177
working holiday in Africa 156–7
"World Affairs" (Kamoze) 134
"World Beat" tour 174

World Cup 1998 183
"World in Trap" 133
World Music Festival 138
"World of Peace" 88
world tour 1980 123–8
"Wound May Heal, The" (McKay)
    97
Wynder K Frogg Band 59

"You Are Never Too Old" 36
"You Can Get It If You Really
    Want" 69, 77, 82, 180, 199,
    200
"You Can't Be Wrong and Get
    Right" 91
"You Can't Keep a Good Man
    Down" 155
"You Don't Have To Cry" 149
"You Left Me Standing by the
    Door" 118
"Your Reward" 57
"You're the Only One" 101
Youth Consciousness concert 139
"You've Got a Friend" (King) 185
Yugoslavia 69

Zaire 156–7
Zambia 133, 137
Zimbabwe 123, 133, 138